The Greek Plays 2

Other Books by Ellen McLaughlin Published by TCG

The Greek Plays

The Greek Plays 2

Ellen McLaughlin

THEATRE COMMUNICATIONS GROUP
NEW YORK
2024

The publication of *The Greek Plays 2* by Ellen McLaughlin, through TCG Books, is made possible by Mellon Foundation.

TCG books are exclusively distributed to the book trade by Consortium Book Sales and Distribution.

Library of Congress Control Numbers:
2024007567 (print) / 2024007568 (ebook)
ISBN 978-1-55936-991-6 (paperback) / ISBN 978-1-55936-944-2 (ebook)

A catalog record for this book is available from the Library of Congress.

Book design and composition by Lisa Govan
Cover design by Kitty Suen
Author photograph by Raisa Desypri

First Edition, September 2024

Contents

Preface

By Ellen McLaughlin

It's been exactly thirty years now since I began, with my adaptation of *Electra* in 1994, my encounter with the ancient Greeks in these versions of their literature and myths. The sister volume, *The Greek Plays*, published in 2005, includes the first six adaptations I wrote, involving plays by the three great tragedians, Aeschylus, Sophocles, and Euripides, as well as a version of Aristophanes's comedy *Lysistrata*. This volume similarly contains adaptations based on plays by all three tragedians, but also includes a music-theater piece, *Penelope*, inspired by Homer's *Odyssey*, and a short play, *Conversations at the Return of Spring*, the source of which is the myth of Demeter and Persephone.

The work included in these volumes makes up a great part of what I have done as a playwright over a long career. But with this second volume of work inspired by the Greeks, I feel I'm bringing a rich conversation that has lasted decades to a close. I can only be grateful for the way these meetings with the dead have sharpened my sensibility, awakened my instincts, and challenged my skills. With every assignment I've taken on, the Greeks have taught me crucial lessons about my craft and given me insights into myself I would not have received elsewhere.

Ajax in Iraq, the first play in this volume, was written in 2007–2009 during the bloodiest years of the Iraq War. *The Oresteia*, the last and most recent play, was finished in 2019 amid the Trump presidency. These have been tumultuous times for the world, terrifying for democracy, and hard to navigate as a citizen, let alone as an artist. But the Greeks have helped me. It has been a comfort to remember that they made their great work as their world buckled and heaved with its own bad times and that what they created endures beyond the politics and crises of their era.

What the Greeks have given me as a writer is courage and size. If you're dealing with the Greeks, you can't just make little plays that stay safely within the bounds of what's easily achievable. I've found that liberating. Scary in the right way. There is nothing tidy, nothing settled, at the end of a Greek play. These aren't nice pieces of literature you savor with your glass of sherry; they bleed all over the floor if you try to bring them inside the house. There's an exhilaration to the ambition, the chutzpah, of the Greeks. I wanted to engage with that and so I let the Greeks lead me where they did.

I'm always struck by just how disturbing Greek plays are. At the center of each one there is an unthinkable thought, a terrible image that is designed to jolt us into a struggle with the ethical conundrum that the play circles but can never resolve. As a writer in conversation with them, I have found that the only way to encounter these plays authentically and fruitfully is to embrace their difficulties, to head toward the darkness. When students I teach find the ancient plays off-putting and hard, I don't try to convince them otherwise. They are. I advise them to value and pay attention to the aspects of the work that confound and disturb them. These plays were not intended as academic exercises or to be mastered through analysis. They are intended to shock, to defy logic, to move deeply into the psyche and do their work. When writing in response to one of these plays, I have to stop dithering on the surface and just drop down into the cave of it, enter the depths, and see what I can discover there. It takes time, sometimes years, but I will find something, an odd dreamlike fragment that is born of these works but is also passionately and undeniably mine. Once I find that, I can begin.

To write each of these plays, I had to wait for some image to break in me that refused analysis and lifted me away from an intellectual, dutiful stance into creative urgency. Antigone in a 1930s housedress knocking Morse code on a wooden floor; Odysseus as a brain-wounded veteran sitting in an armchair looking out to sea, waiting for his own return; the gray ribbon that Mercury ties around the wrists of the dead when he takes us to the Underworld—those were some of the tickets to the rides these plays took me on.

In my preface to the first volume of *The Greek Plays*, I wrote that I found Greek plays uniquely useful when addressing war, both its majesty and its horrors. But in looking at the plays assembled for this second volume, I realize that what they share has less to do with my continuing desire to address war and its effects than with my personal history over the past years, which has included a reckoning with death and loss—a subject that the Greeks treated in all their literature and about which, as with war, they were exquisitely, searingly eloquent.

There is an ancient belief that the gods send us sorrows so that we will have stories to tell, and every human life will eventually tender its stories of loss. Losing, as Mercury says in my play *Mercury's Footpath*, is all we mortals ever do. "From the moment of your birth you begin scattering your possessions like so much seed—baby teeth, innocence, hopscotch pebbles—right up until the moment of your death, when you abandon pulse, sky, color, music, life, life, life." My father died in 2005 and my mother died in 2016, and those losses, different but crucial, have informed and deepened my work over the time that this volume spans. They have endowed me with my own stories but also stirred in me a need for the stories of others, and the Greeks tell some of the best. All these plays involve encounters with the dead or the suicidally death-bound, and all of them attempt, as the Greeks so often did, to grapple with the mystery of death and the two great questions it inspires: What do we owe to life and what do we owe to the dead?

The play in which these questions are most starkly weighed is *Antigone*—which I adapted as *Kissing the Floor*—but the Greeks were considering them throughout their literature and culture.

They were a people of the present tense, as is apparent in their vital embrace of life, with all its sensual thrill, bitter anguish, peril, and passing delight. Their idea of death was as bleak as any I can think of. Nothing so vivid as a heaven or hell in store for them. They foresaw an eternal existence of aimless wandering in silence and shadow, homesick for the sharp air and sunlight to which they could never return. Sure, there are the Elysian Fields for the few and famous, but even there, where warriors might stride about in their clanking armor forever, there was nothing to quicken the heart or engage the spirit. When questioned by Odysseus at the mouth of the Underworld, Achilles says memorably that he would rather live a brutal life as the slave of a hard master than spend the rest of eternity as the king of the dead. This view of death has always struck me as bracing and right, and I find their queasiness in contemplating the return of the dead to the living world reasonable. No matter how much we ache to bring our loved ones back to life, whenever that desperate wish is actually granted, in play after play, myth after myth, it does not go well. People who live in the present understand that all we can ever know, whether it is through suffering or joy, can only be known while we live.

What do we owe the dead? I've faced this question personally through these plays, but I realize that it's also an issue that is at the heart of any conversation with the literature of the past. There's a necessary struggle in creating the new while honoring the old, the essential artists we venerate whose work has determined so much of our aesthetic and shaped our sensibilities. Reverence—awe—is important. If you had never felt it, why would you want to make art in the first place? But there are limits to reverence; there comes a point when you have to transcend it in order to take your own work as seriously as you take the art that inspired you to do it. When it comes to the dead poets who wrote the ancient plays I have spent so much of my life trying to reckon with, I want the audience to understand what's happening on stage, not at a safe distance, but as close as breath. These plays should be as disturbing, beautiful, and immediate as they ever were in what they demand from us. That is what I think we owe the dead. We must meet them where they stand and take up their challenge to find our own ways toward what they do, which is to articulate on the highest level what it is to be human.

It's not surprising that the Greeks, with their highly attuned sense of the fleeting moment, invented the theater as we know it. Because theater people are also people of the present. We know that once the brief run of a play is over, it's gone from the world. That is the heartbreaking and piquant lesson of every final performance. Our short, bright existence above the ground is all we have. Let us pay attention, let us revel in it, now, now, now, while we can.

Acknowledgments

Every writer racks up debts over the course of a long career, but playwrights are particularly beholden to a host of people, from actors, directors, and dramaturgs to designers and stage managers and everyone in between, not to mention other playwrights, friends, and family. I cannot possibly do justice to all the people who have been part of the making of this book, but a few do demand special mention.

Brian Kulick, dramaturg, director, professor, all-round egghead, and mensch, got me started on all this back in 1994 when he asked me to write a version of Sophocles's *Electra* for a new *Oresteia* he was presiding over at the Actors' Gang in Los Angeles. Then throughout my career, he has steered me to provocative and fruitful paths of inquiry, including Euripides's *Helen*, which he suggested when I was severely blocked, and most recently, when he, as artistic director of Classic Stage Company in New York, commissioned me to write a play based on a fragment of a lost Euripides play called *Protesilaus*. The play that emerged as *Mercury's Footpath* would surely never have happened without that strange assignment, and it is dedicated to him as belated thanks for the small but steady flame he lit under me so long ago.

Michael Kahn commissioned the most recent major adaptation I wrote, *The Oresteia*, as his last project at the Shakespeare Theatre Company, the theater he created in D.C. and which he led for nearly four decades. It was an extraordinarily ambitious and challenging commission and I'm still a little stunned that he trusted me with it. I was deeply proud of what we, and everyone who worked on that production, accomplished and I will always be grateful for that experience. Michael's soaring leadership and his generous treatment of me throughout have led me to dedicate that play to him.

Lisa Rothe has directed more of my work than anyone else and I have felt fortunate beyond measure for her unflappable intelligence, humor, and grace as a director, as well as for her warmth and kindness as my trusted friend. *Penelope*, which she directed both in workshop form at the Getty Museum in Los Angeles and in its premiere at PlayMakers Rep in North Carolina, is dedicated to her.

Jane Lincoln Taylor has been my dear friend since college and, all of my writing life, has been the best first and last reader for anything I have done. Her sensitive, astute, and meticulous textual care never fails to astonish me. She is an extraordinary editor and the finest of friends. She has made me a better writer and a better person. *Kissing the Floor*, most of which I wrote while staying in her family house in Maine, is dedicated to her.

Finally, there's Rinde Eckert. An inspiration as an artist and my spirit's home.

Ajax in Iraq

Introduction

What is the meaning of the Trojan War? If you want an answer, don't go to the ancient Greeks for it. They will provide only a fistful of paradoxes and a twisting, confounding beast of a story in which characters you come to love sometimes do sickening, ignoble things. You don't know what to feel about any of them, but you can't look away either. The heroes are defined by the size of their flaws as well as by the heights of their passions, but it is their suffering that draws us to them and makes it impossible for us to turn our backs.

I never intended to write an adaptation of Sophocles's *Ajax*. I didn't think I'd ever be able to cope with the horror of that opening image—Ajax's mad slaughter and torture of docile animals while he's in the grip of a delusion that he is taking revenge on the men he thinks have betrayed and shamed him. Those men are his generals, Agamemnon and Menelaus, as well as Odysseus, who Ajax thinks has unjustly won his rightful trophy, the armor of the dead Achilles. Ajax's butchery of the innocents—never seen but all too present in the closed tent center stage—is an image I've always found abhorrent in a way that none of the other brutality conjured by the Greek tragedians has ever been for me.

Sophocles hurtles us into the thick of that savagery at the start of the play, letting the sun come up on it after Ajax has been at it all night. Throughout the opening scene, we look at the closed tent, listen to the grunts and ax blows, and imagine what must be going on inside. When the horrified Odysseus enters, following a trail of

3

blood to his former comrade's tent, the goddess Athena appears to him and explains that she drove Ajax mad in order to protect his intended victims. Our first glimpse of Ajax is as a blood-crazed man interrupted in his butchery when Athena, pleased with herself, calls him out of his tent. She wants to exhibit the mania into which she has driven him to the very man Ajax thinks he is presently torturing, Odysseus. She is surprised that Odysseus doesn't share her pitiless glee at the abasement of the enemy who hates him, but Odysseus disappoints her by wanting to be spared seeing the wretched transmutation of a man who had been, mere hours ago, not only his trusted, steady comrade but one of the greatest heroes the world had ever known. When Athena asks Odysseus why he is so squeamish, in my version, Odysseus says:

> I can't hate him as he is now, Goddess.
> I look at him and I feel nothing but pity.
> That could be me.
> That could be any one of us.
> He's what we all look like to you, I guess.
> Flickering shadows, settling dust, that's all we are.
> I see that now.

Though Odysseus knows that's what human beings must look like to the gods, still the vision of the glory of humanity degraded to that extent is unbearable to him.

And so it has always been to me.

But when I took it upon myself as a playwright to address the American military presence in Iraq, I found myself returning to Sophocles's Ajax: his sense of betrayal, his bitterness, his descent into insanity, and finally his clear-eyed suicide. I went back into that thorny thicket of a hero, almost against my will, precisely because his claims on me are so hard to honor.

Ajax in Iraq was born of a particular moment in the Iraq War—2007 and 2008—and a particular group of collaborators, the class of 2009 at the A.R.T./MXAT Institute for Advanced Theater Training at Harvard University.

Though by then I had already written many adaptations of Greek plays, when I went into the process at A.R.T., I did not intend this play to be one of them. All I knew was that I wanted to write about the Iraq War, which I felt compelled to address as we entered its bloodiest year and there seemed to be no end in sight.

I wanted to collaborate with the graduate acting students not just as actors but as fellow artists. This was partly a function of the material, with which I needed their help. I told them that it seemed to me that the current war was their war rather than my war, in the sense that my generation was essentially sending their generation to fight its battles. I knew what I felt about it all, but wanted to know what it meant to them, and I told them that I would work with the material they generated to make something that addressed their ideas as much as my own.

The director, Scott Zigler, and I led the actors through a series of workshops over the next six months. Initially, I simply asked them to bring in theatrical material of their own devising that related to war in any way at all. Their research led them from the mythology of war and the history of the military to current soldiers' blogs and YouTube videos. They all did interviews, in some cases with their grandparents, who told them stories the students had never heard before about their experiences of World War II. Homeless Vietnam veterans on the street were also interviewed, as were returning soldiers, some of them the students' relatives or childhood friends. The presentations ranged from scenes and monologues to dance pieces to various forms of performance art.

Much of the work was beautifully realized, subtle, and smart. After the first round of workshops, the students had generated about thirty hours of material so wildly diverse in subject and tone that I was overwhelmed and unsure of how to organize the piece, particularly since I didn't want to just co-opt their work and sign my name to it. I needed to find an overarching structure and a means of transforming all the disparate pieces into some sort of new whole I could have control over and legitimately claim as my own. As I have done for many years now, when in doubt, particularly about structure, I turned to the Greeks. And as we began to look directly at the war in Iraq, I found that it was Ajax's terrible story that resonated best with the brutal mess we were investigating.

Much of the research material dealt with the psychological toll the current war was taking on its veterans. Specifically, we were identifying a trend, now an epidemic in the military, of soldiers committing suicide, sometimes during their tours of duty, sometimes once home and returned to civilian life. Military psychiatrists now use the term "moral injury" to describe the common phenomenon of soldiers wounded less by the trauma of battle than by their feelings of shame and guilt related to moral injuries, the damage done to deeply held beliefs about right and wrong—what the Greeks would have called *themis*. This psychological crisis can lead to suicide, but it can also lead to berserking—soldiers turning on innocent civilians, on prisoners in their care, or, with increasing frequency, on their own troops. The common theme for so many of these suicides and psychotic breaks seemed to be a loss of faith in commanding officers, a sense of betrayal, and, most importantly, a feeling of having been shamed—"thrown away," as one suicide's note said—by the American military they had once been proud to serve.

Possibly because there were more women than men in the group, we also started learning about the rampant sexual harassment of, predation on, and rape of female soldiers by their commanding officers or their comrades. Rape as an act of suppression and domination is an unsurprising if horrific outcome of the aggression war can unleash, as all military history teaches us, but what is relatively new in the world is what happens when so many female soldiers (one in six of the active military) are serving on equal terms with men and expecting to be treated as comrades. When such soldiers are subjected to "command rape" or "rape by rank" it is peculiarly traumatic, since they suffer at the hands of people they have no choice but to obey and on whom they depend for their survival. It is betrayal in its rawest form. In one interview after another, women spoke of having been drawn to the military as an unambiguous field on which to seek honor, but then finding that once in Iraq they were viewed as nothing more than sexual objects to be used and shamed by the men with whom they served.

The other theme that kept coming up was confusion. Civilians looked like insurgents and insurgents looked like civilians, which meant that soldiers were bound on occasion to, as they put it, "kick in the wrong doors," leading to yet more hostility in the communities the soldiers were attempting to control. But the greatest confusion for the soldiers in Iraq concerned their mission. No two soldiers interpreted what they were doing in the same way. One soldier who worked almost exclusively driving trucks of army meals around at high speed ultimately felt that he'd been putting his life at stake for a lot of refrigerated soda. This was literally true. Driving trucks, something women soldiers often did, turned out to be one of the most dangerous things you could do in Iraq because of the IEDs—explosives planted in roadsides—which, even more than direct combat, were causing some of the worst injuries. This led again to the sense of betrayal by superiors, since the way to protect yourself from such weaponry is with better intelligence in every sense of the word. You need commanders who know the risks and don't ask soldiers to take them unnecessarily, but above all you need adequate armor, full "battle rattle," equipment that was shockingly late in coming to the aid of soldiers in Iraq, if indeed it ever did arrive.

All these themes—a sense of confusion and injustice, as well as the shaming and betrayal by one's own side that forces so many soldiers to isolation and suicide—led me to *Ajax*. But even though the fit of the material to that classic text was obvious, I found that simply making a modern version of the play with a female Ajax (whom we called A.J.) just didn't seem sufficient to the gravity of the original text somehow. Nor would a relatively straightforward new version of the Sophocles—something that might seem closer to a modern translation—do justice to the complexity and specificity of the Iraq War and the ways we were trying to address it. So I decided to combine two equally weighted, intertwining narratives, classic and modern, each rendering the other richer as we came to see how they reflected and deepened each other. I found that I liked the shimmer of the female/male, modern/ancient, vernacular/poetic double resonance of the tragedy when the two stories chimed against each other in counterpoint.

The figure who presides over both the classic and the modern streams of the play is, unsurprisingly, Athena, Goddess of War. I've always been fascinated by the idea that the Greeks believed that war, that most masculine of enterprises, would have as its primary divinity a female deity. (Ares isn't taken seriously by gods or men.) Athena is also, intriguingly, the goddess of mind and therefore presides over madness as well—rational thought and necessarily the absence of it. What she gives—insight, strategy, cunning—she can just as easily take away. The more we explored PTSD and the more I studied the Sophocles—in which Athena is a frighteningly capricious force—the more it seemed right that she should be the one to frame the material, speaking directly to us with the cynical power of one who knows our darkness and depths all too well. And since we had more women than men in the cast, we were investigating women's particular relationship to violence and specifically to war, so Athena should have sway. It is, after all, as she keeps insisting, her play.

As the play shifts between the modern and the ancient worlds, the chorus belongs to neither world exclusively. They speak to us as amalgams of all soldiers everywhere and have access to some of the elevated language of the ancients while being grounded in the realities of the moment. They speak for us, but also for all the veterans who have ever put their lives on the line for their countries.

In the course of the play, we watch two great warriors—both a modern and an ancient one—descend into the ignominy of beserking. Ajax's, as in the classic text, comes at the beginning of the play, A.J.'s at the climax of it. Once released from their bloody delusions, both warriors are sickened by shame, and the two narratives, which have been running parallel, unite at the end of the play when both the female and the male Ajax are finally alone onstage together. They don't acknowledge each other but share a monologue as they prepare to die.

Ajax's quiet suicide, an actor all alone onstage, was original to Sophocles—nothing like it exists in the rest of the classical literature we have—and was, as far as we know, an innovation in Greek drama. The chill of it is no less shocking and poignant today than it was then, as we mourn the loss of so many disillusioned former soldiers who die in that same solitude and bitterness. Their lonely deaths mark the end of their attempts to make sense of the wars and the countries they feel have betrayed them. Their shame, like Ajax's, prickles inside all of us who have let them walk off into the wasteland of despair alone.

Production History

Ajax in Iraq had its world premiere at the Zero Arrow Theater at Harvard University in Cambridge, Massachusetts, on October 9, 2008, developed with the American Repertory Theater/Moscow Art Theatre School Institute for Advanced Theater Training (Scott Zigler, Director) graduating class of 2009. It was directed by Scott Zigler, who also took part in the production's development. The scenic design was by David Reynoso, the costume design was by Hilary Gately, the lighting design was by Margo Caddell; the vocal coach was Julie Foh, the dramaturg was Heidi Nelson, the production stage manager was Elizabeth Bouchard. The actors/collaborators in the development of the piece were: Emily Alpren, Renzo Ampuero, Skye Noel Basu, Kaaron Briscoe, Sheila Carrasco, Doug Chapman, Shawn Cody, Carl Foreman, Manoel Hudec, Nina Kassa, Roger Kuch, Careena Melia, Paul Murillo, Anna Rahn, James Senti, Lisette Silva, Josh Stamell, and Chudney Sykes.

The playwright is indebted to the passionate and inspired work all of the participants contributed to the process over the course of her sixteen-month residency, and to Theatre Communications Group and the National Endowment for the Arts for the funding that made it possible. Thanks must also go to Ryan McKittrick, Head of Dramaturgy at A.R.T., who was responsible in large part for the project's conception.

Ajax in Iraq had its New York premiere at the Flamboyán Theater, Clemente Soto Vélez Cultural and Educational Center, on June 3, 2011, presented by the Flux Theatre Ensemble (Corinna Schulenburg and Heather Cohn, Creative Partners). It was directed by Corinna Schulenburg. The scenic design was by Will Lowry, the costume design was by Lara de Bruijn, the lighting design was by Kia Rogers, the sound design was by Asa Wember; the dramaturg was Heidi Nelson, the production stage manager was Jodi Witherell. The cast was:

CAPTAIN/THERAPIST/NVG DREAM	
SOLDIER A/FLETCHER*/MINISTER	Matthew Archambault
F/ABRAMS/PATIENT/DEBBIE*	Tiffany Clementi
B/SICKLES/CHORUS/NVG DREAM	
SOLDIER B	Sol Crespo
E/SERGEANT/FIRST MAN IN THE DARK/	
TEUCER	Joshua Koopman
AJAX	Stephen Conrad Moore
A/ODYSSEUS/PISONI/NVG DREAM	
SOLDIER C/LARRY*	Mike Mihm
D/REBO/TECMESSA	Lori E. Parquet
GERTRUDE/CHORUS/JUDY*	Anna Rahn
ATHENA	Raushanah Simmons
A.J.	Christina Shipp
CONNIE MANGUS	Chudney Sykes
C/CHARLES/CHORUS	Chinaza Uche

*Fletcher, Debbie, Larry, and Judy died in rewrites, R.I.P.

Characters

Preshow and opening characters:

ATHENA   Goddess of War and of Mind.

OPENING CHORUS
(A, B, C, D, E, F)   A diverse group of American soldiers, male and female, who are encountered in only one scene and are unlike later characters. Distinct accents and costume pieces are important.

GERTRUDE BELL   Female English archeologist and political administrator who was largely responsible after World War I for drawing the borders for several countries in the Near East and for establishing the state of Iraq. Middle-aged, Edwardian dress. Brilliant, ironic.

CAPTAIN   Male American officer who was part of the initial U.S. invasion. Rueful, clear-eyed.

Female American soldiers in their twenties:

CONNIE MANGUS   A.J.'s closest friend in the company. Thoughtful, tough.

SICKLES   Sharp, critical.

ABRAMS   Warmhearted, anxious.

REBO	Sensitive, if hardened by her experience.
A.J.	Brave, valorous, but struggling profoundly with disillusionment and damage to her sense of self.

Male American soldiers in their twenties:

CHARLES	Amiable, used to being the clown.
PISONI	Seasoned, kind.
SERGEANT	Cruel, but sharp-witted.

Classic characters:

ODYSSEUS	A fine warrior, clever, who has seen too much.
AJAX	A great warrior, broken by the events of the night.
TECMESSA	Formerly a princess, taken captive when her country was invaded. She has been Ajax's war bride for several years.
TEUCER	Male. Ajax's brother.

Additional characters:

CHORUS	At least four soldiers, male and female, who can act as representatives of both ancient and modern soldiers. Their costuming should be based on modern fatigues but contain at least one element that ties them to the ancient world.
PATIENT	A young wife.
THERAPIST	Male. Doing his best but out of his depth.

FIRST MAN IN THE DARK	American soldiers in Iraq, interrogators.
SECOND MAN IN THE DARK	
NVG DREAM SOLDIER A	American soldiers, male and female, dreamers.
NVG DREAM SOLDIER B	
NVG DREAM SOLDIER C	
CHAPLAIN	Male. American.

Place and Time

Iraq in 2007; ancient Troy.

Note on the Text

A slash (/) indicates the point at which the next character should begin to speak, overlapping the rest of the first character's line.

Note on Casting

There are at least thirty-three parts and potentially many more if the chorus is expanded. But the play gives itself over naturally to multiple casting on all the parts except Ajax, A.J., and Athena. The casting for the 2009 Flux production in New York gives an idea of how the parts might be multiple-cast and also of the smallest number the company can feasibly be (twelve). An ethnically diverse cast is strongly recommended.

*The floor of the stage is a period map of the Middle East circa 1890
without any country boundaries drawn but perhaps with some
place names. Patches of sand are heaped to indicate mountains.
The area that will be modern Iraq should be center stage.*

*Preshow: A woman in Edwardian dress, Gertrude Bell, uses a
long-handled rake to arrange the sand to make a topographical
map of Iraq, also creating the boundaries in some way, either with
sand or with lengths of string.*

*The only standing structure on the stage is a small canvas tent.
Sounds come from within, difficult to discern. Shadows are cast
against the walls from a figure (figures?) inside. Gertrude exits
and the lights change. All we can hear is whatever is going on
inside the tent. Still unidentifiable, but disturbing.*

*Athena enters. She should look suitably martial and impressive,
recognizable as the Goddess of War, perhaps complete with helmet
and lance. She speaks to us.*

ATHENA

(Referring to the tent) You don't want to go in there. Terrible stuff
happening in there. Can you hear it? Not really, right? But you can
imagine. He's been at it all night.

It's OK, no one's going to make you go in there. Well, I won't anyway.
You've been outside this tent before, haven't you? It's familiar, isn't
it? The not knowing, the not wanting to know.

15

Still, every now and then, you can't help it, you get a glimpse. Some grainy, jumpy, hard-to-see thing taken from somebody's point of view. It's never long, just a few seconds. And even though you can't really hear, not quite, what anyone is saying, and you can't see what *exactly* is going on, it's enough for you. Isn't it? That's all you need to know.

(Sound from within.)

Screaming? You think? Nah. Could have been something else. Any number of things.

(Sound from within. She smiles.)

OK, so that was, *had* to be . . . What the heck is going on in there? That's what you're thinking. Or rather, that's what you're trying *not* to think. Who wants to think about this stuff? What's going on right now? Nobody.
Yeah, it's bad. In fact it's worse, it's worse than what you're imagining right now. Or even right now. I don't blame you for not going in. Who in their right mind would?
What's his name? Ajax. It's a play by Sophocles. It's about what I did to him. Because I could.

(End of scene.
Choral section. Modern male and female soldiers speak to the audience, as if being interviewed. They represent all ranks and different eras in the Iraq War.)

A

Yeah, we help people. People are in need and we step up, over and over. But the bottom line? We're soldiers. We take lives, that's what soldiers do. So you better get clear on what that means to you. Because for the rest of your life, that's what walks with you.

B

You just live in fear all the time.

C

It's just, the noise, it never stops: gunfire, explosions, rockets—they kinda hiss when they—and RPGs, it's a, like, a rushing / sound . . .

D

There's so much adrenaline pumping through you all day / every day.

C

You're jumpy every second because there are no people anywhere in this country you can rule out as threats. Shit, man, there are no *things* in this country you can rule out. A paper bag by the side of the road, a dead dog, a tin can? That could be where the IED that's going to kill you is hidden. That *thing* could kill your sorry ass.

A

Were there accidental casualties? Well, yeah.

B

We can't talk to them, they can't talk to us. It's a situation. We're, like, screaming at them, "We're here to help you!" while we're pointing guns at them and scaring the shit out of / everybody.

C

How do you know who the insurgents are? I don't know, man.

D

They hate us. And there is nothing we can do, no amount of— We are genuinely trying to help them. And they just keep trying to kill us. Are they crazy? Are we crazy?

C

Should I shoot him? . . . How about / him?

E

At least with the Iraqis you can see the pure struggle of their lives, day after day. Even when I hate the motherfuckers, I get it, why they're doing what they're doing, because I can see their lives and they just suck.

C

How about that guy? What's that guy doing?

E

But when I get home I look at all these fat idiots wandering
around the malls and I start feeling just, I don't know, contempt?
So that's not good.

C

After a while it got to be: If you killed him, that was an insurgent.

F

Seems like our job is to get shot at sometimes, 'cause you have to
draw fire in order to legitimize firing back in a civilian situation,
which is, let's face it, this entire war. We're the only ones in
uniform here, you know?

E

When I'm in a firefight I'm really happy, really calm. That guy
who's shooting at me? I can kill that guy with no hesitation at all.
Thank you! Everything else I do, I'm telling you, *everything else
I do* with these people I have hesitation.

D

I'm going in to try to talk to a bunch of chieftains and shit about
how they need to let us set up checkpoints? I got one translator for
the whole unit. Even *he* can't speak this particular local dialect all
that well, apparently. But he's all I've got. He's *it*, you know? And
I can't even trust *that* motherfucker.

F

It's this feeling of all of us, the Iraqis and the American soldiers,
we're all being just hung out to dry.

A

From the beginning, when Bush was saying things like "Mission
Accomplished," and then, Christ Almighty, "Bring it on" . . . "*Bring*

it on"? When the troops didn't have armor, shit, we didn't have full
battle rattle until, like, well, do we even have it *now*? It was pretty
clear the people in charge didn't know what they were doing.
We were taking casualties we never should have taken because
we were going on nothing, no real intelligence, not enough
translators, no gear, no *water* sometimes—I'm asking my troops
to function without sleep for days in 120-degree heat, passing a
single bottle of water around six guys. I don't know who I'm more
angry at, / the enemy or—

D

So what's the mission anymore? Remember when it was about
WMDs? That's why I was here. That's what I was told the mission
was. OK, so it turns out there weren't any, no WMDs, weren't ever
any. When we heard that, we were like, so what the fuck are we
doing over here? Then we hear that the mission is the security of
the Iraqi people? Suddenly that's what we were here to provide?
That was a big surprise to us. The day I heard this, I remember,
I'm standing in what used to be a government building but now,
I mean, between the invasion and the looters—there's nothing
there, I mean *nothing*, no furniture, no files, no phones, no ceiling
tiles, fuck, they even stripped the copper wires out of the walls, the
place is a fucking shell. We've disbanded the army, there's no police
force; all day, all night, all you can hear on the streets is screaming,
and now . . . Oh, hang on everybody, turns out we're here to give
you a brand-new democratic country? Built out of what? You ever
tried to make a living cow out of a cooked hamburger?

F

When you're back in the States, you hear, "Bring the troops home,
bring the troops home" all the time. But see, how's that going to
work? If I get to go home, who doesn't? You know? How am
I going to live with that? And I don't just mean Americans at this
point, I mean Iraqis. There are people I don't want to leave behind.
I can't just walk away from them at this point. I can't. Don't ask
me to do that.

C

So when you say that you disagree with this war, OK, that's your right, and I can deal with the idea that I'm basically putting my life on the line to protect your right to say that.

D

I've been back and back. This is my fourth. I can't stay home. I don't feel like I mean anything except here.

C

But I know people who died, people who lost arms and legs . . . It has to have been for something, OK? Don't tell me I did this for nothing. Don't tell me that. That makes me crazy.

A

This war, man . . .

B, C, D, E, AND F

This war, man . . .

A

It'll fuck you up.

B

When I go home, I can't stand the people I'm supposedly fighting for. They just seem obsessed with a lot of stupid crap, and all I want to do is get back here, and then I get back here and I go, right, oh fuck, *this* place, and I can't wait to get out of here and go . . . Well, where am I supposed to go at this point? I mean, really. Where the fuck am I supposed to go?

(One of the soldiers begins a jody call—e.g. "I'm a steamroller, baby . . ."—and the soldiers march out with it.
End of scene.
Gertrude and Captain enter. During the scene, Gertrude will continue making adjustments to the borders of the country. Both speak to us, referring to the map beneath their feet.)

GERTRUDE

Perhaps, looking back on it, we were doomed from the start.

CAPTAIN

I guess it should have been obvious what would happen, but in the rush to war, no one thought past the invasion and the transfer of power. Once we'd effected the regime change there was no sense that we might have to stick around.

GERTRUDE

We rushed into the business with our usual disregard for a comprehensive political scheme.

CAPTAIN

No one had thought through what it might take to help the Iraqi people make the transition to a workable democracy. Hell, a stable functioning government of *any* kind.

GERTRUDE

I believe I was the one who articulated the plan. It went something like this:

CAPTAIN

Something they still don't have, by the way.

GERTRUDE

"Mesopotamia would have a good British father in the high commissioner, she would be nannied by British advisors, and she would be mothered by me. Like any tractable, well-reared child, she would return the favor in kind. Her general sentiments would be ones of gratitude and loyalty, as well as a natural obligation to protect the parental route to India, giving us the wealth of her agriculture, archeology, and oil."

CAPTAIN

The only project anyone was interested in was taking out Saddam. We would protect the oil but that was the only thing the American military was committed to protecting. The looting, the destruction of the culture, the squaring off of rival ethnic and religious factions, the whole, well, the whole *mess* that followed the invasion . . . If anyone had cared, it all could have been anticipated. It wasn't. We were supposed to be able to take the country from Saddam and then just turn it over to a bunch of Iraqis we picked to run it. As if everybody would be just fine with that . . . It's like no one had ever read a book about the place. Or even just rented *Lawrence of Arabia*.

GERTRUDE
We sat in our ornate room, day after day, a mass of men and me, alone of all my sex as it were, carving up the Eastern world between us. All the vast holdings of these former empires—Austro-Hungarian, Russian, and of course the Turks—the seat of civilization, to be divvied up by the victors. It is the Garden of Eden after all, that green cradle between the Tigris and the Euphrates. It is where it all began.

CAPTAIN
But then the whole thing unravels, we're standing in rubble, the country is in chaos. We start trying to make some sense of what we've done.

GERTRUDE
When these men referred to the people of the country we were chopping into bits, they spoke of monkeys and barbarians and worse. They said this of a people who were writing great poetry and making great art when *their* ancestors were still sitting in the mud.

CAPTAIN
Turns out we're supposed to build a new country from the ground up. Someone else's country. That's when it just becomes this ludicrous improvisation.

GERTRUDE

(Referring to the map at her feet) The Sunni nationalists want an Arab kingdom, the Shiites want an Islamic religious state, and of course the Kurds in the north want an independent Kurdish entity.

CAPTAIN

Basically, it was up to us to justify doing the thing after we'd done it.

GERTRUDE

No one can agree on what they all want except that they don't want us.

CAPTAIN

So, yeah, we create havoc and then we want to be thanked for it.

GERTRUDE

We had promised them an independent Arab government with British advisors and what we gave them was a British government with Arab advisors.

CAPTAIN

It's the American delusion. We always go into these situations with a kind of toxic combination of confidence, naivete, and a will to power.

GERTRUDE

We would allow them to advise us on how we were going to run their country.

CAPTAIN

Military occupations go wrong, they just do. Even when they begin with the best of intentions. The reason is that you always have to do the same things to occupy a country. You have to come in with force, which is always going to hurt some people you don't intend to hurt, and then because you don't know the territory, the language, or the people, you have to set up your network of local informers. You become completely, cripplingly dependent on those locals. And those locals will do the wrong thing sometimes, for any number of reasons. Maybe they're using the opportunity to settle scores, maybe they just make mistakes. People make mistakes. But when you're kicking down the wrong doors, when you're arresting the wrong people—and you really can't avoid this—harming the innocent, doing damage, however limited, local resentments are inevitable, local resistance grows, and then, well, what happened before will happen again. The country will shake the occupiers off. And it doesn't matter what kind of benefits the occupiers might have brought in along the way. What matters in the end is the damage they did, the mistakes they made. Because that's what will be remembered.

GERTRUDE
Ibn Saud once challenged even the notion of national borders. Iraq, he said, was a fiction in which none of his people would ever believe. He called it a made-up place, as indeed it is. He said, "My people do not think as you do. You draw marks on a piece of paper you call the desert. We don't see those marks, we see only the horizon, which shifts as we journey toward it. We are nomads, you are mapmakers."

CAPTAIN
The occupying force is the one that won't last. Everybody knows this but no one knows it better than the Iraqis. They've done it for centuries. They know it's just a matter of waiting it out.

GERTRUDE
I said to Ja'far Pasha that complete independence was what we ultimately wished to give. "My lady," he answered—we were speaking Arabic—"complete independence is never given; it is always taken."

CAPTAIN
We're the ones who leave. That's what they know.

(End of scene.
Connie Mangus enters. She speaks to us.)

MANGUS

You get tired of the whining. I just wasn't interested in whether somebody missed their family or their favorite TV shows or whatever. If you're really a soldier, you just suck it up. And if you're a soldier with *tits* the pressure is just unbelievably immense to, not to . . . If you, even for a second, can be seen to be, like, indulging yourself, having a little pity party . . . I don't know, I just have no patience for people who need a lot of attention for just doing the job they signed up for. But there were things I didn't see, people who I just didn't . . . I didn't take in how badly it was going for them and that, well, I'm just going to have to live with that.

(Mangus, Abrams, Sickles, and Rebo, women soldiers, are sitting around playing poker, five-card draw. Cards have just been dealt by Rebo. A.J. is sleeping off to the side. They take their hands up and begin arranging them. They use different types of bullet casings as chips. The women are comfortable with one another, the joking rapid and offhand, the concentration on the game minimal.)

ABRAMS
So anyway, then he starts going on about how he was related to some Choctaw warrior—

SICKLES
Oh, please.

MANGUS
He's like the whitest person I've ever known.

SICKLES
Totally glow in the dark.

ABRAMS
That's what he said.

REBO
(To Sickles) You in?

SICKLES
Yup, betting five.

ABRAMS
And that's why he's so ferocious in battle.

MANGUS
Did he actually say that? "Ferocious"?

SICKLES
Not 'cause he's a total / tool?

REBO
Just 'cause you shoot forty times as many bullets / as you need to,
doesn't mean—

ABRAMS
And then he tells me that's where he learned that insane battle cry
he does.

(They variously imitate it.)

REBO
Oh, for god's sake—

ABRAMS
Five? What the heck.

(She puts in her chips.)

REBO
I'm staying in.

SICKLES
You know he got that off some old Western movie.

MANGUS
I'll take three.

SICKLES
Some rerun of *Little House on the Prairie.*

ABRAMS
Two.

SICKLES
Can't you just see him sitting in front of the TV in his little fringed vest and cowboy boots?

REBO
I'm taking two.

MANGUS
Hey, don't be mocking cowboy boots, I *loved* my cowboy boots.

SICKLES
Two, please.

MANGUS
Little red ones. I cried when I grew out of them.

SICKLES
No, three.

MANGUS
I wore them with my feather headdress.

ABRAMS
Unclear on the concept apparently.

MANGUS
And my dashiki.

(They crack up.)

SICKLES
So what'd you do? Run around the backyard stabbing yourself
with an arrow?

(They laugh. A.J. turns in her sleep.)

ABRAMS
We should keep it down.

SICKLES
I don't know why, she can sleep through anything lately.
Ten.

MANGUS
(Throwing in her ten) Why's she so tired?

ABRAMS
Ten? Really? Oh, all right. And I'll raise you ten.

REBO
Why shouldn't she be tired? I'm always tired.
Aw, I'm out.

MANGUS
She's never been like this.

ABRAMS
I know, she's usually like Miss NoDoz.

SICKLES
Seeing that ten and raising it another ten.

MANGUS
Oh, you bitch. All right, I'm a-calling you.

ABRAMS
I'm so very out.

(Sickles and Mangus put their hands out.)

MANGUS
Three fours.

SICKLES
Three nines.

MANGUS
WHAT? Let me see those cards, she's got to have put some secret-ass magic marking on them.

(They start to mock-wrestle, laughing. A.J. wakes.)

ABRAMS
Sleeping Beauty's up.

SICKLES
Oh, sorry.

REBO
Are you OK?

A.J.
What time is it?

ABRAMS
It's like two in the afternoon.

A.J.
It is? How'd that happen? Didn't I do roll call?

SICKLES
That was yesterday. You've slept, like, fourteen hours.

REBO
Are you sick or something?

A.J.
No, I . . . I just can't seem to get enough sleep.

REBO
You keep missing meals. You must be starved.

A.J.
No, I've got some power bars around here somewhere.

ABRAMS
When did you last have a meal?

A.J.
I'm fine, I'm fine. Is there any water today?

REBO
Maybe like a bucket's worth.

A.J.
Well, I'm gonna dump it on my head or something.

(She leaves. Little pause. A sense of unease. Sickles starts gathering the cards, which were scattered when they wrestled.)

SICKLES
Have you noticed her nails?

REBO
What do you mean?

SICKLES
She's chewed them down, bitten them, the tips of her fingers are raw.

MANGUS
Really?

ABRAMS
Something's up with her.

MANGUS
She's OK.

REBO
She's the toughest person on this base.

ABRAMS
Was. Not anymore.

MANGUS
I know, she scared the shit out of me when I first got here. So hooah.

SICKLES
Well, yeah, she had to be. Until we showed up, she was the only woman in the unit. It was like months. She must have taken unbelievable shit.

REBO
Well, she never talked about it.

ABRAMS
Of course she didn't, would you?

REBO
She's been first in line every time for anything going out, she's got nothing to prove, / that's for sure—

SICKLES
That doesn't mean that she's doing all that / well—

REBO
Maybe she's just tired.

SICKLES
(End of discussion) Maybe she is.

*(Sickles shuffles the cards in silence for a while.
Charles and Pisoni, men, come in.)*

CHARLES
Strip poker? I'm in.

PISONI
Yeah, we're here to help.

ABRAMS
(Sarcastic, but relieved) Oh, terrific.

CHARLES
You know, you have any problems getting your bras off or /
anything . . .

PISONI
We're trained experts.

REBO
Sickles here has been whipping our butts in five-card draw—

MANGUS
Only 'cause she's been / marking the cards up—

ABRAMS
The most boring poker game / going—

SICKLES
(Objecting) Hey, hey, / hey—

CHARLES
Five-card draw? Who taught you how to play poker? My
granddaddy?

PISONI
It's Texas Hold'em or nothing for me.

REBO
/ You're so butch.

SICKLES
Just 'cause you guys are incapable of mastering the subtleties / of—

PISONI
Where's A.J.?

MANGUS
She's in the shower.

PISONI
(Mock earnest) You think she might need some help / with that?

CHARLES
You mean she's actually conscious? I haven't seen her awake for like a week.

PISONI
OK, let's get down to business, I'll deal. *(Takes the cards)* Who's in?

(Abrams nods.)

MANGUS
I'm out.

REBO
Sure.

SICKLES
If I must.

CHARLES
Seriously though, what's wrong with that bitch?

MANGUS
Don't you mean that whore?

SICKLES
Well, no, if she was a whore she'd have slept with him.

REBO
Whereas, a *bitch*, as we all / know—

ABRAMS
"A whore is someone who sleeps with everyone, / a bitch . . ."

ALL THE WOMEN
(Joining in) "A bitch is someone who sleeps with everyone but you."

PISONI
Bitter, bitter, bitter . . .

CHARLES
(Good-naturedly) Bunch of dykes.

MANGUS
Ah, the third option.

ABRAMS
Gotta be a bitch, a whore, or a dyke.

REBO
"And dykes / aren't worth screwing anyway."

SICKLES AND MANGUS
". . . aren't worth screwing anyway."

PISONI
Are we going to play cards, or what?

SICKLES
What do you mean, "What's wrong with her?"

CHARLES
Forget it, I'm not talking to you people.

SICKLES
No, really.

CHARLES
You'll just jump down my throat.

PISONI
Are we playing cards?

SICKLES
I'm just curious.

CHARLES
It's just, I've noticed, forget it.

ABRAMS
What?

CHARLES
Just, well, last week, she was outside, we sometimes used to go
out the side exit there and smoke together, just bullshit a little,
you know, nothing much, but I hadn't seen her out there lately,
so I was surprised when I got out there and she was there.

*(A.J., unseen by the others, enters close enough to overhear this.
Her hair is wet.)*

It was a few nights ago, really late, and she hadn't seen me, and
I was about to say something, but then I realized she was, like,
banging her head against the wall. Not really hard, but hard
enough to, I could hear it, smack, smack, smack, and I said, I don't
know, something dumb, you know, "That's not going to improve
your looks, you know," or something and she goes—

A.J.
"Like I give a shit about looking good for you."

(Long pause.)

CHARLES
Yeah, that's what you said.

(Awkward silence.)

A.J.

What is it, poker? Don't let me stop the game.

PISONI

Nobody's playing. The cards have been dealt for like a half an hour here.

A.J.

Too busy gossiping.

CHARLES

(To Pisoni) Come on, let's get out of here. They're all on the rag or something.

SICKLES

Chickenshits.

(Pisoni and Charles go.
A.J. looks around at the women with disgust. She lies back down as if to go back to sleep. Pause.)

SICKLES

Five-card draw?

(It doesn't get much of a laugh, and no one wants to play anymore anyway.
End of scene.
Athena enters and speaks to us.)

ATHENA

Remember—boy, those were the days—remember when Achilles was giving everybody the business? Wasn't that something? Achilles and Hector out there swinging away? Spectacular. But of course it was just a matter of time before it all went to hell. 'Cause first Achilles killed Hector and that was an ugly, sordid business, and then that putz Paris killed *him*—Achilles—I still can't believe it. And suddenly it all seemed just so pointless and paltry. A bunch

of guys hacking at each other and yelling. And god, it was so hot.
Dust and sand getting into everything, storms of it blinding you.
The bugs crawling around your sweaty skin beneath all the armor.
Awful. And for what? Can anyone even remember?
The only thing that had a little shine to it anymore was Achilles's
armor. It lay there bouncing light around his empty tent and
waiting. Guys would go in and look at it. They'd see their own
faces in it and think, oh, if only . . . Not that there was much
suspense. Everybody knew. It was Ajax's. He was the next in
line. Sure, he wasn't maybe all that bright, not a sparkling
conversationalist. But, by God, he got the job done.
There was a contest for the armor, votes were cast, and maybe,
well, *maybe* there was some funny business with the ballots, I'm
not saying, but surprise, surprise, he didn't get the armor, Ajax,
no, it went to my boy Odysseus.
And it's not like everybody thought Ajax would be *fine* with that,
it's just that no one expected him to go completely bananas. Well,
they didn't. I did. I knew exactly what would happen. 'Cause a
guy like him, he's got a rudimentary but absolutely infallible
sense of justice and when you take away the thing he's spent his
whole life earning, you better duck. KABLOOEY! He's running
around his tent in circles working up a head of steam that's going
to send him off to kill, well, everybody, it's a long list. But the top
of the list is Agamemnon and Menelaus, joint chiefs of staff, and
Odysseus, of course. But he doesn't just want to kill Odysseus, he
wants to torture him all night, and *then* kill him. Well, I can't have
that. So when night falls, I drive him crazy. I've got him frothing
at the mouth and I point him toward the corral and watch him
run headlong into a flock of sheep and goats and cows. He spins
there, plunging his knife and slicing, blood of his slaughter roping
through the air, falling like veils over him as he works through
the night. Neck by neck, he opens every animal. But when dawn
comes, he's not done yet. He drags some of his victims back into
the tent with him and he begins to torture them. Each one is
another Odysseus. Ajax gets to make Odysseus suffer again and
again. He smiles with every bellow beneath his knife.

(Odysseus enters, tracking Ajax. During this scene, A.J., alone, cleans her rifle.)

ATHENA
What are you doing here, Odysseus?

ODYSSEUS
Athena! Dearest voice in my ear!
I hear you but can't see you.

ATHENA
Are you tracking something?

ODYSSEUS
Well, yes, in a way. But how can this be? It doesn't make sense.
Could it have been the mighty Ajax who did this terrible thing?

ATHENA
What terrible thing is that?

ODYSSEUS
Last night someone fell upon our captured herds and killed them
all. I have followed the trail of blood, but how could it be that the
wet red tracks have led me here?

ATHENA
Ah, but it's true.

ODYSSEUS
He did this?

ATHENA
Yes. You've found your man.

ODYSSEUS
Why?

ATHENA
The armor of Achilles.

ODYSSEUS
Because it went to me instead of him?

ATHENA
It was a night raid and you and the brother generals were the prey
he was stalking.

ODYSSEUS
But he killed the animals.

ATHENA
He thought he was killing you.

ODYSSEUS
Greeks? He was trying to kill *Greeks*?

ATHENA
He got to just outside the tent of the brother commanders.

ODYSSEUS
What stayed his hand?

ATHENA
I did. I flooded his head with madness, dimmed his sight. I reached
down and turned his roaring head to look at the penned beasts and
then just let him loose. I watched him hack away for hours, happy
in blood. Finally he brought the last suffering victims back to his
tent to finish them off. He's completely crazy in there. Want to see?

ODYSSEUS
Oh, no.

ATHENA
(Calling) Ajax? What are you up to? Come on out here!

ODYSSEUS
What are you doing? Please don't call him out.

ATHENA

Why not? It'll be fun. Don't you want to see your enemy drunk
with delusion?

ODYSSEUS

No, Lady. Please. Leave him where he is.

ATHENA

What are you afraid of?

ODYSSEUS

I don't want to look into the eyes of a man who could do what he did.

ATHENA

He won't even see you. He's far gone. I can do that. He's locked
inside the black box of his insanity. Let me show you. *(Calling)*
Ajax! Don't you hear? It's me who is calling you.

(Ajax, bloody, comes out of the tent.)

AJAX

I see you, Daughter of Zeus! I shall glorify you with the bloody
trophies I'm making for you.

ATHENA

You look like you're enjoying yourself. Did you kill them well?

AJAX

No one could have killed them better. Let them try to rob me now!

ATHENA

What about Odysseus?

AJAX

Oh, I saved him for last. He's my favorite. I wanted to take my time
with him.

ATHENA

What are you doing to him?

AJAX

Oh, so many things. Whatever comes to mind.

ATHENA

You go too far, you should let him die.

AJAX

I'll do what you want in other matters. But not this.
This is mine. I shall have my pleasure.

ATHENA

Well, let your pleasure have its way.

AJAX

You know me well, you know I will. *(Looks up at the sky)* No rest
for the weary, back to work.

(He exits into the tent.)

ATHENA

And to think what a sober scout he once was. Now look at him.
Isn't it amazing what the gods can do if we have a mind to?

ODYSSEUS

I can't hate him as he is now, Goddess.
I look at him and I feel nothing but pity.
That could be me.
That could be any one of us.
He's what we all look like to you, I guess.
Flickering shadows, settling dust, that's all we are.
I see that now.

ATHENA

That is what it is to be human. Only the gods are deathless. You
people forget sometimes and talk too loud, step too far. You see
what happens when a man crosses that line. All it takes is a day
to make the difference between you and whatever that is in there.
Remember that.

(End of scene.
Minutes after the poker scene, Pisoni and Charles return to their
quarters. Sergeant is there, listening to "Friends in Low Places.")

PISONI
Dude, my ears are crying, could we give Garth a rest for a minute?
Or at least turn it down?

(He turns the music down.)

SERGEANT
What's wrong with you? This man is a genius.

(He sings along to the song as the scene continues.)

CHARLES
(To Pisoni) It's either that or Drowning Pool these days. His playlist
is like two songs long. Yodeling or screaming.

PISONI
What is it with everybody lately? The whole place is, like, chewing
glass—

SERGEANT
This song was written for me. This is me at my girlfriend's wedding.
Did I tell you? During tour number two, I leave her at home
supposedly planning our wedding.

PISONI
Yeah, you said . . .

SERGEANT
I get the letter: Turns out, she's getting married, but not to me.

CHARLES
Yeah, it stinks, it's the great saga.

SERGEANT
Same time, same day, same fucking *dress*, only difference is the
chump in the tux.

PISONI

Yup. Well, count your blessings, man, she sounds like a real piece of work . . .

SERGEANT

But the best part is I kept my leave. Did I tell you that? I showed up anyway?

CHARLES

Yeah, cut to you in the parking lot of the reception, too drunk to get out of the car.

SERGEANT

(Laughing at himself) I wake up in my fucking truck at two in the morning, everybody's gone. I go and puke in the flower bed.

CHARLES

Well, that showed her.

PISONI

(About the music) Seriously, man, please?

(Sergeant turns off the music.)

SERGEANT

So why're you guys so pissy?

PISONI

Just got back from the lady tent and it's icy cold.

SERGEANT

Maybe you just don't know how to talk to them.

CHARLES

Give me a break, man, like you're making time with anyone.

SERGEANT

I don't have to ask. They're begging for it.

CHARLES
The only way any of them would beg you is if you put a gun to her head.

SERGEANT
You underestimate me.

PISONI
So how do you do it? They just go weak in the knees for all your shiny medals?

SERGEANT
It doesn't hurt, I have to admit, that I outrank 'em all.

CHARLES
So the only action you can get is command rape?

SERGEANT
Hey, don't knock it 'til you've tried it.

CHARLES
(Not sure if he's serious) And you don't worry they'll report on your ass?

SERGEANT
Please. My word against hers and where's her evidence?

PISONI
Come on, we'd know it if you were making time.

SERGEANT
Stealth and cunning, my friends. I know how to put all that training to use, that's all.

PISONI
Who is it?

SERGEANT
One very lucky lady is all I can say.

CHARLES
You're just bullshitting us, right?

PISONI
Right?

(Pause. Sergeant smiles.)

SERGEANT
Yeah. What kind of sergeant would I be if I scored off my own troops?

CHARLES
Well, if you want some action from me, you *are* going to have to put a gun to my head.

PISONI
'Course I'm easy. You just have to offer me candy.

SERGEANT
I'll bear that in mind, Pisoni.
Now here's the real shit.

(He puts on something abrasive and loud, like System of a Down's "B.Y.O.B."
End of scene.
Music continues as we see the women's quarters at night, perhaps just indicated by women lying separately on the floor. Music stops. A.J. snaps awake. She looks around, checks that all the women are asleep, and then carefully sneaks out between the sleeping women. As close to a blackout as possible. We hear voices:)

SERGEANT
You're late, Soldier.

A.J.
I can't do it anymore.

SERGEANT
Of course you can. Look, you're doing it right now.
You know you want it.

A.J.
I don't want anything. Except for this to stop.

SERGEANT
It's your fault. You drive me crazy.

A.J.
Please.

SERGEANT
Please what?

A.J.
Sergeant. Please, Sergeant.

SERGEANT
Please, what?

A.J.
Sergeant. Please, Sergeant. Let. This. Stop.

(End of scene.
Athena enters, then watches as the chorus enters, coming through
the audience. They cautiously approach the tent. Athena speaks
to us.)

ATHENA
Buddies. What does it take to make a buddy turn his back on you
in wartime? Lots. You've got to go pretty freaky. After all, they
came over here with Ajax. They're from his hometown island,
Salamis. What are they going to do if the guy who brought them
here is completely bonkers? They've heard the rumors. This is
bad, bad news.

(Lines should be divided among members of the chorus. Overlapping is fine.)

CHORUS

Do we go in?

How can we?

What if it's true?

What if he's crazy?

I can't believe it.

You saw what he did to the animals?

I'm not going in there.

Is he alone?

She must be in there.

Who?

Tecmessa, his war bride.

You mean she had to watch him do that all night long?

All night long.

She must have been there; where could she go?

How could she get out?

God, to be alone with that.

(They crouch, looking at the tent. A woman patient in civilian dress is talking to a male therapist.)

PATIENT

He doesn't go out. He doesn't talk. Since he got back this time. He's just . . . I mean, it's not like he was ever, you know, Mr. Party, even before. But that was because he was shy. I used to sort of like that. But it's a whole different . . .

THERAPIST

Is he sleeping with you?

PATIENT

Oh, no. He hasn't slept in the same bed with me for, oh, it's been a long time. There are a lot of reasons. Nightmares for one thing, he screams, most nights he has them, but other things . . .

THERAPIST
There are other things keeping him from staying in bed with you?

PATIENT
Well, he's . . . he's got . . . I don't know if I should say this.

THERAPIST
Is he armed?

(She nods.)

Knife? Gun?

PATIENT
He's got a gun. I don't, you know, understand it. Why he can't . . .
I keep telling him you're safe now, it's not, nobody's gonna mess
with you. But he can't, he knows it but he can't *believe* it, you
know? He just, I make him, you know, lock it. At least that. It's got
a safety, and he keeps that on. But I can't, I just can't sleep in the
same bed with that.

THERAPIST
Does he understand?

PATIENT
No. Yes. He does, yes. Sort of. Not really. But yes. I don't know . . .
I don't think he wants to sleep with me anyway, in the same bed.
Not really. I mean, we . . .
(Cries) He doesn't want to be like this. I know that.

*(Tecmessa, spattered with blood, begins crawling out from under
the side of the tent, trying not to make any noise.)*

(Stops crying) He can't even . . . He doesn't want to be left alone
with the children anymore. At first I thought it was because he
didn't think he could handle them, the noise and stuff, but now . . .
now I think it's because he doesn't trust himself with them.
He loves them, but he actually thinks he might . . . I don't know.

We used to be able to like *laugh* about things, you know? Even
after he'd been over there. The first two times, he'd come back,
and you know he was a little different but not, you know, he was
still *him*, the guy I married. We could still have a good time. But
now, no, no, it's just, I don't know . . .

TECMESSA
Homesick comrades, bad news.
The mind of mighty Ajax was broken in the night.

THERAPIST
Do you think you're in danger?

PATIENT
From him?

THERAPIST
Yes.

TECMESSA
He became a madman, sick with blood
Killing and torturing innocent creatures
Thinking he was slaughtering Greeks.

PATIENT
I don't know. I don't know anymore. I started locking my door.
I still can't believe it. I didn't even used to lock my *front* door
sometimes, that's the kind of place we live in. All the time he was
over there, I always felt safe. Now he's home and I'm locking my
door. My bedroom door. Against him.

TECMESSA
Please, please, talk to him.

CHORUS
But how can we speak to him now?
He is untouchable.
He is no longer Ajax.

TECMESSA
No. The storm is past.
The house of his mind flattened
He sits on the wreckage and looks around
At what the tornado left behind.

THERAPIST
Do you think he's in danger?

TECMESSA
He is in awe of the horror of his own sick rage.

PATIENT
Like is he going to hurt himself?

THERAPIST
Yes.

TECMESSA
I talk to him but he can't hear me.

PATIENT
Could be.

TECMESSA
Won't you try to reach him?
Call him back to himself.

PATIENT
Every night I come home from work and I think . . . Maybe this
time, I'll come in and . . . It could happen. I think it every night.
Every night.

THERAPIST
How would you feel?

TECMESSA
He doesn't remember who he is.

PATIENT
Unsurprised.

(Ajax cries out from within the tent.)

TECMESSA
Oh, it's awful.
I've left him alone in there with everything he's done.

(Another cry.
End of scene.
Athena enters and speaks to us.)

ATHENA
I know what you're thinking. But I'm not a sadist. Well, I don't think I am. Of course that's exactly what a sadist would say, right? But I'm not doing anything anyone else wouldn't do if they had the chance. OK, so maybe they don't actually *do* it. But they *think* about doing it.
You do. Even you. You know what I'm talking about. Even if you've never acted on it. The thought has occurred to you. It's like this:

(The women's barracks. Women are lying in rows, occasionally moving in their sleep. Between the rows of women sleeping, men low crawl. Music. A.J. is having a nightmare; she thrashes in her sleep, making sound periodically.)

Some mud creature lifts itself from the silty bottom of your spirit, blinks its mud eyes open and starts to slither up the insides of you, until its scrabbling head is nuzzling up your throat and then birthing itself into your mouth. And then it stands on the plate of your tongue and looks up. It lifts a long, narrow finger, like a tendril from an old potato in the dark, and it puts it there, just there, that hairline crack on the roof of your mouth. And then oh, it's so quiet and so quick, the entrance into you, climbing up the ladders of your nerves until it's in every room of you. It used to be that there was nobody home but you in that head of yours, but now there are two of you. You and it.

And you share the house. You and cruelty.

(The men crawl off, just as A.J. wakes with a gasp and looks around her. The other women continue to sleep.)

So don't get too pleased with yourself. The difference between you and the person who can do unspeakable things? Not so great. Believe me. I can turn you in an instant.

(A.J., panting, continues to sit there, looking into the dark.
End of scene.
Darkness. Two men are talking quietly. We should only barely be able to make out where they are.)

FIRST MAN IN THE DARK
You mad at me about something?

(Pause.)

SECOND MAN IN THE DARK
No.

FIRST MAN IN THE DARK
Seems like, I mean, I don't know—

SECOND MAN IN THE DARK
No, I'm—

FIRST MAN IN THE DARK
You just—

SECOND MAN IN THE DARK
It's not—

FIRST MAN IN THE DARK
You kind of turned away and I was asking you, I guess you didn't hear—

SECOND MAN IN THE DARK
No, I—

FIRST MAN IN THE DARK
And then Eisley came in and I didn't see you for, like, hours, and
I thought, 'cause when I saw you next, you were like . . . Are you
sick or something?

(Pause.)

SECOND MAN IN THE DARK
Yeah.

FIRST MAN IN THE DARK
You're sick?

SECOND MAN IN THE DARK
Why'd you have to do that?

FIRST MAN IN THE DARK
What?

SECOND MAN IN THE DARK
The guy told us everything he knew. He didn't know shit. You know
that. We all knew that. It was pointless.

FIRST MAN IN THE DARK
I didn't know that.

SECOND MAN IN THE DARK
Yes, you did. He was nowhere near the place.

FIRST MAN IN THE DARK
(Emphatic) I did not know that.

SECOND MAN IN THE DARK
He's not the type.

FIRST MAN IN THE DARK
What do you know about "he's not the type"? Like you know that about any of these / people—

SECOND MAN IN THE DARK
I know that, you know that, we all know that. You just know.

FIRST MAN IN THE DARK
(Muttering) Well, I didn't.

SECOND MAN IN THE DARK
It's the kind of thing you're doing all the time now.

FIRST MAN IN THE DARK
Everybody's doing that, you think I'm the only one?

SECOND MAN IN THE DARK
Not everybody, man. Not every / body.

FIRST MAN IN THE DARK
It's common practice. *(Vicious)* Grow up.

(End of scene.
Athena enters and speaks to us.)

ATHENA
You knew he was bonkers because it was all so uncharacteristic of Ajax, the whole business. I mean, it was a night raid. Sneaky stuff. Not like him at all. Because Ajax only ever had one prayer. He prayed for light. There was one time. It was in the thick of battle and Zeus decided to blot the sun out. And as the darkness swallowed the battlefield you could hear Ajax shouting, "Father Zeus, make bright the air! Give us back the day! If it is your pleasure that we must die, let us be killed in the light!" So what was he doing in the dark?

(Green light. Three soldiers, all wearing night-vision goggles,
move in a slow-motion dance, as if underwater, holding rifles.
Sound swarms as they narrate a dream together.)

NVG DREAM SOLDIER A
In my dream, I'm wearing the NVGs

NVG DREAM SOLDIER B
Night Vision / Goggles

NVG DREAM SOLDIER C
and I'm looking out at that sort of aquarium light / you see. The green film over everything?

NVG DREAM SOLDIER A
And the black figures, the black figures, all the living things are—

NVG DREAM SOLDIER C
black figures moving in this green light.

NVG DREAM SOLDIER B
And these sheep,

NVG DREAM SOLDIER A
there are all these sheep, you know?

NVG DREAM SOLDIER B
And they're looking at me and they've got / this fear,

NVG DREAM SOLDIER A
they're backing into each other and panicking,

NVG DREAM SOLDIER C
and I'm moving through them

NVG DREAM SOLDIER A
and they're just stampeding each other / to get away from me and all the time I'm feeling this kind of *rage*

NVG DREAM SOLDIER B
to get away from me

NVG DREAM SOLDIER C
and all the time I'm feeling this / kind of *rage*

NVG DREAM SOLDIER B
this *rage* moving up inside me

NVG DREAM SOLDIER A
and I've got my M16

NVG DREAM SOLDIER B
and I begin butting / at them,

NVG DREAM SOLDIER A
bam, bam, bam, but it's not doing it for me,

NVG DREAM SOLDIER C
bam, bam, bam,

NVG DREAM SOLDIER A
you know and then I'm shooting / into the herd,

NVG DREAM SOLDIER C
bam, bam, bam,

NVG DREAM SOLDIER A
just shooting and even then, it's like I can't / kill enough

NVG DREAM SOLDIER C
it's like I can't kill / enough of them,

NVG DREAM SOLDIER B
it's like I can't kill enough it's not / *feeling* like—I mean,

NVG DREAM SOLDIER C
it's not *feeling* like—I mean, there's just not / enough

NVG DREAM SOLDIER B
just not / enough *real death*

NVG DREAM SOLDIER C
just not enough *real death* that I can *feel*,

NVG DREAM SOLDIER A
it's just not enough, no matter how much I shoot.

NVG DREAM SOLDIER B
And the blood, because of the goggles, / it's not the

NVG DREAM SOLDIER C
it's not the right color,

NVG DREAM SOLDIER B
and I can't *hear* everything right either,

NVG DREAM SOLDIER A
it's like when you're in a firefight and you can't hear everything
right because it's all just this storm?

NVG DREAM SOLDIER C
And the anger,

NVG DREAM SOLDIER B
I don't know where it comes from but / it just doesn't stop,

NVG DREAM SOLDIER C
I don't know where it comes / from

NVG DREAM SOLDIER A
But it just doesn't / stop,

NVG DREAM SOLDIER B
it gets deeper / even,

NVG DREAM SOLDIER C
it just doesn't stop,

NVG DREAM SOLDIER A
I'm wading through the bodies I'm making,

NVG DREAM SOLDIER B
the only thing that slows me down is reloading / and even that

NVG DREAM SOLDIER C
and even that,

NVG DREAM SOLDIER B
And then it's like I don't even have to reload

NVG DREAM SOLDIER A
I can do it without the bullets stopping

NVG DREAM SOLDIER C
I can do it without / stopping.

NVG DREAM SOLDIER B
Because the bullets never stop.

NVG DREAM SOLDIER C
And even while I'm doing it,

NVG DREAM SOLDIER A
even in the middle of this fucking storm of whatever I'm in the
middle of, there's this voice that's saying to me, "What are you
doing? What the fuck are you / doing?"

NVG DREAM SOLDIER B
"What are you / doing?"

NVG DREAM SOLDIER C
"What the fuck are you doing?"

NVG DREAM SOLDIER A
And I can hear it, it's me saying that,

NVG DREAM SOLDIER B
but I don't care.

NVG DREAM SOLDIER A
I'm going, "This is what has to happen."

NVG DREAM SOLDIER C
So I'm making it happen.

NVG DREAM SOLDIER A
Because that's what I'm supposed to do.

NVG DREAM SOLDIER B
And the whole time, I'm thinking,

NVG DREAM SOLDIER C
/ so this *has* to be a dream, right?

NVG DREAM SOLDIER A
so this *has* to be a dream, right?

NVG DREAM SOLDIER C
I'm going to wake up from this.

NVG DREAM SOLDIER B
And I know, or I think I know that I'm dreaming.

NVG DREAM SOLDIER A
But also,

NVG DREAM SOLDIER C
and this is the thing,

NVG DREAM SOLDIER A
I'm also thinking,

NVG DREAM SOLDIER B
oh, God, when I wake up and look around at what I've done, this is
all going to be so bad,

NVG DREAM SOLDIER C
so incredibly bad,

NVG DREAM SOLDIER B
in the light of day, you know?

NVG DREAM SOLDIER A
Like the dream is also the truth, what I'm actually *doing*. I'm not
only dreaming this but I'm also actually doing it.

NVG DREAM SOLDIER C
It feels real.

NVG DREAM SOLDIER B
And I'm thinking, when I come to, / you know,

NVG DREAM SOLDIER A
when I come to, you know,

NVG DREAM SOLDIER C
when I come to, you know,

NVG DREAM SOLDIER A
when I take off the goggles,

NVG DREAM SOLDIER C
this is going to be bad.

VOICE
And that's when you wake up?

NVG DREAM SOLDIER A
I guess.

(End of scene.
Mangus enters and speaks to us.)

MANGUS
It was a bad time. Lots of mortars coming in, we couldn't figure
out where they were coming from. We'd go take out a house,
two houses, three, sweep through a whole neighborhood, pick
up dozens of weapons, arrest several suspects, think we must've
solved the problem that day and then that night we're getting
pounded again. People are going a little nuts. They're talking
about just taking out the whole village, like they could just kill
everybody, nuke them, you know. It's how people get.
And then A.J. goes out on a routine mission . . . She's driver for a
team that's going out again, house to house, watching from the

Humvee while the fire team goes into a house, kicks the door down. Suddenly two things happen: Something goes off inside the house, some sort of explosion, and at the same time a sniper starts firing on the Humvee. The other soldier, the gunner in the Humvee, is hit right away, they take the head off him, so she's alone with the vehicle. Now she's under fire, calling some help to the area and trying to get her sights on where the sniper fire is coming from, but also driving the Humvee to some kind of protection so she can be there if anyone comes out of the house. She gets the Humvee to this wall near the house and that's when the house just explodes, completely goes up, there's just no way anyone in there could survive the blast. What's incredible is that she survived it, but that's just because she got herself behind the wall. So what's she going to do? The understandable thing would be to just split, get the fuck out of there, let people come back and deal with the situation later, but she does this thing, which is that she goes into the burning building and drags out every single body from there, just in case somebody's alive. Nobody is, but she keeps going back in to find them and bring them out and she's still under fire while she's doing it. It isn't until she's bringing the last body out that she finally gets relief from another unit that comes in and takes out the sniper and takes over recovering the bodies. Now soldiers in this unit have done some remarkable things, heroic stuff, you know, it happens here just like anywhere else. But no one's ever done anything like that.
Back at the base, she's called into the sergeant's office.

(Mangus exits as A.J. enters. She stands at parade rest, looking out. Sergeant stands. Pause.)

SERGEANT
Been a long time since I've seen you alone.
Cleaned yourself up, I see.

A.J.
Yes, Sergeant.

SERGEANT
I thought you'd come in here looking like a little blood-and-guts
girl Rambo. Rambette.

A.J.
No, Sergeant.

SERGEANT
I'm so proud of you, Rambette. You're my little hero.
Come here. Let me smell you.

A.J.
Sergeant?

SERGEANT
Come here, Rambette.

A.J.
I . . .

SERGEANT
Get your ass over here, Soldier.

*(A.J. takes a step toward Sergeant. He grabs her and spins her
around so that he has her pinned from behind, clamping her
throat with his hand, breathing into the back of her neck.)*

Yeah, that's it, that's the smell I miss so much.

A.J.
This isn't what I deserve.

SERGEANT
Sergeant.

A.J.
Sergeant. This isn't what I deserve, Sergeant.

SERGEANT

Huh. So you really thought I was going to pin a medal on your tit? Is that what you thought when you came in here?

A.J.

No, Sergeant, not you.

SERGEANT

Thought you rated a special little something.

A.J.

No, Sergeant, I know I don't rate anything with / you.

SERGEANT

And you were right. 'Cause I've missed you so much all this time you've been holding out on me, and when I heard that you alone of all those fine men walked out of there, I said to myself, "Hallelujah, she's coming back to me."

(He releases her. She holds her throat, doesn't look at him. He unzips his fly.)

Take your pants down.

A.J.

(Disbelieving) Sergeant?

SERGEANT

Pants down.

(Neither moves.)

Off.

(Suddenly A.J. goes for the door. He has been expecting this, swiftly grabs her from behind, takes her pants down, and enters her from behind. It is fast and brutal and over in seconds. She makes no sound at all, staring out, simply enduring it. He zips his pants up.)

Well done, Rambette. Welcome home. Isn't life wonderful?

(A.J. numbly pulls her pants up and gets herself together.)

Dismissed.

(A.J. is suddenly by herself. She has some difficulty breathing. As her breathing evens out, it becomes a sort of panting. She gathers her strength. The other women enter and fill in behind her, panting in unison. A.J. begins a ritual invocation of Kali, Hindu Goddess of Death and Destruction. The women dance. The women chant with her on the word "Kali.")

A.J.
KALI, you, the Devourer,
KALI, you, Time!
All things are brought forth by you, KALI!
All things are destroyed by you, KALI!
In the Mouth of Creation, KALI!
We shudder to look upon Mother End, KALI!
BRING YOURSELF FORTH IN ME, KALI!
GODDESS, LET ME SWING YOUR BLOODY AX!

(The entire company of soldiers is now onstage, men and women, behind A.J. They chant together, performing a Māori haka, or war dance. The dance ends in a shout and a blackout. In the darkness we hear panting and unidentifiable cries, violence being done. Sudden silence.
End of scene.
We are at the closed tent again. Tecmessa speaks to the chorus.)

TECMESSA
It's time. You must look at this.
He can't be left alone with it anymore.

(She lifts the tent flaps to reveal Ajax, covered in blood.)

AJAX
Look hard, Fellas,
Here's your old hero

Slick with the blood of farm animals.
What a joke.

CHORUS
Oh, Sir.
How has it come to this?

AJAX
I listened to my father telling war stories all my life
How he came out here and got himself some glory
So I came back to do him proud.
Oh, I did. I did for a while there.
The great warrior
Second only to Achilles
Bulwark of the Greeks
The man who rescued the fallen Patroclus
And went one-on-one against great Hector
Hero of the battle of the ships
One mighty tale after another
I show up in all of them.
What was it all for, if this is where I end up?
I'm ashamed of myself.
So are you. I can see that.

CHORUS
What can we do for you, Sir?

AJAX
Kill me.

(A.J. has entered and sits on the ground, covered in blood. Mangus approaches her.)

A.J.
Who is it?

MANGUS
It's me.

A.J.
Who?

MANGUS
Connie.

A.J.
What do you want?

MANGUS
I just want to know.

A.J.
What?

MANGUS
Why'd you do it?
I thought you loved animals.

A.J.
I do. I did. I do.

MANGUS
You've wiped out his whole flock.

A.J.
I did?

MANGUS
What was that for? What did that shepherd ever do to you?

A.J.
Thought they were someone else.

MANGUS
Who?

A.J.
A whole lot of someone else.

MANGUS
I don't understand.

A.J.
I don't either.

MANGUS
What happened to you?

A.J.
I don't know. I just became . . .

MANGUS
What?

A.J.
While I wasn't looking, I went off and became a person who could do this.

AJAX
Where is my son?

TECMESSA
I sent him away.

AJAX
Why?

TECMESSA
When you were at the peak of the madness, I thought, I thought you might . . .

AJAX
Oh. Yes.

TECMESSA
Did I do wrong?

AJAX
No, he wasn't safe with me.

MANGUS
You're in so much trouble.

A.J.
More than you know.

AJAX
No one is safe with me.

MANGUS
I don't know who you are.

AJAX
Least of all, me.

A.J.
Neither do I.

(Ajax and A.J. stare out.)

AJAX
Where can a man run to when the person he flees is himself?
/ Look what I've done.

A.J.
Look what I've done.

MANGUS
Everybody's freaked. No one knows what to do with you.

A.J.
Well, when they figure it out, they should let me know.

AJAX
How can I ever live past this?

A.J.
'Cause I'm stumped, gotta say.

AJAX
I was so very busy with my knife.
Somewhere in this mess of bodies
Is the man I once was.
I killed him too while I was at it.

A.J.
Huh.
It's just meat after a while.
The only difference is there's meat with a pulse and meat without
a pulse.

(She puts a finger on her neck.)

I've still got one. Banging away in there.
For a while anyway.

MANGUS
They'll send you home. It'll be OK.

A.J.
Yeah, that'll work. I can just see it.
Hey, Mom, hey, Dad! Guess what I did in the war?
They'll be so proud.

AJAX
The Mighty Ajax.
When I am remembered now.
It will be for this. This.

A.J.

No, I ain't going anywhere. This is where this ends.

AJAX

I cannot escape this.

What can I do?

No, there is only one choice.

If you can't live well, you have to die well.

I'll take this thing into my own hands.

What am I waiting for?

TECMESSA

For me, you can wait for me.

Remember me and so remember yourself.

I did not choose this life.

I was once a free woman.

But that was before my parents died,

And my country fell to you.

Then you took me because you could.

But I have made the best of it.

And you have been my only protection.

In return I have given you my life and my loyalty.

I have shared your bed

Given you pleasure there

And borne you a son.

Have you thought of what will become of us without you?

Doesn't it matter to you that we would be slaves?

Haven't we earned the right to your care?

Think on us.

You have known kindness from me.

That should mean something if you are a man of integrity.

A man who doesn't value the kindness he's received is not worthy

of such tenderness to begin with.

AJAX

I'm beyond such things.

A.J.
What's the point of me at this point?

AJAX
Death is all I want now.

A.J.
You got any bullets?

(Mangus shakes her head.)

AJAX
Just to dip this red horror in the black stream of nothingness.

A.J.
I'm out.

AJAX
Hermes, dear messenger, come to me now.
Your shining helmet alive with the blur of wings
Your gray eyes searching out the dark corners
Let me take your cool hand
And follow in your swift flight
Down to invisibility.

A.J.
It's time for me to go.

AJAX
Tell my brother to see to things.
Give him the child.
Let him rear him in the shadow of me.
Let my son be like me in all ways except in luck.
In that, let him be my superior.
Sweet darkness.
I am longing for you.

TECMESSA
No, Sir, / not you.

CHORUS
No, Sir, / please.

A.J.
Help me go. I gotta get out of here.

MANGUS
No, I just can't, A.J. . . . . I'm sorry.

TECMESSA
Please don't leave / me.

AJAX
Quiet, woman. Let me think.

(Ajax exits back into the tent while the chorus and Tecmessa disperse but stay onstage, watching the tent. Sound of sirens.)

MANGUS
The MPs are coming.

A.J.
Well, then you gotta do something for me.

MANGUS
What?

(A.J. fumbles under her clothes for a photograph; it's laminated, a small school photograph. She wipes blood off of it.)

A.J.
Keep it for me.

MANGUS
What is this?

A.J.
It's my kid.

MANGUS
Your kid?

A.J.
My son.

MANGUS
You never said you had a son.

A.J.
He doesn't know. My sister's got him. Tells him he's hers. It was better that way. But he's mine.

MANGUS
What do you want me to do?

A.J.
Tell him. Tell him that . . .

MANGUS
What? Tell him what?

A.J.
Tell him that I had that photograph of him on me. OK? That's all he needs to know. Tell him that's the only thing personal I was carrying. It's all I ever carried. Just him.
OK?

MANGUS
Yeah. Got it.

(Two MPs enter and stand watching; one has handcuffs.)

A.J.
You tell him that. Swear to me.

MANGUS
I swear.

A.J.
OK.

(She starts over to the MPs, who will take her off.)

MANGUS
OK.

(Ajax comes out of the tent to address the chorus and Tecmessa.)

AJAX
Nothing surprises me anymore.
Things want to come to light.
They rise like fish from deep black water
The circles of their mouths working
They stare at us.
They dare us to look back at them
Before they fall away into invisibility again.
The mind of the world moves like the beam of a lighthouse.
In time, everything is laid bare.
At last I can see clearly.
I'm going now to wash the blood off of me
and bury my sword for good.
I'll put everything away.
My anger
My glory
My old-fashioned sense of justice.
It's time to stow that ancient gear and get on with things.
Everything gives way eventually.
Up in the northern mountains in the early spring
the sound of the ice cracking is like gunshots
Cannons echoing in the ravines

Until the new water pelts down from the cold heights
into the sea-searching rivers.
No one has to worry about me anymore.
When my brother comes
Tell him I've finally sorted myself out
And I'm on my way home.

*(He exits. The chorus and Tecmessa watch him go. The chorus
speaks to us, dividing the lines among them.)*

CHORUS
How many years have I been out here in this desert?
My life plays itself out
Shimmering in the heat
I hear the distant buzz of the television you are watching
The jumping square of light
Tiny loudness
Yammering in the other room of the world
Speaking to you.
While all your life continues
Mine stays here.
Do you remember why you sent me here?
It was something that you wanted done.
But not so much that you would do it yourself.
I'm the one you sent.
And so I live here inside this impossible job
The job of war
It is, you say, never-ending.
And so I dream
And when I dream I dream of:
Greenness
Fragrant
Cool shade
My body naked, but not punished
Naked but not cringing
Naked for love

Love
   Silence
      Kindness
         Safety
A clear horizon on a country road going no place bad.
But then I wake up and I'm here again
Squinting in the blinding light
Waiting for the mortars to fall
The bomb to burst under my wheels
The sniper fire from the rooftops.
Waiting for the worst to happen.
Inside the war you sent me to
All those years ago.

(They exit.
End of scene.
Mangus enters and speaks to us.)

MANGUS

Why do we fight? I don't mean, you know, are we fighting for the
oil or democracy or Diet Coke or whatever. None of that is why
I'm fighting. I don't think it's why anyone's fighting. But then why
am I? I've had to think about it. I've had the time.
There's this thing that happens with time in Iraq. It just doesn't
go by. When you're being mortared, the seconds happen so slowly
that they expand to where you can walk around in each one of
them like it's a cathedral. Each detail is important—the angle of
my hand on the wheel, the shape of the white cloud of the blast
twisting up from the road—it's all there to be looked at, thought
about, as you circle every little thing of it.
And then there's the rest of the time. Days when nothing's ticking.
The clock forgets how to move. So you think about your life, how
long you've been here, how long you've got to go, and how maybe
you're never going to leave this place or even this particular long,
long second of your life because the time just fucking won't go
by. So what's your life, measured up against that eternity? And

what are you, measured up against the size of the desert? You and all your buddies and your guns when all that sand stretches out in front of you? Just another army. Just another beetle crawling across it all. And that's about how long it's going to take. And that's about how much it'll matter. So what the fuck are we doing? Why are we fighting this thing? I finally figured it out. It's just brothers and sisters. You're fighting for the soldier who fights beside you and that soldier is fighting for you. And I think it's been that way since people first picked up stones and started throwing them at each other. You might hate the son of a bitch when nothing's shaking, but still you love the soldier who fights next to you. You will lay down your life for the person who would lay down their life for you.

TEUCER
(Offstage) Where is my brother?

MANGUS
That's all I got.

TEUCER
(Offstage) I have come for my brother.

MANGUS
So when you betray that trust?

(Mangus shakes her head and exits. Teucer enters. Tecmessa and the chorus enter, having heard his call.)

CHORUS
Teucer, you've come at last.
Your brother has gone.

TEUCER
Gone?

CHORUS
Off. Out.

TEUCER
Where?

CHORUS
To bury his sword, he said.

TEUCER
Then it's over for him.

CHORUS
Why?

TEUCER
If he'd only stayed with his people. Not gone off alone. The curse would have passed and he could have gone on with his life.

CHORUS
He is cursed?

TEUCER
Athena. She drove him mad and even when he came out of it he was still under her thumb. But only for the day. By sunset she would have lost interest, left him alone. Her rage is fleeting.

CHORUS
But he seemed so calm.

TEUCER
It's only because he knew at last. No more hesitation.

(Tecmessa has been watching all this.)

TECMESSA
(Suddenly understanding) He had decided to die.

CHORUS
And he had to get away from all of us to do it.

TECMESSA
We have to find him.

CHORUS
If we can stay his hand—

TEUCER
Keep him breathing until sunset.

TECMESSA
Just an hour more.

CHORUS
By sunset he'll be free.

CHORUS
Just an hour more.

TEUCER
Just a single brick can prop open the iron door.

(They head off in different directions to search.
End of scene.
Ajax and A.J. enter with their weapons; a sword for Ajax, an M16
for A.J. They are calm. They should not look at each other but they
are together, perhaps sitting side by side or back-to-back. Ajax is
sharpening his sword and then propping it up at an angle, the hilt
buried in the sand. A.J. is cleaning an M16 and loading it. They
speak easily, as if as one person.)

AJAX
In the end of it, shame

A.J.
Shame is just one of the things I say goodbye to. / There is also

AJAX
There is also the river I fished that morning,

A.J.
tossing the light around on its surface as it rushed over everything
it contained. / And

AJAX
And there is the smell of the fire cooking what you will eat.

A.J.
There is also the sound a baby makes when it wakes up in the
morning / and nothing is wrong.

AJAX
and nothing is wrong. There is the day I saw hail

A.J.
Hail / for the first time

AJAX
for the first time

A.J.
and my mother put a battered ball of whiteness in my mouth,

AJAX
so I could taste,

A.J.
so I could taste, she said, / the sky.

AJAX
The sky.

A.J.
These things are also part of me.

AJAX
These things are also true. I thought

A.J.
I thought

AJAX
I thought I was protecting them

A.J.
I was protecting them.

AJAX
But they

A.J.
But they were protecting me. I lose them now

AJAX
I lose them now

A.J.
I lose them now

A.J. AND AJAX
in order to keep them.

(Ajax stands, about to jump on the sword. A.J. puts the gun in her mouth. They both inhale. Sudden blackout. Silence.
End of scene.
Lights up on an empty stage. Mangus enters and speaks to us.
During the following, two soldiers come in and plant the barrel of A.J.'s rifle in the sand, her helmet is placed on the butt, her boots on the ground beneath.)

MANGUS
I don't know how she got the gun. But she was pretty canny. And nothing was going to keep her from doing what she'd decided to do.

The ironic thing was she only had a few weeks left on her tour. The war was over for her. It wasn't long until she would have been home free. The rest of us had months to go. We'd envied her. Maybe that's what made us so blind.

(All the American soldiers assemble for the memorial service. Heat. Everyone stands.)

CHAPLAIN
We're here today to mourn the death of a soldier.

(He begins to quietly intone the 46th Psalm. Athena appears and speaks to us over the prayer.)

God is our refuge and strength, a very present help in trouble.

ATHENA
Well, of course, it's different in my play.

CHAPLAIN
/ Therefore will not we fear, though the earth be removed, and though the mountains be carried into the midst of the sea;

ATHENA
Ajax kills himself about halfway through and the rest of the thing is about everybody wrangling over what to do with his corpse.

CHAPLAIN
/ Though the waters thereof roar and be troubled, though the mountains shake with the swelling thereof. Selah.

ATHENA
Of course, he's a suicide, which is always a tricky business.

CHAPLAIN
/ There is a river, the streams whereof shall make glad the city of God, the holy place of the tabernacles of the most High.

ATHENA

But let's not forget: This is a guy who very nearly killed his commanders in chief and a fellow hero of Greece, Odysseus.

CHAPLAIN

/ God is in the midst of her; she shall not be moved: God shall help her, and that right early.

ATHENA

By anybody's standards, this isn't your garden-variety hero.

CHAPLAIN

/ The heathen raged, the kingdoms were moved: He uttered his voice, the earth melted.

ATHENA

Menelaus and Agamemnon are determined that, far from honoring him with a funeral, the body of the guy who'd just tried to kill them shouldn't even be buried.

CHAPLAIN

/ The Lord of hosts is with us; the God of Jacob is our refuge. Selah.

ATHENA

It all comes down to Teucer, Ajax's bastard stepbrother. He's got to take everyone on.

CHAPLAIN

/ Come, behold the works of the Lord, what desolations he hath made in the earth.

ATHENA

Teucer pleads with Menelaus and Agamemnon to let him bury his brother as a fitting end for a man who had been, up until the night before, the right arm of the Greek force. They shout him down, threaten him, sneer at him. It's an ugly business, this haggling, it goes on for a long time and neither side comes off looking all that good.

CHAPLAIN
He maketh wars to cease unto the end of the earth; he breaketh
the bow, and cutteth the spear in sunder; he burneth the chariot
in the fire.

ATHENA
And as the men argue, Tecmessa and Ajax's little son cower next
to Ajax's body, as if, even dead, the great man might be able to
protect them.

CHAPLAIN
Be still, and know that I am God:

ATHENA
But then the strangest thing happens.

CHAPLAIN
I will be exalted among the heathen,

ATHENA
Odysseus, Ajax's greatest enemy, shows up.

CHAPLAIN
I will be exalted in the earth.

ATHENA
And he makes an eloquent plea for Ajax's burial.

CHAPLAIN
The Lord of hosts is with us;

ATHENA
He says it's what a hero, however flawed, is owed.

CHAPLAIN
the God of Jacob is our refuge. Selah.

ATHENA

And, with an ill grace, the generals bow to his persuasion.
They tell Teucer he can bury his brother.

CHAPLAIN

Does anyone have anything they want to say?

SICKLES

Listen, I'm just going to talk about what I think we're all feeling,
which is, yeah, loss, sadness, I guess, but it's also . . . I feel, I think
we all feel, betrayed. 'Cause, let's face it, when you kill yourself . . .
We've all thought about it. We all have. It's one way, an easy way,
out of a bad situation. But you don't do it because it's not just you
you're destroying. It's everybody. It's a selfish act.
And I'm supposed to, what? *Honor* that? I can't do that. I hate it.
I hate the whole thing. I don't know. And I guess I hate her for
making me look at it.

PISONI

Well, we have to look at it. She was one of us. But she did this
anyway. That's the kind of pain she was in. There must have
been a thousand times she tried to signal that pain. We didn't
see it because we didn't want to. To say that her killing herself is
a betrayal of any of us just keeps us from seeing how much her
killing herself is about our betrayal of her. We should have paid
better attention. She was one of us and we didn't take care of her.
Yeah, it's hot, and yeah, I don't want to think about this. But we're
the only ones who can. No one back home will do this for her, they
just don't know. We do. So let's give her that. It's too late and it's
not enough and she won't get anything out of it. But it's all we can
do for her now. And it's all we can do for ourselves.

ATHENA

And, at the end of the play, everybody leaves and Teucer asks the
chorus to help him dig the grave.

(Sergeant calls the company to attention. "Taps" is played, during which Athena exits while the rest of the company stands. When "Taps" is finished, the company exits, leaving Mangus, who turns to us.)

MANGUS

A.J. put her sister down as the next of kin. The two officers who went to notify her had a hell of a time with that detail. Apparently the sister wouldn't let them in the place. She slammed the door in their faces and kept screaming that they had the wrong house. They keep knocking but she throws the locks and goes on yelling at them. They're standing there trying to figure out what to do when they see this little boy in the window. He's motioning them around to the side. They go to the back door and knock. He opens the door. He's got these huge old eyes, he's like, six. Five or six. They don't know it, but he looks just like A.J. He lets them in and he turns and calls, "Mommy, the war is in the kitchen. They want to apologize."

I'm going to go out there. If I ever get out of this desert. I'm going to take myself out there.

I want to meet that kid.

END OF PLAY

Kissing the Floor

For Jane Lincoln Taylor

Introduction

I've been looking over a couple of years' worth of notes on Sophocles's *Antigone*, trying to track the process that led to my odd response to it, and I ran across a Muriel Rukeyser poem called "Easter Eve 1945," a fragment of which I had copied into my notebook:

> Whatever world I know shines ritual death,
> wide under this moon they stand gathering fire,
> fighting with flame, stand fighting in their graves.
> All shining with life as the leaf, as the wing shines,
> the stone deep in the mountain, the drop in the green wave.
> Lit by their energies, secretly, all things shine.
> Nothing can black that glow of life.[1]

Perhaps I have misread this poem, but what it conjures whole for me is the mind of Antigone, her obsession with the death in life, the life in death. Late in the play I have my character Annie say to her sister, "Just listen. Ah, God, it's here, they're all here, shining in the air like mist. Death is the element we live in, it's so obvious. Even the most commonplace things are speaking to us, always, and always about the dead, murmuring constantly, these walls are singing, the filaments in the lights are humming with it, you just

---

1. Muriel Rukeyser, "Easter Eve 1945," in *Out of Silence: Selected Poems*, ed. Kate Daniels (Evanston, IL: Northwestern University Press, 1994).

have to listen. Everything is always telling us about the beauty of death, the beauty of the dead."

Which is precisely what has always been the problem with Antigone for me.

But then I suspect that from the start Antigone has made the rest of us feel uncomfortable. Such exemplars of radical idealism always do. Antigone is, after all, the woman who chooses to give up her life for a gesture. She dies because she has defied the king, her uncle Creon, by ritually throwing dirt on the corpse of her brother to whom the king has forbidden burial. She has much to live for—she is loved not only by her sister but by the young prince Haimon, Creon's son, who expects to marry her before she decides to sacrifice her life by committing what she knows will be a capital crime. She maintains that any alternative is unthinkable because not to bury her brother would be an offense to the gods and would relegate him to an eternal spiritual limbo. Her rigidity of principle is mostly admirable when she is faced with her uncle's secular political arguments, but it is unnerving when she is confronted by those who love her and are simply begging her to embrace life instead of death. Her sister Ismene in particular makes a singularly wrenching plea, which Antigone harshly mocks as cowardly. However much one may respect such a character, she doesn't inspire affection. Probably because she doesn't seem quite human. Antigone's name, which can translate to something like "instead of" or "anti" generation, is apt. With her death she effectively brings her own family line to an end. She forgoes procreation and becomes a bride of Hades when she chooses to bestow her life and love on a dead brother rather than on a living husband. But she is very much her father's daughter, and Oedipus's grotesque distortion of the generative process through parricide and incest is her blighted legacy.

And then there's her brother.

What seemed clear to me as I thought over the Sophocles play in translation was just how morally compromised Polynices is in that text. By anyone's standards, Polynices is an ethical nightmare—a traitor who would rather destroy his own city than allow his brother to continue ruling it. When Antigone treats that treason as irrelevant, and indeed goes so far as to die to protect her brother's spirit from what she believes it would suffer if his corpse lay unburied, she is pursuing a logic to its end in a way few mortals could manage. We never realize what ethical relativists we are until we are faced with a person who is blind to context and deals only in abstract ideals.

Kissing the Floor is the ninth play I wrote directly inspired by a Greek text, and though it wanders farther from its source than any of the work I'd done up to that point, it is still along the lines of a modern rendering of the Sophocles. I've always approached the adaptation of Greek plays aslant, privileging intuition over intellect and allowing the plays to disturb and disarm me before I make any moves to find my own way in.

I have found time and again that there is an emotional knot or psychological conundrum at the heart of each of these plays, some fundamental mystery. That knot is probably different for each reader, but until it's discovered, there's no point in putting pen to paper. With the Greeks, I'm always looking for the thing I can't understand or that gives me bad dreams. Like the grain of sand the oyster makes into a pearl, there must be the necessary problem it takes the writing of a play to resolve. In this case, what kept me up at night was my ambivalence toward the title character, my suspicion about her motives, and my discomfort with her ultimate decision. I began to have some insight into her character when my own father died and I realized how much of my life was now spent with my ear to the ground, metaphorically speaking, constantly in conversation with a man whose responses to my questions I could no longer hear. I felt a kind of panic as I realized that with every day he became more and more my own creation as the reality of him slid further into the past. A growing certainty that I would never see him again, not only in life but after life, made the loss just that much harder to bear than it had been when I didn't have to think through what I really believed death must be. It was in this state of mind that I found myself beginning to understand Antigone at last. And when the image of a woman kneeling on the floor to tap in Morse code to her dead father came to me, I trusted it.

Then the problem was what to do about the dead brother. It seemed clear that Paul, as he became, should be alive because I wanted the siblings to be able to talk. But more importantly, I wanted to put the same kind of pressure on my Annie as Sophocles puts on his Antigone; I needed to test my character's devotion and sense of duty to her brother as severely as he does. Was there any human action universally recognized as so contemptible that a sister's loyalty to a brother who committed such an act would be morally debatable? I decided there was.

I let Ismene become the person telling the story, framing the play for us, since it was her agonized impotence to prevent her sister's tragedy that always moved me most in the Sophocles. I dispensed almost completely with Creon, feeling that his argument had already been thoroughly explored in other adaptations—Jean Anouilh's comes to mind. A trace of Creon's secular and rational authority remains in the figure of Brennan, the man who runs the island prison where Paul is held. I wanted someone older than the siblings and outside the family to be able to see their actions objectively. He functions a bit like the chorus in the Sophocles; he is our way in, someone able to speak for us and articulate the issues clearly. I also liked the idea of having some figure tell the story of Oedipus and Jocasta, so I recruited (and resurrected) Polynices's brother, Eteocles (Eddie), simply to walk onstage and address us directly as Paul's identical twin. I find it theatrically satisfying to see the actor playing Paul transform into Eddie. Each of these stunted souls is the other's fraternal counterpart.

As these notions fell into place, the play began to take on an idiomatic life, and fragments of it started to show up in my dreams. Images of Depression-era America kept occurring as I wrote, and when I happened upon James Thurber's 1934 piece "Lenox 1734" from the New Yorker archive, about the abandoned and dilapidated Pulitzer mansion, once so splendid, now the home of mice and pigeons, with its "gray and dismal" ghostly crystal chandeliers, the world of this play bloomed whole for me.

I'm always grateful to the Greeks for their insistence on posing the hardest questions. They force us to consider the mystery of blood kinship and ask: What do we owe each other? How far must that obligation and loyalty extend? Past what is unforgivable? Past death? Does it never quit? Does the demand of blood beseech us without end, even as we peer blindly into that darkness which is the darkness that awaits us all? The character of Antigone still haunts and disturbs me, but now she is all too familiar, the sister I never had, speaking to me just out of earshot. She's impossible to ignore because now I think I know what she's likely to be saying. But it seems she's with me for good and I will always be listening for her, even when I've successfully silenced her.

Production History

The world premiere of *Kissing the Floor* was produced by One Year Lease Theater Company (Ianthe Demos, Artistic Director) at Theater Row in New York City on February 23, 2023. It was directed by Ianthe Demos. The set design was by James Hunting, the costume design was by Kenisha Kelly, the lighting design was by Driscoll Otto, and the sound design was by Brendan Aanes. The assistant director was Nadja Leonhard-Hooper, the movement director was Natalie Lomonte, the production manager was Omri Bareket, and the production stage managers were Vanessa Rebeil and Melissa Sparks. The cast was:

IZZY	Akyiaa Wilson
ANNIE	Christina Bennett Lind
PAUL/EDDIE	Leon Ingulsrud
BRENNAN	Rinde Eckert

Characters

IZZY, thirties

ANNIE, Izzy's somewhat younger sister

PAUL, Izzy's somewhat older brother

EDDIE, Paul's twin

BRENNAN, Irish accent, fifties or sixties

Place

Izzy's head.

An island prison.

A radically dilapidated nineteenth-century mansion.

Time

Depression-era America.

Set and Staging

The set should be as minimal as possible, with places indicated principally through light and sound. (For instance, the entire kitchen scene at the end can be staged using only sound effects.)

It may be that the only pieces needed are a table and a few chairs. The play should have the fluid, surprising feel of memory and nothing should impede the flow of storytelling.

That same seamless quality should be true of the staging, one scene bleeding into another without distinct breaks. Since the play is taking place in Izzy's head, she might be onstage and watching through much of it until the last scene between Paul and Annie, when they should be alone. Eddie should also have the stage to himself when he appears.

Note on the Text

A slash (/) indicates the point at which the next character should begin to speak, overlapping the rest of the first character's line.

In the dark, we hear a tapping—rapid, assured, and quiet. Slowly,
we begin to see. Dim light. Annie is crouched on the floor. She is
engaged in a conversation conducted in Morse code, tapping, then
listening, and tapping again. Izzy stands to the side. Izzy speaks
to us. Annie speaks to herself, preoccupied and intermittently
listening for responses to the questions she asks the floor.

IZZY

So, it's this night again. She's asking the questions. She was always
asking these particular questions. Even when we were kids. It was
a sort of game, I guess. But since she never told you the rules, it
was a game she played *on* you rather than *with* you. You were
helpless to protect yourself. You never knew precisely *how* you'd
betrayed yourself, just that you had somehow. You could feel it,
see it in her eyes. But all you were doing was answering these
questions of hers. It was a sort of story you went on together.
A journey you took. You always started in a forest.

ANNIE

It's the beginning of a journey. You're in the middle of a wood.
Describe it to me. Describe it to me like I'm standing next to you
and I'm blind.

IZZY

And you were off. There was a bear, there was a body of water, there was a house, there was something else, several other things, it took some time. There was lots you had to do, decisions to make, places to think up, until you got to the last question, which I knew was coming, but could never prepare for.

ANNIE

You've reached the end of the journey. Tell me what you see.

IZZY

But I never could. Because as soon as she said that, I saw nothing. Blank nothingness. You couldn't even call it darkness, it was just the end of sight. It terrified me.
It wasn't until I was all grown up that she told me what I was trying to look at.

(She watches Annie for a moment.)

Yes, that's her. Well, this is how I see her anyway. It's this particular night again. I keep coming back to this. The last night. And she's waiting. For him. I'll get to that. Him. I'll get to that.

ANNIE

Early morning. Yes? A ferryboat? Across what? Lake? River? Midpassage. Thin rain.

(She continues inaudibly.)

IZZY

What's she doing? She's talking to the dead. They're a chatty lot, apparently. All except for the one she really wants to hear from, the one who never answers that last question of hers. Our father. Who is also our brother. Long story. Bad story. You've probably heard it.

ANNIE
Something running? A horse? Horses running in the field above
the shore. Beauty? Beautiful? Beauty.

IZZY
Yeah. That's the dead talking.
(To us) Can you hear it?

(Silence, while we listen.)

Yeah, neither can I. Nobody can.
It's Morse code. Tippity-tap. She thinks the dead know it.

ANNIE
He did.

IZZY
Well, my father did in fact. Learned it in the trenches.
They came in handy, the things he learned in the trenches.

ANNIE
He was magnificently . . . capable.

IZZY
But still he blinded himself when he found out. It was kind of an
odd thing to do.
And then he lit out. Took her by the hand and never let go. She
drove that old Buick down back roads day after day, month after
month, years they drove.

ANNIE
Didn't talk much. Just played the radio.

IZZY
It was the way he liked to figure out where they were.

ANNIE

"Don't tell me, don't tell me. Just turn on the radio, Annie."

IZZY

Local polka shows, country music with yodeling, recipes, call-in advice for the lovelorn. There was always a giveaway, a sound that could only happen there.

ANNIE

And he would always, always guess right.

IZZY

They told the time by waiting for the moment when the neon motel signs came on with a jiggle of light, like an irritated eye fluttering. He liked to hear the names.

ANNIE

Stop-a-Mo Motel, Buster's Bait and Bide, Auntie Cupcake's Hideaway.

IZZY

In the cool of the evening, they'd start to slow as they passed each one.

ANNIE

No Vacancy, No Vacancy, No Vacancy . . .

IZZY

Until at last she'd be clapping her hand down on some forsaken tinny bell somewhere and waiting for the missus or the mister to come out and survey the strange couple the night had flung in. Grimy girl with finger-combed hair and no lipstick holding the hand,

ANNIE

always holding the hand,

IZZY

of the old gentleman at her side. No one could ever describe him
well afterward because once you'd had a glimpse of those hollow,
blackened eyes flayed with vivid scars, you weren't about to look
his way again. It was too terrible. But you did take in something,
some awful certainty about him, his height, a military stance,
even then, in that ragged hank of a coat, and a kind of clarity of
mortal taint that came off him like the steam rising from him on
a wet cold night when they'd come into the overheated lobby from
the sleet outside. He was remarkable and appalling.

ANNIE

Both at once. Even when they couldn't describe him later, they
never forgot him.

IZZY

She'd sign for them both and then stoop for the one scuffed red
suitcase, all they had, and lead him down the hall. Twin beds,
I guess. That's how I picture it anyway. Pushed together so that
he could reach her.
See, long experience had taught her not to drop that hand in sleep
or he'd wake up screaming and thrashing. So their clasped hands
would ride together in the gap between the beds, hers prickling
with the blood drained away, but she learned how to endure it.
And at night sometimes she would wake to feel him tapping into
her hand in her sleep.

ANNIE

Morse code.

IZZY

Wake to stare up at the darkness of the motel ceiling, trying to
hear the message he was sending her in his dream.

ANNIE

Dit DAH dit.

IZZY

He taught her. It's not like they had a whole lot else to do. Days
bleeding into weeks into years, remember, travel as relentless as it
was aimless.

So I picture the two of them, listening to the radio, driving the
blue highways all that time. Her left hand on the wheel, and into
her right hand, which is cupped to receive it, like a nest lying on
the cracked leather of the Buick's front seat, into that hand he is
murmuring with his left until she catches him gently by the wrist
and he turns his hand like an ear to take her tapping.

ANNIE

"Describe it to me, Annie."

IZZY

So she tells him about the towns they pass, churches and pool halls
and gospel tents lit up with the shadows dancing and that moose
who stood like a homely building in the middle of a shallow lake.
It was so easy to teach her. She picked it up fast and soon could
go like lightning. His face would crease with harsh pleasure as he
nodded, listening to her in his hand. He said he was glad he taught
her. Said it might be useful for her when he was finally gone.

ANNIE

And he was right.

IZZY

Because now, she thinks, that's how he talks to her.
She won't say how he died. Nor where.

ANNIE

I drove all the way home with his dust in the creases of my hands.

IZZY

Won't tell anyone. We just know he's dead and that's the end of it.
We hadn't spoken, we hadn't laid eyes on each other in years, still
the first thing she asks when I open the door:

(Annie is up from the floor, in a scene with Izzy.)

ANNIE
Where's Paulie?

IZZY
He's in jail. Been there for a while now.

ANNIE
Was it a little girl?

IZZY
Well, no. Breaking and entering. But really, yes, a little girl. Pammie McAfee.

ANNIE
What'd he do to her?

IZZY
Looked at her.

ANNIE
Just looked at her? That's all?

IZZY
Well, from the foot of her bed.

(Annie exits. Izzy continues, to us.)

She'd seen him before, Pammie had. He was the one, his fingers twined through the chain-link, always looking at her in the playground when she was playing Duck, Duck, Goose. And then this one night, Pammie wakes up and there he is, that same man, but now he's standing at the foot of her bed, staring at her like that. Annie visits him in prison. She's the only one who does. He hasn't seen a soul else since they put him in there.

(Prison visiting room. Paul is seated, Annie across from him.
Annie is having difficulty breathing and she can't stop shaking.)

PAUL
What'd you do to your hair?

ANNIE
I don't know. Did I? Do something to it?

PAUL
It's different somehow.

ANNIE
More'n likely. It's been years.

PAUL
Years? Nah.

ANNIE
Yes, Paulie. Long time gone.

PAUL
What you shaking for?

ANNIE
I got the closets in here.

PAUL
Oh, right, the closets. Poor old Lynx Cat. Afraid of closets. Right
down to her little cat bones.

ANNIE
Yes.

PAUL
Iddy kitten Lynx Cat.
Eddie locked you up in the attic closet. Said you were bad and
that's what became of bad girls. People had to lock them in closets
and just walk away. Remember that?

ANNIE
Not much. I remember screaming.
No one heard me.

PAUL
'Cept me. I heard you. About sunset, it was. Opened the door and there you were, shiny cat's eyes blinking in there. Teeth chattering like earthquake teacups in a china cabinet.

ANNIE
I can't remember.

PAUL
Splinters under your cat's claws from where you'd been going at the door.

ANNIE
I can't remember. It was too late by then.

PAUL
How old were you? Little biddy thing.

ANNIE
Five. I was five.

PAUL
My best girl after that. Yes, you were. Thought the moon rose in my eyes.

ANNIE
The sun.

(He looks nonplussed.)

What rose in your eyes. I thought the sun rose in your eyes. Clichés, Paul, you gotta get them right.

PAUL
Jeez, we had some good times, Annie. You were my little lynx cat.

ANNIE
I was.

PAUL
I petted you and you would purr.

ANNIE
Paul?

PAUL
Lifted your little chin and I would scratch it. Kitty, kitty.

ANNIE
Tell me what you were going to do to her.

PAUL
Who?

ANNIE
Pammie McAfee.

PAUL
Is that what you're here for?

ANNIE
What?

PAUL
Same as the others? *(Does an officious voice)* "Just a few questions, Paul, this won't take long . . ."

ANNIE
I wanted to hear it from you. Describe it to me like I'm standing next to you and I'm blind.

PAUL
Just wanted to know which one.

ANNIE
Which one what?

PAUL
Which one of her stuffed animals she slept with. I heard her talking
to this other girl, said she liked all of her animals but there was
only one, *only one* she could ever sleep with, 'cause he was special.
That's all.
Just wanted to see that for myself.

ANNIE
Which one was it?

PAUL
(Trying to remember) Lion?

ANNIE
(Unsettled) Lion?

PAUL
(He's sure now) Yeah. Sad old lion with matted hair, looked like it'd
been cried on.

ANNIE
I'm sure it was.

PAUL
Yeah, that one.

ANNIE
So why'd you leave the van running?

PAUL
Did I? Stupid git.

ANNIE
And you had the clothesline to tie her with looped over your
shoulder, the length of cloth tape for the gag stuck to the front of
your shirt.

PAUL

I had to come prepared.

ANNIE

In case what?

PAUL

In case she didn't want to come with me.

ANNIE

Come with you where?

PAUL

The tree house.

ANNIE

Our tree house?

PAUL

Thought she'd like it there.

ANNIE

I see.
But she didn't want to come?

PAUL

No. She woke up and saw me. She made a sound.

ANNIE

Started screaming?

PAUL

Her mouth got so wide. Big, I thought, for a little girl. Never saw such a big mouth on a little girl.

ANNIE

You could have left. You still could have made it. The window was open. First floor, you wouldn't even have had to jump. Why didn't you leave?

PAUL

'Cause I wanted to look at her. Touch her. I knew I'd never be able to touch her if I didn't right then. But she was all squirmed up in the corner of the bed. And I couldn't think straight because of the sound coming out of her.

She couldn't hear me. I kept trying to talk to her. Trying to calm her down.

ANNIE

What were you saying?

PAUL

I don't know, just, you know, "Kitty be good. Kitty be quiet. Kitty come here," like that.

ANNIE

(This is all too familiar) Yes, right.

PAUL

And then as soon as I get my hand to her face—I just want to pet her, you know—she bites. Fangs she's got. Right down into my finger there. Still got the mark of it. Look.

And then I see her daddy in the doorway. Got a shotgun long as your arm catching the glow from her night-light. And that was that. And all I wanted was to see, you know, to see which one it was she slept with.

(Pause.)

ANNIE

The lion's name was Lennie. I got him on a trip to Heywood Falls. Yes, his mane was matted. Lots of tears.

PAUL

(Vaguely) Oh, I remember that.

ANNIE

Lots of tears.

(Pause.)

I can't do this anymore. I got the closets too bad. I have to go.

(She gets up and begins to exit.)

PAUL
(He barely notices) Big difference, Lynx Cat. You never bit.

(She's gone. He smiles.)

Lennie the Lion.

*(End of scene.
Izzy, who has been watching, turns to us.)*

IZZY
She sees him twice a week for months, even though every second she's in that cell with him, she's tasting her lunch at the back of her throat. Not to mention that she can't stop shaking.

(Annie crosses, as if walking out of the prison to a cliffside overlooking the river.)

ANNIE
There's nothing I can do, it's just the animal. She shakes.

IZZY
But that doesn't stop her seeing him.
And she starts noticing things. Marks on him. A way he keeps shaking his head, like the way you shake a stopped watch. Trying to unconfuse himself, she thinks. She goes to see the warden. She asks to meet outside, looking out over the water from the island prison.

(Sound of wind. Buoys, tankers passing. Brennan, an older man with an Irish accent, enters and joins Annie, looking out.)

BRENNAN
Surprised you wanted to meet here on this hill.

ANNIE

It's where I always come after the visits. Clears my head.
Only place I can breathe on this island.

BRENNAN

So you don't know what you're standing on I guess.

ANNIE

What do you mean?

BRENNAN

It's potter's field we're standing on. This. It's where the city's
unclaimed dead go, stacked like tins of mackerel, hundred-fifty to
a grave. The prisoners bury them.

ANNIE

How many are here?

BRENNAN

Got it all down in a book. Call it the Doomsday Book, inherited it
from the fellow before me. A few hundred thousand anyway. All
on this hill here.

ANNIE

Pretty spot, really. The view across. The green hills on the other
side.

BRENNAN

I've often thought so myself. A bit crowded, though I don't suppose
they mind at this point.

ANNIE

This their headstone?

(He nods. She "reads"—though there needn't be an actual headstone.)

"And He shall call His own by name."

BRENNAN
Nobody else will, that's for sure.

ANNIE
Who were they?

BRENNAN
Who knows? That's the thing. Poor sots found under bridges,
in sewers, hit by trams, washed up in the river. Lot of babies, of
course, left in the parcel room of the train station, back of a city
bus, side of the road.
Entire people thrown away like empty matchbooks. Keeps the
boys busy, I tell you, burying them all. Boats come in twice a
week, about six thousand bodies a year now.

ANNIE
So many. Can there be so many unloved people in the world?

BRENNAN
(Laughs) You're asking the wrong fellow. That's my entire
acquaintance, dead or living. The sons of bitches no one's ever
loved. Excuse my language.

ANNIE
That's not true. Not always.

BRENNAN
Ah, yes. That's why you're here.

ANNIE
My name is—

BRENNAN
I know who you are. Of course.

ANNIE
And my brother—

BRENNAN

Him I know. Know your man quite well. As well as anyone could stand to know such a person.

ANNIE

What do you mean by that?

BRENNAN

What you think I mean? Got over two thousand of the scum of the earth in my care and he's the least popular of the lot.
They've tried to kill him every day he's been here. Every blessed time I turn around, I have to break up some dogfight he's in the middle of, curled like a baby, taking the kicks from the billy boots.

ANNIE

Ah. That's about what I thought was going on. You can't protect him any better than that?

BRENNAN

If you'll pardon my saying so, Miss, it's not my job to keep your brother in a world that doesn't want him much.
And my interest is flagging in the project. As it is, during the day I have to shift him out to the auld loons and cripples, the ones who've been in so long they don't remember who they are anymore. I let him make brooms with the droolers out in the shacks, just so I don't have to spend every waking minute looking after him. But they're getting wise to the situation and it's just a matter of time before he won't be safe there either. Those that still have teeth in their heads will bite the nose off him once they figure out who he is.

ANNIE

You know they couldn't make the charges stick, don't you?
They only got him for breaking and entering?

BRENNAN

Well, the boys don't care too much about the legal fine points.
That's not their area of expertise. They put things together in their

own way, these fellas, and the verdict came down without the benefit of a single law degree. They just want him dead.

ANNIE
Is there anything I can give you? Something you need? Something that would—

BRENNAN
—bribe me, like, to coddle your little prince 'til he can get out and do the same again? Is that it?

ANNIE
Yes.

BRENNAN
It's girls like you I can't figure out. Look at you. You might have a decent pitch at life if you put yourself together and looked the other way. You're not ugly. But you come out here, regular as my da's gold watch, to stare into the eyes of a waste of food like that brother of yours. What is the living point of that? You know what the monster's done.

ANNIE
Yes. Better than you.

BRENNAN
This is your life going by, Miss. For him. Such a man.

ANNIE
He's my brother.

BRENNAN
Ah, Miss. We're standing on a mountain of brothers. Nameless bones and dust. All the glory of creation, to end up here. The waste of it, it's past thinking of. Little mite gets left like a bundle of snot-rags in a bus station lost and found. He's just a stone chucked into a pond. Over before he's even started it up. He didn't have a

KISSING THE FLOOR / 117

chance at it, that mite. No one put the choice to him: Here's your life, do you want it or not? You think you have the right, Miss, in the face of that, to throw yours away for a man like your brother? It's an insult to every single soul whose body you're standing on. Weep for them. Visit them. It'll make as much difference. It'd make as much sense. Some of them must have been decent folks at least. Somewhere in this mountain of poor souls, there are bound to be a few worthy of your tears.

ANNIE
But he's my living brother.

BRENNAN
Yes, Miss, he's above ground, for the nonce anyways.

ANNIE
I'm grateful to you.

BRENNAN
Don't be. Last couple of times I saved his neck was just luck on his part. I happened to come by.
Why shouldn't he be dead? What's the use of the life of a shite like that? I hate your man at least as much as any of the rest of them do. Maybe more, now that I'm thinking. I got two little girls of my own.

(He looks at her with contempt.)

Your brother.

(He leaves. Annie hears something. She kneels on the dirt, listening for the dead.)

ANNIE
Yes? I can hear you. Yes. You're high up . . . yes. You dropped a gold coin through the slats? Yes, it's shining down there in the mud, you can see it. And now you're scrambling down somewhere. Under a bridge? Yes. And the light on the river is like . . . what?

Metal? Hammered tin . . . Wait, wait. Oh, someone else . . . You
want to talk about the last moments? Yes?
The wind of the train as its headlight comes out of the tunnel. The
heat, it's a hot night, and, yes, you're holding something, a piece
of paper, the wind of the subway flutters it like a what? A moth, a
moth's wings, the paper you're holding, yes, and . . .
I can't hear you anymore. Who is this now?
Wait, wait, oh . . . yes? You're wrapped, swaddled in, what? A quilt.
Brown and black diamonds on it, yes, wrapped too tight, your feet
are—wait, I can't, a dog barking, yes, and then . . . ? It's too, there
are too many voices now, I can't . . . wait—

(Suddenly she can hear one voice clearly.)

Ah, hello, love, who are you? Something about stars? Yes? Turning
like . . . what? Doorknobs. Shining. Black, black night, and the stars
are turning, bright, turning, yes. Opening the door to . . . what?
This. Where we are now. Yes. Yes.

(Izzy, who has been watching, turns to us.)

IZZY
It's hard not to believe her, isn't it?
It's like she's throwing a party. And she's a marvelous hostess,
attentive, curious, she has a knack. So much better with the
dead than with us, the living. For us, she only has the handful of
questions. And we never answer them right.

(Annie is now back in the prison with Paul.)

ANNIE
You're starting a journey. You're in a wood. Describe it. Describe it
to me like I'm standing next to you and I'm blind.

PAUL
Black trees, no, it's black stuff hanging from them. Bats. It's bats.
They're hanging upside down. Sleeping.

ANNIE

So we won't wake them up.

PAUL

We just gotta be quiet.

ANNIE

Right. So we're past that. Past the bats. Now we come to a body of water. Describe it.

PAUL

Body of water? Lake, pond, river, what?

ANNIE

Sure, anything. Just water. Water of some kind. You choose.

PAUL

Well, maybe there's a hose. Someone left a hose on somewhere.

ANNIE

Uh-huh.

PAUL

So there's this stream, well, not a stream, hose water, coming down this bank of mud. Looks like a snake.

ANNIE

Uh-huh. And now I'm supposed to ask you . . . you cross it somehow—

PAUL

What do you mean "supposed to ask me"? Is this a test?

ANNIE

Well, kind of.

PAUL

I hate tests. You know that, Annie. Why you giving me a test?

ANNIE

It's not a test like you mean. It's just for fun. Psychological, you know. You find out things about how you think.

PAUL

Why do you want to find out things about how I think?

ANNIE

Not, you know, specifically *you* so much—

PAUL

Why you giving me a test?

ANNIE

Like, there are these symbols in it. Like you get asked, there's a bear, what is the bear like, what do you do to the bear, you know? And the bear means . . . it's a symbol, the bear . . .

PAUL

Gotta kill it, right?

ANNIE

Not necessarily—

PAUL

'Cause you got this *bear* standing in your way, you can't just *walk around it*, even if it's just like a story, you have to, right, kill it? No choice.

(Pause.)

So what's the bear, you know, what does it *mean*?
You were going to say.

ANNIE

Your father. It's the symbol for your father.

PAUL

Well, jeez. You should have told me.

ANNIE

Well, see, that's kind of the point.

PAUL

'Cause now I can't do it. I'm all self-conscious. I'd be thinking, "Ooh, can't give myself away. Ooh, did I just come off as some sick bastard? Was that the *right answer*?"

ANNIE

It's just for fun. It doesn't really mean anything.

PAUL

Well, sure it does. Sure it does. Surprised you didn't bring your notepad, jot this stuff down.
(Imitates her) "Oh dear, *bats*? Did he just say 'bats'?"
So, yeah, OK, what was that first part?

ANNIE

The forest?

PAUL

Yeah, getting off on the right foot *there*.

ANNIE

It's just, you know, where you feel you are at this point in your life right now. It's just the present tense.

PAUL

Uh-huh. And the water? You had a question about it? The "body of water" from the hose?

ANNIE

Well, it's just, um, how you get across it, which in this case is pretty—

PAUL

Well, whoever left it running, you got to find the spigot and turn it off, right? Turn it off at the source, right?

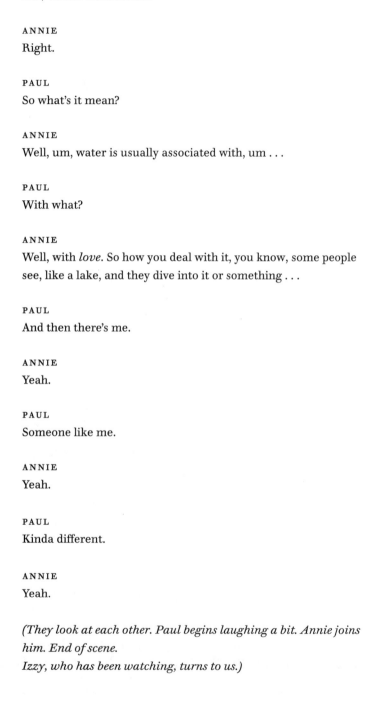

ANNIE
Right.

PAUL
So what's it mean?

ANNIE
Well, um, water is usually associated with, um . . .

PAUL
With what?

ANNIE
Well, with *love*. So how you deal with it, you know, some people see, like a lake, and they dive into it or something . . .

PAUL
And then there's me.

ANNIE
Yeah.

PAUL
Someone like me.

ANNIE
Yeah.

PAUL
Kinda different.

ANNIE
Yeah.

(They look at each other. Paul begins laughing a bit. Annie joins him. End of scene.
Izzy, who has been watching, turns to us.)

IZZY

She's still going to the prison. She's never been a cook, but
she spends the day before going through my mother's dusty
cookbooks, the bindings coming off in her hands sometimes,
looking for difficult recipes. Usually sweet. Then she brings it in
for the warden. Never anything easy. Blackberry cheesecake one
time, blackberries picked from our own rock slopes. She comes
home one afternoon with a bucket full of them. She's got bruises
and scratches up and down her legs and arms, blood and flattened
mosquitoes dotting her forehead. If he ever ate the stuff, which
I sincerely doubt, I'm sure the warden could always taste it like
ashes in his mouth, the joyless work she put into the things. But
I suppose that was the point for her. Penance or something.

*(Another day in prison. Paul sits across from Annie, who is now
wearing white gloves, a headscarf, and sunglasses. She is still
dealing, to some extent, with the shaking.)*

PAUL
You look like a movie star.

ANNIE
Well, sure. That's me.

PAUL
What's with the sunglasses?

ANNIE
There's something in my eyes.

PAUL
What?

ANNIE
Poison ivy. Also my hands.

PAUL
How'd that happen?

ANNIE
Picking blackberries.

PAUL
Why were you picking blackberries, Lynx Cat?

ANNIE
Something I made for your warden, Mr. Brennan.

PAUL
What do you want to do a thing like that for?

ANNIE
He's been kind to you.

(Pause.)

Hasn't he?

(Pause.)

Hasn't he?

(Pause.)

Paul? Have they laid off at all?

PAUL
I wish you hadn't talked to him.

ANNIE
Well, I wanted to know. You wouldn't tell me.

PAUL
I'm all right.

ANNIE
Of course you aren't.

(Pause.)

PAUL

You do, you look like a movie star. Ruth Champion, *Bicycle Built for Two*. Must have seen that twenty times.

ANNIE

Why that one? It's so hokey, that one.

PAUL

You saw it?

ANNIE

All that grinning.
I couldn't stand it.

PAUL

Well, then you know. You remember they're having that party, they're dancing and singing, "Daisy, Daisy, give me your answer do," and this little girl comes down in her nightgown and everyone's saying, "What are you doing up?" and, "Go back to bed, Kitty," but she's, you know, *determined*, she wants to stay up, she wants to *sing* and first it's this sort of racy song that she suggests, "Where Were You Last Night, Brother?" or something, and they all shout her down about that, but then she talks Ruth into doing a song and dance with her, right there in her nightgown with everybody watching. And she's got dimples, and then she gets a little tired and someone picks her up and takes her up the stairs to bed, just carries her up the stairs because she's so sleepy and she's limp in his arms and she's smiling because she had such a good time down there in her nightgown. There's a kind of, it's a perfect thing. That little girl, I don't remember her name.

(Pause.)

ANNIE

(With a new intensity) I'll tell you what I'm worried about, Paul, when you get out—?

PAUL
(Suddenly remembering) One of the times I saw it, you know? It
was one afternoon, a matinee? There was this girl's birthday party
there. Must have been seventeen little girls there and they've all
put on their best dresses and they're squirming around on their
seats and giggling a lot and whispering to each other. No parents
or anything, just the little girls. And they smell like, you know,
cake, and I'm watching them watch it, you know, and when it gets
to / the part—

ANNIE
(Carefully, disturbed) How do you know what they smelled like?

PAUL
'Cause I was sitting right with them. It was cake with chocolate
icing, she had it on her fingers.

ANNIE
Who?

PAUL
Jeanette? Suzette? *(He's sure)* Jeanette. She let me lick it off her
fingers.

ANNIE
Where did you do that? Lick it off her fingers.

PAUL
I helped her. She had to go to the bathroom, so I helped her.

ANNIE
Oh, yes?

PAUL
And then she helped me.

ANNIE
She helped you.

PAUL

She wanted to. Said she did it for her brother. Said she liked it. *(Off her look)* She *liked* it.

ANNIE

And then what happened?

PAUL

What? Nothing. We went back to the movie. Saw the whole thing. I held her hand.

(Pause.)

ANNIE

(Quiet, roiling, rapid) Will it never stop? Will it never stop? Will you *never stop?* Will there ever be a day when thinking about you and what you might have done, what you might do doesn't . . . ? When you don't . . . *worry* me?

PAUL

I told you I'm all right. And I get out in a month. I'll be back home with you. You don't have to worry about me. Not me. We'll have us some fun, Annie Lynx Cat.

ANNIE

Yeah, we'll have fun. High times in the old house.

PAUL

We'll go to the pictures. That's what we'll do. Take in a flick.

(End of scene.
Annie, alone.)

ANNIE

I put out my hand to the bear. He lays his heavy dry paw into it and we wander farther and farther into the woods as it gets darker and darker. I think at first that I'm leading him, but it turns out he's leading me. His step is sure, if weary. There's a light—yellow,

just a pinprick bouncing between the branches. It gets brighter as
we get closer. It's got to be coming from behind a lit window.
I think, oh, he's taking me to his house, which I immediately
realize is ridiculous, I mean, he's a *bear*, it's not like he's going
to live in a *house*, right? But we are getting closer and closer to
it, hand in hand. And you're right, it's just like you imagine it.
Thatched roof, curl of smoke coming out of the chimney. It's got
a softness to it, this house, a *rounded* thing, like a cat sleeping in
a little patch of green grass. Nothing bad could be inside such a
place. And we stand outside it, he and I, and it belongs to neither
of us, such a place. Of course. We can't even imagine the kind of
people who would live such a blessed life—certainly no one we've
ever known. The windows are steamed up with the warmth of their
lives, whoever they are, and we can't see in. The glass reflects us
back to ourselves. Our hollow eye sockets, the stupid expressions
of woe and exile. And it's getting colder and colder. He can feel
me shivering next to him and he puts his arms around me, the
gray-brown fur is coarse against my cheek. I know he thinks he's
comforting me. And knowing that, he thinks that I am content.

(A door opens. Paul is there, home from prison.)

But the journey is not over. Not yet. And we go on.

(End of scene.
Izzy alone.)

IZZY

That was the closest he ever came to being caught, Pammie
McAfee, because that was the only time he went so far as to break
into a girl's house. But that was all they could get him for. You
can't put a man in jail for staring at a little girl, no matter how
hard he's doing it.
And the goings-on in the tree house? Maybe all they did up there
was have tea parties. That's all he said they did anyway. The only
people who knew different were the little girls, who weren't so

little anymore, most of them. All the Susies and Sallies and Evies
sunk now into adulthood with married names and children of
their own tugging their skirts in the grocery store. Except of
course there was Annie, watching from behind the cart as she
wheeled it down the aisles. There were women of a certain age
who would catch a glimpse of Paul as he stood perusing the
canned goods, and they would flinch, almost imperceptibly.
They needn't have worried. Even if he looked up at them, his eyes
would just roll over their faces like a wave. He never remembered
them. They had become invisible to him. It was their daughters he
could see now. The little towheaded girls burbling monologues,
patting at their mothers' hips as they pointed longingly to
whatever looked sweetest on the shelves. The girls would crane
their necks as their mothers yanked them away, trying to wave
back to the nice man with the gentle eyes.

On the way home Annie and her brother don't speak as they wheel
the wire cart down the street.

And the home they're headed toward? It's a mansion. An American
palace. A ballroom, a billiard table, twenty guest rooms, a dining
table that once sat three dozen people, with delicate gilt chairs that
took the weight of tycoons and duchesses, admirals and foreign
royalty. To say that the place has been neglected, however, is to put
it mildly. The slate roof has fallen into three of the five great attics
and the sound of squirrels and other wildlife in the upper rooms
can be quite distracting on a still day. Beds have become burrows
for mice and the horsehair from the silk upholstery has been
strewn through the halls in bird flight as the sparrows carry it for
their nests in the rafters of the ballroom. Chandeliers, wrapped in
muslin dust covers years ago, look like enormous hornets' nests,
bearded and ribbed with gray dust, streaked with grime. Ivy has
sealed all the windows, closing the entire house in a dappled green
aquarium light.

I decide at last that it is time. I've got to get her out of there.

I search for tracks through the scat and dust on the parquet
floors. Human tracks, as opposed to the skittering marks of the
animals on their errands. I follow the ones I think are hers as they

thread through the hallways until I reach the ballroom, an empty vastness, the air animated only by the occasional flight of birds to corners and high rafters. The floor is a sea of dust, down the center of which is the seam of her bare footprints leading to where she stands in the center, lost in thought.

(Annie is barefoot.)

ANNIE
Hello, stranger.

IZZY
Hello.

ANNIE
To what do I owe the pleasure?

IZZY
Just stopping by the old hearth and home.

ANNIE
Home sweet home.

IZZY
I'm only surprised it's still standing. You must have mice running over your face all night.

ANNIE
It's not so bad.

IZZY
I didn't even look for Paul's burrow. Where is he holed up?

ANNIE
Where do you think?

(Izzy thinks for a moment and it's obvious.)

IZZY
The nursery?

ANNIE
Got it in one.

IZZY
Isn't it teeming with wildlife? I thought the roof had caved in up
there.

ANNIE
He likes them. He feeds them Kellogg's. He's up there like Francis
of Assisi, covered with blue jays. He's a picture.

IZZY
Well, I hope they peck his face off.

ANNIE
They won't, they're crazy about him. He sings to them.

IZZY
(Curious in spite of herself) What does he sing?

ANNIE
Pretty sappy stuff. From movie musicals mostly. He's quite a
crooner.

IZZY
Shirley Temple numbers?

(Bad little pause.)

ANNIE
Did you say why you came?

IZZY
I thought it was time.

ANNIE
Time for what?

IZZY
Time to get you out of here.

ANNIE
You've made the decision, is that it?

IZZY
Yes.

ANNIE
You consult with Eddie about this?

IZZY
Of course I didn't. Why would I talk to Eddie about anything?

ANNIE
I thought you two were tight.

IZZY
We're barely on speaking terms.

ANNIE
So it was just you, all on your own-ee-o, decided enough was
enough?

IZZY
It is, you know it is. You've done enough for him. If he wants to
live in this palace of rats, that's his lookout, let the place cave in on
the son of a bitch, good riddance, but not you.

ANNIE
This is my home.

IZZY
Of course it's not.

ANNIE
It is. I feel entirely at home here.

IZZY

So you wander the hallways, remembering the good times, is that it?

ANNIE

There were some good times.

IZZY

Were there?

ANNIE

Parties they threw? People dancing. Right here.

IZZY

We weren't allowed down.

ANNIE

No, but we'd sit at the top of the stairs and listen. You could imagine it. The musicians playing over there, the ladies lifting their arms and . . .

(She dances.)

It wasn't all terrible.

IZZY

You want to know one of my first memories? Father running after Mother, trying to stop her screaming. Him bunching her dress in his fist to pull her down. That's when I realize how old she is. She's so exhausted, I think, from running such a short distance. The way she was panting. But what made her think she'd ever get away from him? Then he's holding her down on the floor, his hand over her mouth. I don't know how long it lasted. How long he had to wait before she'd get up and go on with it all. Being his wife.

ANNIE

I saw him kiss her fingers.

IZZY

You did not.

ANNIE

They were standing in the garden. It was before a party. She'd just picked a white flower for his buttonhole and put it on him. She patted his chest. He put his hand over hers on his chest / and then—

IZZY

You know that didn't happen. You saw it in a movie.

ANNIE

You're so hard on them. They couldn't help being what they were.

IZZY

Is that right? Is that what you say to Paul? "It's all right, Paul, I know you can't help being what you are?" That must be a comfort to him.

ANNIE

That's not what I say to him.

IZZY

No? What do you say?

ANNIE

I just tell him, you know, that he has to try, as hard as he's ever tried to do anything . . .

IZZY

Try . . . ?

ANNIE

Not to, you know, ever, ever . . .

IZZY

What?

ANNIE

Never again. I tell him, you just have to try as hard as you've ever tried to do anything not to . . .

(Izzy won't help her.)

Not to touch them. The girls. Ever. Ever again.

(Pause.)

IZZY
Pathetic.

ANNIE
It's the best I can do.

IZZY
No, the best you can do would be to leave him.

ANNIE
He wouldn't be able to take care of himself.

IZZY
So what?

ANNIE
He might, if I don't watch him, he might . . .

IZZY
Yes? So this time they might put the bastard away for good. Get him off the streets at last.

ANNIE
They'd kill him. In prison. They almost did as it was, even without—

IZZY
Would that be such a terrible thing? His death?

ANNIE
Yes.

IZZY
Why, Annie? Look at what he is. Why are you doing this?

ANNIE
He's my brother.

IZZY
He's my brother too. I wouldn't cross the street to spit in his face.

ANNIE
I owe him.

IZZY
What on earth do you owe him for?

ANNIE
You want to know *my* first memory? I'm looking up, I must have been in a crib, and he's just grinning at me. And he's got a peacock feather, it's green and blue, you know, and he's running it over my legs and arms. It felt delicious. And every time I try to catch at it, he gets it away. I guess he was tickling me.

IZZY
It's the way you play with a cat.

ANNIE
(Realizing it, somewhat taken aback) Yes.

IZZY
You were his little lynx cat.

ANNIE
Yes.

(Pause.)

IZZY
I wish I'd known what he was when we were all kids together. I'd have stood up in my playpen and wrung his neck.

ANNIE
He deserves love.

IZZY
Of course he doesn't.

ANNIE
Everyone deserves love.

IZZY
That's the stupidest thing I've ever heard.

ANNIE
He *has* my love.

IZZY
You can't mean that.

ANNIE
I do. I love him.

IZZY
(Appalled) This is sick. You've become sick with this. Him.
Please, please, Annie, come away with me.

ANNIE
I can't.

IZZY
It's time. You know it is.

ANNIE
I can't. I can't leave him.

IZZY
Yes. You can. You have to.

ANNIE
What will happen to him?

IZZY
I don't know. I don't care about him. I care about you.

ANNIE

If you care about me, help me with him.

IZZY

I can't.

ANNIE

Well, then that's all we can say to each other.

IZZY

Please, Annie. *(She puts her hand out)* You're done. It's finally finished. No one could ever have done more for him.

ANNIE

No.

(Pause.)

Not yet.

IZZY

When?

ANNIE

I have to figure it out. I'll figure it out. Then I'll come. I promise.

(Izzy leaves. Annie watches her go, then exits.
End of scene.
Eddie enters; he's Paul's twin, played by the same actor. He is elegantly dressed—a tuxedo? A cigarette in a holder? He smiles as he speaks directly to us.
As far he's concerned, this is now his play.)

EDDIE

No, I'm not him. I'm the other one. Eddie. Not that anyone's ever been all that crazy about *me* either. I'm quite a peach. Locking little sisters in closets and so forth, you heard about that. And that ain't the half of it.

But at least I'm not him. That's pretty much all I've ever had going for me. That I'm not him.

So you're thinking, what gives with this family? How come they're all nuts? And I'm the boy to tell you. You want to know what happened here?

At first it's just a romance novel, one of the racy ones. The girl from the wrong class—Josie, the Irish scullery maid—hooks the heart of Lloyd, the millionaire's son. Pretty hackneyed stuff at first. He gets her pregnant, oh dear, but Daddy never finds out, 'cause Lloyd invents a dying mammy in the home place Josie's gotta go tend, so she's safely out of sight somewhere when she has the thing, then it's rushed off for adoption lickety-split.

Josie comes back to work looking like death on a soda cracker, and anyone with two eyes in his head can figure out why, but no one, not even the folks below stairs, knows the whole sordid story. And you'd think that'd be the end of it, right? It's the sort of thing happens every day of the week, often in the best families, and no one's the wiser. But no, not with this pair. 'Cause, what do you know, he's nuts about her. He knows he can't keep her in the house anymore but he's got to keep her someplace. He fires her himself, makes a terrific show out of it, but almost ruins it by winking at her as he slams the door of the cab on her.

Thing is, the cab takes her and her tiny trove to a nice little apartment several neighborhoods away, where she gets to stretch out for him on a good wide bed with soft sheets, while the pretty lace curtains are closed up tight. Splendid, right? But no. He knows how this is supposed to work: He's supposed to find some thin-lipped blue blood to marry and then the pressure's off—everybody's happy, his parents, his wife, his mistress in the pleasant apartment. Nothing could be easier to pull off, in fact, he's quite a catch. Every time he turns around, some eligible girl is dropping her fan at his feet in an opera box or bumping into him at the dances and apologizing prettily, but he can't stay interested. He spends the nights dancing forgettable girls around his daddy's ballroom and all the time he's thinking about the one who used to clean the floor, skirt hoisted up above her red knees. Pretty

soon he's dropping his cigarette on the front steps and telling her
address to the cabbie as they trot away. He looks back at the place,
it's lit up like a ship, music pealing from the tall open windows. He
doesn't care. He just wants her.

Pretty soon his parents start looking at him funny when he tosses
his coattails behind him to sit down at dinner. It's a silent trap of
a house, this place, and he can't see his way out of it. He's on the
verge of confessing everything and blowing his inheritance, the
whole shebang, when the most amazing stroke of luck occurs.
Scare headlines on the society pages: a sudden storm, a boating
accident. The rest of the party survive it, but his parents drown
together.

He wears crepe for a year and then brings his bride home from
a quiet wedding out of town. No one knows her. Well, that's not
true. There is one old servant, the one Lloyd couldn't bear to fire
when he took over his daddy's house, and the old man has to look
the other way when she walks past because he doesn't trust his
face not to betray him. It has been years now and she's changed,
God knows, but he knows Madam for what she is. What she was.
Thing is, she's no dummy. And she's a stunner, there's no dispute
about that. Those who thought her crass when she first arrived
come to find her charmingly direct as the years go by. Her
husband can't believe his luck when he looks down through the
candlesticks at her. He thought he'd just live off the pile his father
left him, but she convinces him to keep the business going; she
chivvies him into deal after deal, and she's never wrong. She eyes
the competition over the turtle soup and then tells him in bed at
night what she picked up while dancing with an ambassador or
playing whist with some senator's wife.

Then one night there's a young comer down at her end of the
table. This is the kid who's been making quite a splash downtown.
He comes from nowhere as far as anyone can figure out, did his
bit in the trenches and then came home and started his little
empire with a fistful of money. He's got no refinement whatsoever.
Nobody's dear old granddad is safe from him, nor is granddad's
heap of dusty dollars. He's a killer. And not bad to look at. They hit

it off right away, and by the end of the evening, whenever he puts his mouth close to her ear to speak over the din of the china and chatter, she gets a shiver of lust running through her, lights her up like a Christmas tree. She's never felt like this. And the thing of it is that neither has he, and him being such a forthright fellow, he tells her right to her face that night, just as he's taking her out on the dance floor one too many times to be quite discreet.

Well, it's a disaster, of course. But what can they do? She's lying so much to her husband that even he gets suspicious, the dear old goat. She's never home now, and every time she gets in late from the ladies' auxiliary, or wherever she said she was, her eyes are just a mite too bright. Lloyd's having the worst luck all of a sudden, the business starts going belly-up. Her tips aren't so foolproof anymore, and there's one company that's gunning for him now, he can't get out of their crosshairs. Every time he beefs about it to her, she goes quiet and looks flushed. She's got no advice for him, so the poor fool decides to trust his own instincts, which are not to be trusted.

Then comes the morning when he realizes what's been done to him. The kid, that boy who ate right out of his silver spoons not so long ago, that punk as good as owns him. The whole thing's gone kaput. But that's not the end of his day. He gets home that night to find she's gone, the wife, left that very night with the kid himself. He could pursue them, they haven't been gone long. He plays out that awful scene in his head, the one that takes place in the lovebirds' swank cabin on the ship about to sail, where the champagne is on ice and the negligee is draped across the bed. He can picture it so easily. But what he couldn't bear would be to look into her face and see what hasn't been there for him for years, he realizes it now, years he hasn't seen it.

There's only one thing to do. He doesn't have to think about it more than a few seconds. He goes down into the gun room, cocks his best one, puts it into his mouth, and pulls the trigger.

When the widow remarries and almost immediately gets pregnant, you'd think that she'd be the happiest woman on Earth, right? But she's acting funny, pacing the floor at night, talking to herself. People assume it's just the pregnancy, but when she gives birth to healthy twin boys, she's no better. Sure, they throw parties every now and then, lavish affairs that would pauper just about anyone else in their circle, but the guests show up as if at gunpoint and no one seems to have any fun. And she's not the dependable hostess she once was. She gets herself pie-eyed at her end of the table and starts talking a blue streak until she's suddenly sobbing into her napkin, or she can't stop laughing, which is almost worse. The house begins to fall apart, roof slate starts collecting in the unweeded garden. Rats start rummaging in the pantries. Nobody's paying much attention. The help gets harder to keep; word on the street is that the whole household gets fired every six months. Except one. The old geezer her first husband couldn't fire. She keeps him on board, no one knows why. All he does is glare at her.

The two girls follow us twins and we're pretty much left to ourselves. When we pass her door, we can hear our mother sobbing or talking to herself. It becomes a rare event even to glimpse her in the halls. Shocking too—she looks like hell. We study her portrait, that sleek woman with the limpid eyes, and we see nothing of her in the bent shadow with a ducking head that our mother has become.

Every week or so, dinner with Nanny is interrupted when Father steps into the nursery. No one, including him, quite knows what to say, so he goes around the table, absently patting heads and smiling unconvincingly until he leaves and we can go on eating. He's just another stranger, just one more person who has nothing to do with us.

So no one sees it coming when one morning the upstairs maid finds Mother has hanged herself. The cry goes up and Father is running down the hall in his nightshirt. Then there's complete silence. It goes on for a long time. Long enough, we find out later, for him to read her note. Then there's the sound. It's not really human, but it's definitely coming from an animal, and it repeats, like an engine turning over and not catching. Paul and I run in there and see him at it. He's stabbing at his eyes with the pins of her brooches, the diamond ones he gave her back in the good old days. The ones she could never bear to keep in the safe and tossed like loose change from her pocket on her dressing table at night. The blood is spattering all over her bed, the carpet, and also her bare feet, which are swinging, pale and bony, right near his face. He didn't even cut her down. The girls are screaming and Paulie's just standing there with his mouth open. And now the servants are running in and trying to cope with it all. Which is when I see the note, sliding from the bed to the floor. I read it later, after he's taken off with Annie and the house is finally quiet except for the weeping below stairs.

It's about what you'd expect. She knew, you see, from pretty early on. She even thinks, she says, she might have known it from the very beginning, though she can't stand to think about that. There was something familiar about him from the start, something she recognized. But she couldn't help herself. Flesh of her flesh, but she couldn't help herself. And over the years, the truth she kept swallowing back—that snake in her belly?—in the end, it just wouldn't stop its battering against her clenched teeth. It wanted out. So it drove her crazy, hanged her, then slithered out into the dying rooms of this dying place and took up residence for good. But here's what I think: There were a lot of snakes in this house and she could smell every one of them. Her husband wasn't the only one of her sons who worried her. After all the lying she'd done, she was a connoisseur of deceit. Could sense it anywhere. Oh, you know she only had to walk into that nursery and look at my brother to see what he wasn't saying shining like wet paint all over his face. Not to mention the little girl gnawing her fingers in the other corner of the room. But what could she do? She knew it was all her fault. The children are bound to pay when they're the spawn of such a marriage.

(He smiles.)

We're all monsters, see? Not just him, not just me. Every single one of us. That's what my sister can't seem to tell you about.

144 / ELLEN MCLAUGHLIN

We should none of us have ever seen the light of day. What can we expect from life? Love? Happiness? Fulfillment?

(He laughs.)

It can't go well for the likes of us.

(He leaves. End of scene.
Annie is alone, tapping and listening. It feels like it did at the top of the play. Izzy comes in and speaks to us.)

IZZY
Familiar? Yeah, here we are again.
I just want to tell you where she is. It's the old kitchen. This is where she spends most of her time. Making meals for two in a kitchen fitted out to feed a banquet hall. It hasn't seen a lit match for years, but you could roast a good-sized boar on a spit in the fireplace there, it's that big. There's a radio that's something of a conundrum—either that or a miracle, depending on your view of things. It should be kaput, the thing, mice gnawed through the wires long ago. It shouldn't work, right? But sometimes it does. Mostly it doesn't though. It's like the demented dowager in the corner everyone's given up on 'cause she hasn't spoken in years who suddenly tells you a plausible story about going boating with Thomas Edison. Disconcerting, if mildly entertaining. My brother's been out all night, so she's talking to my father while she waits for him. It's the usual set of questions, the ones she's asked us all, except my father's the only one who might be able to give her the real goods, at least on that last one. So far he hasn't.

ANNIE
(Tapping) You've reached the end of the journey. What do you see? Describe it to me. Describe it to me like I'm standing next to you and I'm blind.

(Silence. They listen.)

IZZY

All the lines go dead. Happens every time.

(Silence. They listen.
Izzy steps toward Annie and talks to her. Annie doesn't look up at
her.)

This is the part where you start to wonder, don't you, Annie? You
start thinking, have I ever really heard anything? Anything at all?
Or have I just been ruining my knuckles all these years, tapping
messages to someone who never tapped back? Some dead man,
who's, you know, *dead.* Was I making all that up? Just fooling
myself? Hearing what I wanted to hear?

ANNIE

Shut up! I can't hear.

IZZY

No, you can't, can you? But really, honestly, did you ever?

ANNIE

Just because *you* can't, / doesn't—

IZZY

My question is: OK, even if he exists, somehow, somewhere, dead,
even if he's out there, *down* there somewhere, even if that's true—
why would he want to talk to you? I'm very unclear on how this
Underworld of yours works. So he's just sitting around waiting for
you to call him? You can just summon him and he'll come like a
well-trained dog? Don't they have anything better to do, the dead?
Isn't death, I don't know, *grander* than that? Why wouldn't he just
forget you, forget all of this, move on to bigger things?

ANNIE

(Controlled) I don't know how it works, all right? I wish I did,
I spend my life trying to . . . I just hear things. I can't argue with
you about it because there's no logic to it. He speaks to me.

IZZY

How do you know it's him? Couldn't it be, I don't know, like listening in on a party line in some rural telephone exchange? Just voices in ether, wires crossed?

ANNIE

It's him.

IZZY

How do you know?

ANNIE

Because always, always, there is this sense of . . . I don't want to tell you, you'll just . . .

IZZY

What?

ANNIE

Love. A sense of that. His love for me. It's something I know.

IZZY

Uh-huh . . .

ANNIE

I knew you wouldn't believe me.

IZZY

It's not a question of believing you, I'm just—

ANNIE

He hasn't forgotten me.

IZZY

He's dead, Annie, it's not like / he—

ANNIE

(Emphatic) He hasn't forgotten me. He's waiting for me.

(Pause.)

IZZY
(To us) Yes, well, that's a conversation we didn't have that night. But I guess that's how it would have gone if we had. But I wasn't there. And this is what happened.

(Izzy leaves. Silence. Suddenly, Paul enters. He's startled to see Annie.)

PAUL
Sheesh, Annie, what you doing up this late?

ANNIE
Just waiting for you.

PAUL
How come?

(Pause.)

ANNIE
You been in the tree house all this time?

(Pause.)

PAUL
Think I might want to move out there when it gets warm again.

ANNIE
Throw some tea parties?

(Pause.)

PAUL
I saw a girl yesterday. Thought I'd ask her maybe. She's got a little gray coat and a little gray hat with a bunny-fur trim. Looks like bunny fur. I might ask if I can touch it.

ANNIE
Paul. Paulie. Do you know that if you touched that girl, even a
little bit, you could go back to jail and never get out?

PAUL
I guess.

ANNIE
Do you, though? Do you really know that?

PAUL
Sure.

ANNIE
It's the truth, Paulie.

PAUL
I know that. I do.

ANNIE
Still you were going to ask / that girl—

PAUL
Just thinking about it.

(Pause.)

She might like it. She looked like she might like it.

ANNIE
Do you know it's wrong?

PAUL
That's what everyone says.

ANNIE
Do you think it is?

PAUL
What if she likes me?

ANNIE
It doesn't matter.

PAUL
It doesn't matter?

ANNIE
No. She's too little, that girl, to know what you're thinking about.
You know that.

PAUL
Yes.

ANNIE
You've always known that.

PAUL
Yes.

ANNIE
Even with me.

(Pause.)

PAUL
But you liked it.

ANNIE
No.

PAUL
You did. You told me so.

(Annie begins to cry.)

ANNIE
I hated it.

PAUL
You said you loved me.

ANNIE
I did. And I hated it.

(Paul looks at her while she cries.)

PAUL
Well, here's a fine how-di-do.

ANNIE
It's never going to stop, is it?

(Pause.)

PAUL
I know what you want me to say.

ANNIE
It's all right. You can tell me. It's never going to end, is it?

PAUL
First time I made a little girl cry, I took her back to the playground
and I gave her a popsicle and we sat together until she stopped
crying. Then I told her to tell her mother she just fell down or
something, but that she was all right. She was fine, wasn't she?
And she didn't have to talk about me, did she? Wouldn't say
anything to anyone? I didn't leave until she said that was so.
I came back here in the late afternoon and I got up on the roof.
I made myself look all the way down, right to the bricks in the
garden path, 'cause I knew that's where I was going to end up
when I jumped. Seemed like the best thing to do. It was all so
clear, suddenly. My whole life. I could see all the way to here,
Annie. This kitchen tonight. And I didn't see the point of it.
Seemed like the easiest thing in the world, just step off, that's all,
like stepping down into a street. How hard could that be, right?

ANNIE
Why didn't you do it?

PAUL
Heard something.

ANNIE
What?

PAUL
Like a kitten mewing. It was right under my feet. Couldn't figure
out what it was for the longest time.

ANNIE
(Realizing) Oh, no.

PAUL
Then I knew.

ANNIE
No, no.

PAUL
That was you in the attic closet. Right below me.

ANNIE
God Almighty.

PAUL
So I went down and opened up that door. Saw you in the dark
there. Your little cat's eyes. Took you in my arms and carried you
downstairs.

ANNIE
Oh no.

PAUL
And I never went back up on the roof again.

ANNIE
It was me.

PAUL
It was you, Kitty. You're what I came back down here for.

(Pause as they consider this.)

ANNIE
Have you ever been happy?

PAUL
Sure, Kitty. Plenty of times. Remember when we went swimming that time, that beach with the starfish?

ANNIE
I don't remember it, starfish.

PAUL
Sure you do.

(She shakes her head.)

You had a green tin shovel, brand new, for building sandcastles, and a sun hat that was too big for you. It kept blowing off and I kept having to run down the beach to get it for you. And every time I took off after it, you'd laugh.

ANNIE
That was some other little girl.

PAUL
No, I remember.

ANNIE
One of your other little girls.

PAUL
It was you.

ANNIE
I can't imagine it.

PAUL

You with your little shovel on the beach?

ANNIE

Me laughing.

PAUL

You laughed all the time, mostly at me. You were happy.

ANNIE

I've never been happy, Paulie.

PAUL

You were happy with me. I know that for a fact.

ANNIE

You have no idea who I am, Paul, never did.

PAUL

I know you, little Lynx Cat, I look in your eyes and I know exactly who you are.

ANNIE

I don't know what you're seeing when you look at me.

PAUL

That little girl.

ANNIE

That girl's been dead a long time, Paul. Years and years. You killed her.

PAUL

Aw, Annie, you shouldn't be like that / with me—

ANNIE

I shouldn't, Paul? You know what? If I had looked down from the roof and seen my life laid out before me like that, the whole damn thing, right up to this moment right now? You and me having this little chat in this kitchen here? I'd have backed up too. But I would have backed up so that I could get a good flying start. Would have gone off that roof like a kid jumping into a water hole on a hot sunny day, windmilling my arms and legs, whooping fit to beat the band.

(Pause.)

If I could have been given to see what you saw. If I could have been given to know what would happen to all of us.

(Pause.)

Do you see the point of it now? Your life?

PAUL
I guess I lost track of it somehow. The point. Or maybe there isn't one. Doesn't have to be.

ANNIE
I think there does, Paul. I think there has to be.

PAUL
Well, then I guess I don't have one. My life, it doesn't have a point.

ANNIE
Well, that's a sad, sad thing, isn't it? Mine neither.

PAUL
Well, of course *you've* got one. A point to your life.

ANNIE
What is that?

PAUL
You're the only thing ever made any sense to me.

(Long pause while they look at each other.)

ANNIE

I went to see a pharmacist the other day. Went clear across the city, found a nice fellow who doesn't know me from Charley's aunt. I walked away with something I've been thinking about showing you for a few days. And the way we've been talking tonight, I'm thinking this just might be the right time.

(She takes out a vial and places it on the table.)

It wasn't hard to get, turns out. I just talked to him about this dog of mine, a "beloved" dog, a "big, beloved dog," "been in the family for a long time," and I didn't want to have to see it suffer anymore.

PAUL

(Thoughtfully) You don't want to see it suffer.

ANNIE

He listened really hard, very sympathetic. Sweet face on the guy. He goes in the back room and makes this up. Says he doesn't normally hand out this kind of thing, but he had to do the same himself one time. Nearly broke his heart, he said, but he came up with this special, dog meant so much to him. His own recipe.

PAUL

What kind of dog, did he say?

ANNIE

Doberman. One of those police-type dogs. Name of Ricky.

PAUL

What was wrong with it?

ANNIE

Well, it seems he was a skittish creature. Man picked him up as a stray and he was in pretty bad shape. What happens is, the dog just falls head over heels in love with him and they had a fine old time for a while there. Until some new neighbors move in next door, folks with a passel of kids. Somehow this gets on Ricky's nerves, he starts snarling at them, baring his teeth and so forth. It was like he was a whole different dog around these kids, that's what the man said. Brought out the absolute worst in him, those kids did. So one day the man's leaving the house for work and don't you know, one of those kids is walking by the house and Ricky barrels past him, out the door like a flash and he's attacking that kid and oh, what a mess.

PAUL
Was she all right?

ANNIE
No, she wasn't, Paul. She was never going to be all right again. So you know what this man felt he had to do? Much as he loved that dog, he knew that dog just couldn't go on living. Because it was just a matter of time before some little girl was going to walk by again and that dog, that dog just couldn't help it, he would go for her. So he came up with this. It's homemade.

PAUL
Homemade's best.

ANNIE
Said it's quick as a wink and it just puts you to sleep.

PAUL
Like a dog you love.

ANNIE
Right. Then it'll do its business.

PAUL
What was it like? For Ricky? Did the man say?

ANNIE

Said they had a nice evening together. And then he poured the stuff into a little bowl of something—plain custard, I think—mixed it up for him well and he licked it right up. Then, he says, the dog just turns three times in a circle, right there at his feet, curls up, and commences to snoring.

PAUL

The dog snored?

ANNIE

For a while anyway, until he wasn't snoring anymore.

PAUL

'Cause he was dead.

ANNIE

That's right. Custard in his belly and a little doggie smile on his lips.

PAUL

Little doggie dead smile.

ANNIE

It was a nice death Ricky had. Don't you think?

PAUL

For a dog.

ANNIE

For anyone, Paul. For anyone. To have someone care so much about you that they take that kind of trouble to make good and sure you don't suffer even a little bit when your time comes.

PAUL

And my time has come. That what you're saying?

ANNIE

Yes, Paul. That's what I'm saying.

(Pause.)

PAUL
So I just drink this?

ANNIE
Just break the wax seal there, see it there? You twist it off and /
then, just—

PAUL
But I'm bigger than a dog, did you / say—?

ANNIE
He told me this could do the trick for a creature of up to two
hundred pounds.

PAUL
Big dog.

ANNIE
Uh-huh.

PAUL
Big "beloved" dog.

ANNIE
Uh-huh.

*(He laughs a little. She joins him. Then silence. They look at each
other.)*

So I'm just going to, um, go to my room, go lie down, you know,
for a while. Leave you alone, let you have the place to yourself.

*(She starts to leave, doesn't know quite how to manage this. Pauses
behind him, almost touches him. Doesn't.)*

PAUL
Annie?

(She is standing behind him.)

Thank you.

ANNIE
You're welcome.

*(She leaves. He senses that she's gone but doesn't want to look back
to check. He stares at the vial in front of him on the table. Quickly,
he reaches out, picks it up, twists the cap off, and then places the
opened vial back in front of him in the same place. He stares at it
fixedly for a few moments. He may lift the vial toward his mouth
but be unable to drink it. He places it back down on the table. He
backs his chair carefully away, as if trying not to wake the vial.
When he gets the chair out from under the table he stands up and
backs away, still staring at it. Then he's still. Suddenly, he turns
his back on it and goes directly over to a corner of the room, where
there's a radio. He turns it on experimentally—it's not supposed
to work, after all—but it comes on, surprising him. It's between
stations, sitting in static, so he fiddles with it until he finds some
kind of music he likes, probably a love song of the era. He might
sing with it, perhaps he sits and tries again to lift the vial to his
mouth but can't drink. Finally, he goes and switches off the radio,
then turns and looks at the vial. He goes back to the table and sits
down again, as if with a terrifying dinner companion. He stares at
the vial. Long pause. Lights change, a sense of hours passing, the
first birds beginning to sing. Annie enters silently and looks at him.)*

PAUL
I couldn't do it.

ANNIE
So I see.

PAUL
I'm sorry.

ANNIE
It was just a thought.

PAUL
I'm so sorry.

ANNIE
I didn't think you would. You've never done anything I asked you
to do, never *not* done anything I asked you not to do. Why should
you start now?

*(With sudden violence, Paul leaps up and grabs the vial and tries
to put it to his mouth, but he can't, he throws it off and we hear it
smash. They look at each other. He starts to cry.)*

PAUL
Goddamn it, Annie, why couldn't you help me?

ANNIE
Help you?

PAUL
You know me. I can't. I can't.

ANNIE
I know. I know.

(Paul sits back down in his chair, his back to her, weeping.)

PAUL
I'm sorry.

ANNIE
I know.

(She starts to move around the kitchen, getting out milk, syrup, a pot.)

PAUL
What you doing?

ANNIE
I'm making us some hot chocolate.

PAUL
Why?

ANNIE
You like it, don't you?

PAUL
Yeah, sure.

ANNIE
You're tired. You've been up all night.

PAUL
I am tired, it's true.

ANNIE
I'll make you toast, cinnamon toast—you like that—to go with your hot chocolate, then you'll go up to the nursery, go to sleep, and then we'll see what happens.

PAUL
We'll see what happens.

ANNIE
We'll see what happens tomorrow. Today.
Looks like it'll be a nice one.

PAUL
Boy, listen to those birds! What a racket, huh?

ANNIE
Guess they're pretty excited about the sun coming up.

PAUL
They always are.

(During all this, Annie has been calmly lighting the stove, pouring milk into a pot, mixing the chocolate into the milk, stirring. Now she gets out a loaf of bread and a large knife. She slices the bread.)

Doesn't matter if it's cold or sunny, it can be miserable out, pissing rain, snow, they don't care, they still sing.

ANNIE
I've noticed that.

PAUL
Don't suppose they know much about anything, they just think, "Oh, life," right?

ANNIE
I guess they know enough then.

PAUL
Guess so. And the thing is, Annie, I've been thinking, you know—

(Without warning, she stabs Paul in the back with the bread knife. He slumps forward, his forehead hitting the table, dead. She's frozen where she stands. Silence. Suddenly, the radio comes on, it's static, between stations. She stares at it, then down at Paul, then at the radio. The static organizes itself somehow into something rhythmic. She stares at the radio. It's like Morse code. Slowly, tenderly, she moves to the table and begins tapping, her hand next to Paul's head. A kind of a conversation ensues. Lights slowly down.
Izzy enters.)

IZZY

And that's how they found her. So it's not surprising, really, the way it all turned out.

I did what I could. I did what she asked me to do.

(Annie leaves the stage. Paul remains slumped, dead, over the table in dim light.
Izzy meets up with Brennan outside the prison, where he met Annie.)

BRENNAN

Can't say I see the resemblance.

IZZY

No, I haven't her courage.

BRENNAN

Is that what you call it?

IZZY

Well, what would you call it?

BRENNAN

Cussedness? Sure, she's mad too, isn't she?

IZZY

So why are you helping her? Couldn't you lose your job?

BRENNAN

I run the damn place, who's going to fire me? You?

IZZY

I don't know why she should trust you.

BRENNAN

Ach. We're old friends.

IZZY
Are you in love with her or something?

BRENNAN
(Laughs) Wouldn't that just fix me? To fall in love with the likes
of her. *(Serious)* No, Miss. That type chills my blood. She doesn't
understand but only the *idea* of things—that's all she can get ahold
of—the *idea* of this, the *idea* of that—never the bloody living truth
of the matter. Poisonous madness, that. I'll steer clear, thanks.

IZZY
So you hate her? That's why you're doing this?

BRENNAN
Hardly. I've gone to some considerable trouble for her, you should
know, Miss. But then, this family of yours, you're a demanding lot,
aren't you? You no less than the rest of them.

IZZY
I'm sorry. I just find this hard. She's my sister.

BRENNAN
Well, it's not up to you finally, is it?

IZZY
No.

*(She takes out a vial, identical to the one from the previous scene,
and hands it to him. He pockets it.)*

BRENNAN
She'll get it tonight. After lights out.

(They stare out at the water.)

Did she tell you, Miss? This is where she wants her ashes sprinkled?

IZZY
Here?

BRENNAN
Quite determined, she is. You know how she gets.

IZZY
(Smiles) I do.

(Pause.)

Well, it's a pretty spot.

BRENNAN
That it is. Strangely enough. And she'll be among friends.

(He exits while Izzy goes to meet Annie, who enters wearing handcuffs and a prison uniform. She shakes uncontrollably.)

ANNIE
Did you get it?

IZZY
Yes.

ANNIE
And you gave it / to—?

IZZY
Yes.

ANNIE
Good. *(She gets perceptibly calmer)* Good.

(Izzy cries.)

Why are you crying?

IZZY

Because I'm angry. So goddamned angry with you. It didn't have
to happen this way, you could / have—

ANNIE

That was not my perception. But we don't need to argue anymore.
That's one thing, isn't it? You'll be free of all my yammering.

IZZY

Yes, you win.

ANNIE

Izzy, come on, stop it. I've been a terrible sister.

IZZY

Yes, you have been. But you're the only one I've got.

ANNIE

And that's our little tragedy, isn't it?
We're all we've got. What a family.

IZZY

What a family. And you're no better than any of us.

ANNIE

I never said I was.

IZZY

Didn't have to. Look at your grand finish. "Downright heroic,"
someone said. I guess I'm the only person who knows this has all
been just a fancy way to kill yourself.

ANNIE

Pretty elaborate.

IZZY

Isn't it? Such a lot of trouble when you could have just dusted
off Grandpa's pistol and stuck it in your mouth; but then people
might have figured out your dirty little secret.

ANNIE

Which is what?

IZZY

You hate life. You always have, and I guess I shouldn't blame you
for that, knowing what I know. But I do, Annie, I do. I mean, yes,
it's a mess, life, start to finish. It's a bad night in the fun house,
the whole damn thing. And death is not. It's clean, right? You're
safe from the world, safe from yourself. What a relief. That sweet
netherworld of yours where there is finally order and peace—

ANNIE

You've always missed the point, Izzy. Death isn't someplace *other*,
the dead don't up and *leave*, where would they go? Where else
is there? They're *here*. We're steeped in their voices. Just listen.
Ah, God, it's here, they're all here, shining in the air like mist.
Death is the element we live in, it's so obvious. Even the most
commonplace things are speaking to us, always, and always
about the dead, murmuring constantly, these walls are singing,
the filaments in the lights are humming with it, you just have to
listen. Everything is always telling us about the beauty of death,
the beauty of the dead—

IZZY

The dead aren't beautiful, Annie, all they are is dead. All they are
is not here. That's all we know about them. That's all we can ever
know about them. *Life* is the element we live in. Life is all we'll
ever know of beauty.
Why could you never see that? And if the dead can speak, they
don't speak to us.

ANNIE

They do. All you have to do is listen.

IZZY

I've never, not once, heard anything.

ANNIE

You haven't listened hard enough. You've never wanted to hear badly enough, you've never really believed me—

IZZY

Will you . . . ?

(Pause.)

Will you speak to me?

ANNIE

Yes. If you listen.

IZZY

(Pause, as she tries to believe it) No, Annie, I'll listen, but you'll be dead. And that will be that, and so I'll never hear you again. And every silence will remind me that you chose this. And not just once, over and over again, you had the choice, and you chose death.

ANNIE

It chose me. It was never my decision, Izzy. Death has taught me everything I know. It has been my kindest companion, always. Where would I be without death? I would never have known love.

IZZY

I've loved you.

ANNIE

I know.

IZZY
I don't want you to go.

ANNIE
Well, I can't stay.

IZZY
I don't know how to think of you, dead.

ANNIE
Oh, but I can tell you. I finally know. Paul told me.

IZZY
Paul?

ANNIE
He told me that night.

IZZY
When?

ANNIE
After I killed him.

IZZY
(Completely confused) What?

ANNIE
The answer to the last question. I asked him: "You've reached the end of a long journey. Tell me what you see."

(Lights up on Paul, dead, who raises his head from the table and speaks.)

PAUL
What do I see? I'm looking down with my dead eyes through the table, through the floor, down through the foundation of the house, then it's dirt, rocks, hardness, but that doesn't matter.

I'm something impossibly heavy and bright and I'm dropped into something impossibly dark and there's no bottom to it. It goes on and on, the falling. I've been falling for lifetimes now, Annie, until this, what's happening now.

ANNIE
What's happening now?

PAUL
I'm back in that forest of yours.

ANNIE
The one with the bats?

PAUL
No, I'm past them now. It's just trees.

ANNIE
What time of day is it?

PAUL
It's dawn, just like it was up there. The birds waking up. Pretty dark, but the sun's on its way. And now, yes, it's a kind of a clearing. No, it's a stone, a big flat stone, smooth. I'm surrounded by the forest. The trees are thick around me, I can't see forward or back.

ANNIE
What do you do?

PAUL
I lie down on it, the stone, it's cool on my back.
I look up.

ANNIE
What can you see?

PAUL
The sky, Annie. Only the sky.

(Pause.)

IZZY
I want to believe him. You.

ANNIE
You don't have to. I know it's true.

PAUL
We're waiting, Annie, we're all here waiting for you.

(Annie stands.)

ANNIE
It's time.

IZZY
Do you remember the teaspoon?

ANNIE
What?

IZZY
When we were little, the questions. You asked me what my body
of water was and that's what I came up with: a teaspoon full of
water. And when you asked me what I did with it, I / said—

ANNIE
(Remembering) That's right. You gave it to me.

IZZY
Because I assumed you were with me—we were always together,
why would an imaginary trip be any different?—and I figured it
would be a long journey, so you might get thirsty. And that was
the best I could do. That's what I had to give you.

ANNIE
(She smiles) You did. You said that.

IZZY
Yes.

ANNIE
You did that. Remember that.

(Annie leaves. Paul exits. Sound of waves. Izzy stands on the cliff looking out.)

IZZY
The funny thing is that if she asked me now, I'd be able to tell her, finally.
This is it. Right here:
Standing on this silent ground, looking out to sea.
Listening and not hearing.
But listening still.
And always for her.
This is where the journey ends.

(Sound of waves.)

END OF PLAY

Penelope

Text by Ellen McLaughlin

Music by Sarah Kirkland Snider

For Lisa Rothe

Introduction

In 2006, I was commissioned by Ralph Flores, the manager of the theater programs at the Getty Villa in Malibu at that time, to write a play for their theater which I might act in as well. He stipulated only that whatever I wrote should be inspired by classical sources since the theater is associated with their antiquities museum. I had the idea of writing something related to *The Odyssey* based on a notion that has circulated for many years in classical scholarship (by no less a scholar than Robert Graves, among others) to the effect that *The Odyssey* was written by a woman, or rather by female bards passing the story down and refining it over the course of centuries. It's an intriguing idea, something that explains how different in structure that book is from, say, *The Iliad*—which is a much more straightforwardly linear work—and how much women matter in *The Odyssey*. Nearly every lesson Odysseus learns and each act of crucial mercy in the book is directly related to a female character. (There is also quite a lengthy description of doing laundry—something no self-respecting man of the ancient world would know anything about.)

I asked the composer Sarah Kirkland Snider to collaborate with me because I admired the beauty and intricacy of her music, and I wanted the challenge of singing a series of songs written specifically for my voice. My collaborator throughout the process, as has been true of so much of my work over the years, was Lisa Rothe, who directed the Getty version and then every subsequent version, including the full production at PlayMakers Rep in Chapel Hill, North Carolina, in 2012. I would never have found this piece without her wisdom and skill as a director, her kindness and support as a friend.

Initially, the plan was to write a piece, perhaps a song cycle, based on the female figures in *The Odyssey*. But then I decided to explore another aspect of the text that I've always found fascinating—that it can be read as a kind of Homeric guidebook to the aftereffects of the trauma of war and that each leg of the journey addresses a different aspect of ancient-world PTSD.

After I wrote the play, I came across the psychologist Jonathan Shay's book *Odysseus in America*, in which he brilliantly analyzes *The Odyssey* in relationship to his work with veterans. There is a reason, in other words, that it takes Odysseus ten years to get home. The long journey from the battlefield is psychological and spiritual as much as it's an adventure tale.

So the piece became a monologue told by the ex-wife of a veteran—a compulsive, if charming liar—who comes home to the house they once shared, traumatized by his experience of a modern war and suffering from a brain injury that's given him amnesia. The songs thread throughout the monologue while, as she puts it, they both wait for him to come home.

In an attempt to understand what he might have gone through, she begins reading him *The Odyssey*, thinking that the book might effect a sort of cure since it's a book in which, as she says, "A poor wounded lying murderer picks his way through the terrible business of his own story, and finally, with the help of several females— in fact they're *all* female characters, every single one—he makes it home, to her. Me, I guess, rechristened as I am, the wife who's still waiting in what was once, long ago, his home." But as she reads, she starts to have a strange experience. She finds she can enter directly into her husband's memories as he responds to passages in the book—moments when Odysseus grapples with various horrors, adventures, and mistakes. She begins to understand what has made this man she once married into the shattered stranger she has taken in.

By the end of the play, as they reach the conclusion of the book, the modern Odysseus does have a partial reckoning with his former self. But the play ends in some ambivalence—as does, I would argue, the book—with a sense that some journeys never find their ends and not all ships come to harbor.

Production History

Penelope received a workshop production at Getty Villa Theater Lab (Ralph Flores, Artistic Director) in Malibu, California, on February 2, 2008. It was directed by Lisa Rothe. The scenic and costume design were by Kate Edmunds. The string quartet was Eclipse: Sarah Thornblade (violin), Sara Parkins (violin), Alma Lisa Fernandez (viola), and Maggie Parkins (cello). The cast was Ellen McLaughlin (Penelope).

Penelope had its world premiere at PlayMakers Repertory Company (Joseph Haj, Artistic Director) in Chapel Hill, North Carolina, on April 25, 2012. It was directed by Lisa Rothe. The scenic design was by Mimi Lien, the lighting design was by M. L. Geiger, the costume design was by Adam Dill, the sound design was by Ryan J. Gastellum and Rinde Eckert, and the video design was by Francesca Talenti. The music director was Rinde Eckert, the dramaturg was Akiva Fox, and the stage manager was Chuck Bayang. The string quartet was: Matthew Chicurel (viola), Virginia Ewing Hudson (violincello), Tanya Schreiber (violin), and Claudia Warburg (violin). The cast was Ellen McLaughlin (Penelope).

Notes on Staging

Penelope is to be performed by one actor and a string quartet on a spare stage.

The quartet should be visible throughout, incorporated into the stage design. Penelope shares the stage with them and tells the story with them. When they aren't playing music, they add tonal effects occasionally—with plucking, glissandos, and various acoustic sounds. Their presence is a constant.

Simplicity of design is to be welcomed, the only furniture perhaps an armchair, a table. Projections are helpful.

The transitions between singing and speaking are unfussy. The feeling is of a woman telling her own story in order to understand it, thinking through a problem in the company of others.

There should be, throughout, a sense of the sea.

Notes on the Text

Roman text indicates spoken text.

Italic text indicates sung text.

Bold text indicates Homeric text to be done as recitative.

Note on Music

Those interested in obtaining the original score by Sarah Kirkland Snider may reach her at her website: www.sarahkirklandsnider.com.

Song: The Stranger with the Face of a Man I Loved

PENELOPE
I have a house
Looks out to sea
And this is where he came
The stranger with the face of a man I loved
To the house by the sea
Long time, long time gone
A sort of home.

It's this house
That what's left of his mind
Seems to have remembered
So what's left of his mind
Claims the house as his
Though it's been mine and mine alone since he left me here.

He left me here
Half a life ago
But this is where he came
The stranger with the face of a man I loved.

It's this house
Where the best of our times
I try to remember
And the rest of the time
I try to forget
The times he lied and lied before he just left me here
In the house by the sea
The stranger with the face of a man I loved
Long time, long time gone
A sort of home.

You'd think it would be a terrible disfiguring gash, wouldn't you? Given the damage it's caused. Something raking across his skull, ugly and hard to look at. But it isn't. Just a tiny dent, a little crater, where something that wasn't his went in and got lost in the intricate meat of his walnut mind. All it takes, or so it would seem, to make the difference between the man I knew and this, this stranger.

I opened the door to find him standing on the threshold.

A woman stood behind him and he was so different, so unknown to me, that I thought the person here I should remember the name of was the woman, who looked familiar, someone local. But then she said, "Look who I found. I thought you'd want him home." And then I looked at him, hard, for the first time. And all I could say was, "Oh, someone's husband." She looked quizzical. So I thanked her, thanked her for bringing whoever this person was to my door. I should have asked her in because then she went away. Leaving me with him.

I knew he'd gone to war, but the divorce was nearly twenty years ago now, we'd lost touch, and frankly, I'd forgotten about him. There have been so many men in my life since then. The summer he returned to me in particular, there were so many men milling around that it was chaos, and totally exhilarating.

I never lied to them. It was a point of principle with me, after all
the lies he'd told me. They all knew about each other. Sometimes
three or more would end up sharing the table at dinner, bumping
hips with each other in the kitchen when warming the bread or
tossing the salad, then eyeing each other as they passed the new
potatoes. Then we'd all drink too much and make sozzled ice
cream runs in the cool of the evening. Usually we'd all end up
lying in the meadow, dizzily trying to make out the constellations.

The summer took its time. Lovers came and went.

I made birdhouses, dozens of them, for the swallows, there're so
many, and they flew in and out of them, like lines of thread passing
through a loom.

But then he came, and all, all of that ended.

I still go out sometimes to the meadow at night and look up.
Orion, the hunter, is the only one I've ever been sure of. Him with
his jeweled scabbard and his sketchy guess of a figure. He reminds
me of Odysseus. Yes, that's what I've taken to calling him. You'll
see why. And of course you can call me Penelope. Why not?

He doesn't know who I am, and I don't know who he's become.

It had nothing to do with me. It was the house he came back to.
There wasn't a trace of recognition when he looked at me, or even
the sense that he *ought* to know who I was. He barely glanced
at me anyway, I wasn't the point, he just made a beeline for that
chair he used to like and sank into it. He looked like a starved,
wounded animal who's finally found sanctuary. It was clear even
then that this was it, this was the last place. He had nowhere else
on Earth left to go.

So that's when he began his vigil in his armchair, looking out to
sea. I sit with him sometimes and watch the horizon with him.

I think we're waiting for him to arrive. Both of us. We're waiting for him to come home.

Days, weeks, months pass as we wait. And there's nothing passive about it. It's quite an active business, this vigil. He sits there in that armchair day in, day out. I'd say he sleeps in it, except I've almost never seen him do that. I come downstairs in the middle of the night and there he is, staring. It's like having a pot forever on the boil, always simmering away in the house. It's hard to leave the place sometimes. The sense that the house is going to blow.

Why am I doing this? You might well ask. All my friends do. Those who knew him say, "But he was such a bastard. Such a liar. Don't you remember?"
And that's a silly question of course.
Oh, I remember. But the odd thing is,

SONG: THIS IS WHAT YOU'RE LIKE

I'd give a lot
I'd give a lot to hear him tell me lies like that again
Tell me much of anything.
It's true, he talks
It's true, he talks, but it's not
Anything like it was then
Anything like it was when he talked the way a bird sings,
Just to sing.

This is what you're like
Try to remember
You lick the mustard off the knife
You are a man who when the music dies away
You keep on dancing
And when there's nothing left to say
You tell me lies.

You are a man, you are a man who told me you loved me
You loved me
You loved my eyebrows and my stomach and my knobby knees
I loved your mouth
I loved your mouth and every story that you told to me.

This is what you're like
Try to remember.
You lick the mustard off the knife
You are a man who when the music dies away
You keep on dancing
And when there's nothing left to say
Left to say
You tell me lies.

So this is what I'm doing: I'm reading aloud. I'm reading him
The Odyssey. I used to know some Greek, now that's all gone.
But I can recall the scent of it, that language, underneath the
translation. So it goes slowly, the reading, because of this. As if
I were making it up as I went along. And it's true, I take liberties.
I do make it up, I guess. I make it mine, I make it his.
I've made it our story.

Sing through me, Muse, tell the story.
Sing of the man of twistings, the man of countless turnings.
Let us sing of his mind of many corners.

He used to be like that. Quicksilver. Plausible. That's the word.
A smoothie. That's the man I loved, God help me. I think of his
brain as I knew it then and I think of tributaries, far remote,
needle etchings on mountain ridges, fragile trickles picking their
erratic way down to join each other, the way they gained speed,
muscled, roaring at last, roping toward the sea.
And now, years later, there it is, right across the room from me,
his mind. Curled like a sleeping snail within that only slightly
flawed pearly shell of a skull. It makes him blink, it makes

him swallow, it makes him whimper at night, that mind of his.
It makes him someone I've never met. I miss him so much
sometimes. I miss him even as I stare at him, breathing the same
air. I think we both miss him, I can see it in his eyes. So that's
what we do all day long. We yearn for the man he once was.

Sing through me of his bitterness, bitter nights and days.
The years spent staring across the depths of the salt dark sea toward
the home he cannot find there on the horizon never changing.

Poor old Odysseus. The wrong island always rising up to greet
him. Never home. Always talking about wanting to see the smoke
of his island's cooking fires threading up into the sky. He thinks,

Song: Home

Home is where I'm going, but never coming.
Home is someplace I can't recall, but head for still.
Across the waste of water, I search for her,
Dear blue land,
Show your blessed curve,
So tiny and only mine.

No, no, you can't go home, she says, the world,
Where do you think you're going?
We're not done with you.
No, no, you can't go home, she says, the world,
Where do you think you're going?
We're not done with you.
The world is never done with you.

The world wants her travelers to stay lost.
The world swats their eyes as they run through it,
She grasps at them, tugging and pulling
She grasps at them
Home.

Horses sense their stables,
Dogs on bloody paws
Lift their heads and begin to sniff, ears forward
Then they are running, they are running
Against the world that wants them to forget,
Lose that scent, un-smell that smell.
The world wants her travelers to stay lost.
She swats their eyes as they run through it.
She tugs their sleeves, pulling and saying . . .

No, no, you can't go home, she says, the world,
Where do you think you're going?
We're not done with you.
No, no, you can't go home, she says, the world,
Where do you think you're going?
We're not done with you,
The world is never done with you.
The world is never done with you.
Not you.
The world is never done with you
Not done with you.

But as soon as I start reading the book to him, I have my doubts. At least once we get to Odysseus. I mean, my god, what a terror he is. No wonder it takes him so long to get home. This is not someone who's ready to walk into any front door, least of all his own. He's an animal, and so are all his men. Look at what they do, the first thing after leaving Troy a smoking ruin behind them. They come across a city, a bunch of people who've never done anything to them, just people living their lives, you know. What do they do?

We fell upon the place and stripped it bare of life.
Killed the men, raped and captured every woman, stole every-
thing in sight. Blinded by the blood they spilled, my men would
not leave off from their slaughter. Sheep after sheep and cow
after cow fell heavy beneath the merciless knives. Nothing could
be heard above their woeful sounds of panic as they died.

I look over at him and his eyes are screwed tight, his mouth working. I can hear the crunch of his jawbones rubbing against each other. And then I take my first journey in. Into him. A memory, his memory, rears up, clear as Technicolor.

SONG: HEAD ON FIRE

I wake up running, my head on fire.
Look at me. I am a windmill.
My arms are slashing blades, a threshing machine.
My head is flaming, open to the sky.
I light the dead I'm making with it.
I watch myself working, making the bodies fall.
Look at this torch
Look at this torch of me,
I am the dead,
The dead making the dead,
Making the dead, making the dead,
Dead, dead, dead . . .

Where have I been? Inside of him. No, really, I was. Later one of his buddies told me about it—what happened to him when he took the piece of shrapnel in his head. He went berserk, running through this little village killing everyone he saw, men, women, children. You name it, he's killing it.

I find that out later, where exactly in his head I'd gone. Directly into that memory. But that first time all I know is that I can do it. I'm terrified for both of us now.

We have a bad night, me and Odysseus. There's no sleep to be had in this house. His muscles have gone so tight I can't even get the clothes off him, so I let him sit there in his chair, hands clamped to his knees. Staring and shivering.

I do, I admit, reconsider the reading material. But I don't know,
I have faith in this book. I think it could work. Because in this
book, this old, old book, a poor wounded lying murderer picks
his way through the terrible business of his own story, and
finally, with the help of several females—in fact they're *all* female
characters, every single one—he makes it home, to her. Me,
I guess, rechristened as I am, the wife who's still waiting in what
was once, long ago, his home.

Lift that grand and battered song again.
Start it anywhere, the story will end the same,
No matter where you join it, the road will lead him home.

I pick up where I left off and pretty soon he's among the lotus-
eaters, who are basically drug addicts:

The honeyed fruit they offered dripped forgetfulness. Those who
tasted it fell where they were, dreaming, their faces smeared
smiling with the sweetness of the end of any desire for home.
I drove them, weeping, to their rowing benches and tied them in,
but still they moaned, straining to look back over their shoulders
at the disappearing shore, like children carried off from their
calling mothers.

His eyes are muddy with memory, so I open the door to them and
let myself in:

Song: The Lotus-Eaters

Down the ward, the men are dreaming,
Drooling in their cots,
Pricks of blood in every elbow.
I am no better.
It's just that I'm awake

It's just that I'm awake
It's just that I'm awake and walking.
Walking.

Hear my footsteps down the hall.
Now I'm smelling the night air,
Crunching gravel as I walk, walk, walk.

Never, never, never, never will I
Never will I sleep like that again
Never, never, never, never, never,
Never will I sleep like that, sleep like that . . .
And I'm lost in this night
I'm lost in this night
I'm already lost, but not as lost as them.

And I'm lost in this night
I'm lost in this night
I'm already lost, but not as lost as them
My sleeping, drooling, smiling men.
I'm not as lost,
I'm not as lost
I'm not as lost as them.

OK, maybe I'm thinking of a movie, or remembering some questionable novel I once read, but this is what I see: He snags clothing from a clothesline, sleeps in stables, steals money from poor boxes, food from market stalls. He jumps a freight train and spends a night in an empty car that smells of panicked sheep. He's bothered from the start by a huge man who gets on at the last minute, then slumps in front of the sliding door. He can't see much of him, just makes out the bulk of him, enormous, looming over there; and the glint of the giant's eyes watching him becomes a sort of torture. He's exhausted but he can't go to sleep, not when that giant is staring at him like that. Morning never seems to come as the train rumbles on. Still, the eyes on him. Something snaps in him and he lunges at the eyes with the knife he has. The creature bellows and grabs for him, but Odysseus is scrambling for the handle of the door and it's open with a flash of sunrise at full speed and he's pitched himself out, out and away from the wheels, tumbling now away from the sound of that blinded creature. He's a mess at the bottom of the gully, probably broke something, he doesn't care, he's hooting, laughing, calling out his name to the roar of the passing train. Until it's gone, not even the sound of it left, and there's just him, standing cradling his probably broken ribs and his certainly empty belly in the blank slate of some pastel state in the middle of nowhere he remembers the name of.

There's a woman I'd like to meet some day. She runs a little empire in the desert. A bar, and above it, a massage parlor; above that she reads tarot cards. The drinks are the equivalent of blunt instruments—no olives, no umbrellas, no ice—just rotgut in smeared glasses.

Enough to make a man want to stagger upstairs and fall asleep as a naked girl massages the money out of his pockets. He wakes up with a pounding headache and his guts seething with angry bats. And if he's philosophical, he'll make his way upstairs to where she's sitting in her own smoke, let's call her Circe, and she'll read his cards, slapping them down precisely and humming under her breath.

But when Odysseus gets to the place, he does it backward. He doesn't even set foot inside the bar, just starts up the stairs like a man on a mission. The naked girls crooking their fingers to him on the second floor don't interest him either; he just keeps trudging up. There he stands, reflecting himself in all the grimy mirrors, alone in the falling dust of the upper room, waiting for the prophetess.

She gets there after him, slightly breathless, turban askew, unused to *this*—a man who wants a reading before he wants a drink or a hump. She fans the cards before him, showing their backs, and induces him to pick. And she knows which one it will be before he picks it, had to be, sure enough it is: the Hanged Man. You know the one. Upside down, he hangs from a tree by one foot. There is a weird placidity about it, though it's ominous and odd. He could be praying, his hair streaming down as he swings there, a slight upside-down smile playing on his lips. Chosen for some reason, for this strange fate.

She thinks of hanging by her knees as a child, looking at the world that way. She thinks of milk money falling from her little pockets to the schoolyard dirt.

He thinks of trip wires and booby traps.

Of the blur of a shocked face rushing backward into air.
She looks at him. He has gone white.

SONG: THE HANGED MAN

"Is he dead?" the Stranger said.
No, she tells him.
Say you bounce a ball.
Have you ever noticed that
Between the business of its going up
And the business of its fall
It hesitates? It just waits.
There's a fraction of a second there
When it's luxuriating in the air
Before its fate rushes it on.

"But he's hanging there."
Yes, he's hanging, yes, but from the tree of life.
"Is he some sort of sacrifice?"

Yes, he's a sacrifice.
He gave himself to himself so he could see.
He gave himself.
"So he could see?"
So he could see as only you can see
When the world is upside down
And you hang from the branch of a tree.

"So that's me?" Yes, it's where you seem to be.
And you hang from the branch of a tree.
"So that's me."
Yes, it's where you seem to be.
"So that's me."

"So that's me."
"So that's me."

I think that's when he cried. It was the first time he'd done it
since the beginning. There it was on his face, his own water in the
desert. And she's just holding him. Seems like the most natural
thing in the world. And his arms go around her too. And they
stand there like that for a long time before she takes him up to the
last floor, where no one goes but her, right beneath the eaves, and
they listen to the birds skittering across the roof above them and
he sleeps with her and without her for a very long time. Circe and
the Hanged Man.

Well, he can talk, but I mean, we don't exactly *converse*. Still, he
does say things sometimes.
We are out in the backyard. The air is alive with the flight of birds;
you can hear the burr of their wings as they pass nearby. It upsets
him, the speed of them, the sound of them. I think, and then
I ask, do they remind him of bullets? Was the sound of it like that?
I don't expect an answer. "No," he says. "Bullets snap." He snaps
his fingers. Then there's a flash of impatience, he's angry with
himself. "No, not like that either." He thinks. "A crack, it's sharp,
and it follows the bullet, just behind, just, just . . ." And the thing

is, his face, it's suddenly open now as he tries to hear it. The eyes
are unfocused, remembering. Just then, a bird flies between us,
a dip, a blur. He flinches. It's gone. The memory. Whatever had
begun to happen. The open face closes. Snap. Shut.

The silence can last for days.

I wake at night and the house is full of the dead.
Not my dead. His dead. I don't even know these people. They
stand about him in the darkness, shifting their weight on the
creaking floorboards. They seem to expect something from him.
Sleepless in his armchair, he looks up at them with terror and
tenderness.
Whatever they are looking for, he doesn't have to give.

Even in the daylight world, I find we're reading about the dead.
It's the passage in the book when Odysseus makes a journey to
the Underworld and sees all the heroes of Troy, his dead comrades
milling around the netherworld like so many vagrants at a bus
station, forgetful of the place they were once going but have long
since lost the means to get to anyway. These meetings with the
dead are muted, stunted things, across a divide too awesome to
acknowledge.

SONG: DEAD FRIEND

Dead friend
Turn your back on me
I beg you
Do not look at me
With those eyes.

Dead friend
I must leave you here
I can't stay
You can't follow me

Where I go.
Where I go.

Dead friend
Turn your back on me
Let me go
I've forgotten you
Forget me.

I've forgotten you
Forget me.

But there is one person Odysseus doesn't expect to meet there.
His mother. And she's the only one he tries and fails to touch.

He says,
Oh, Mother, I am so sad to see you here. I didn't know. What
happened to you?
She says,
I died of waiting. Year after year, I stood the days out, squinting
across the water that never showed your sail. One day my hollow
heart cracked to powder like an old egg, and I fell where I stood,
eyes still clinging to the empty horizon.
Bitter with longing, Odysseus reaches out to his mother. Three
times he tries and three times he fails. She is as untouchable as
smoke.
He says,
"Oh, Mother, why can't I hold you in my arms? Is this some fresh
cruelty the gods devised to trick me?"
She says,
"It is only death, my son.
It is the end we all come to.
You and I had our last embrace long ago, in the sunlit world
above. Such things can never happen here.
Go back, my child.
You will be here soon enough, and that is a return I shall not
rejoice to see you make."

Which makes me think of May, his mother, who must be dead
by now. She visited us once, when we were first married, during
a heat wave. It was a dreadful visit. Kind of a toss-up which of
the three of us wanted it to be over the most. She had no gift
for conversation, or at least not with him; he obviously made
her nervous. But you could see her devotion, her eyes following
him everywhere, like a kicked dog watching her master. Which
only brought out the worst in him. He could be a real bastard
sometimes. A little chuckle here, a slight roll of the eyes.
He could make you feel so stupid.

We were sitting outside, hoping for a breeze, I guess. I'd put some
sort of meal together, even though I knew no one was hungry,
and was hiking back and forth to the kitchen to bring everything
out as the two of them sat there uneasily. Her eyes were flicking
miserably around the yard, looking for something to remark on,
something, anything to say.

Suddenly—and I think she was as surprised as anyone to hear
herself talking about this—she's going on about light, something
about light being different in different places and at different
times of year. And then something about the light in old
photographs, the light of paintings—Impressionism, I think she
mentioned. But then she moves into the idea of remembered
light, what you recall from childhood, and suddenly she's in a very
clear memory of herself in a backyard when she was little, maybe
three or four. She remembered looking at light on a puddle in her
backyard. It was lovely listening to her talking like that—she never
talked like that, not around him anyway. He was leaning his chair
back; I remember the front legs were off the ground and had grass
clinging to them. He was frowning, not looking at her, toying with
a napkin ring, spinning it on his finger. I thought, he looks like a
kid, a sullen teenager waiting to be given something he's decided
he won't like.

I was going back and forth getting bread, plates, spoons, bowls—gazpacho, that was what I'd made—I kept catching bits of this speech of hers each time I came out, until I stepped out into silence. I knew something terrible had just happened. It was so hot and they were both so still. I noticed that he'd brought the chair down and the napkin ring was on the table. His face was red; you could see a vein pulsing in his forehead. But it was her face that shocked me. It was a slammed door, white, hard, wiped clean. All that musing softness gone, completely gone.

I don't know what he said, but I can imagine. It wouldn't take much. Just a slight verbal sneer, just enough to ruin it, that scrap of herself she'd been showing him. I looked at him, that great heavy handsome head of his, and I thought, "Do you even know? Do you know what you just did to your mother?" He looked like a criminal.

She was gone the next morning and we never saw her again, never spoke of her even, it was that awful. I look at him now and I wonder if that's what he's thinking about too. "Do you know what you did to your mother?" Oh, I think he did. I think he does. I think he still does. It turns out we don't have that many chances to be kind in this sunlit world above. And he sure as hell blew that one.

When Odysseus visited the Underworld, he was really there to find Tiresias, the great blind seer, in hopes that he could get some advice about how to get home. That's when the dead Tiresias prophesied for Odysseus, saying:

I know you, Captain, all you want in this world is to see the honey light of your own home at last. But there is more trouble to come for you. Poseidon hates you and your way home is through him. He will make it hard for you yet. But if you can hold fast to restraint, there is some hope.

You shall find yourself sailing past the Island of the Sun God. Helios, who sees all and hears everything. Helios, from whom

**nothing is hidden. See his many cattle, sacred to the world, they
dapple his island slopes like banks of clouds. They are beautiful
and they are holy. But, Captain, let no one interfere with them,
even if you're starving. If any man so much as touches them,
everything will be taken from you, all your men, your last ship,
everything. And then you shall be lost indeed, your fine mind
will be useless against the fury of the sun.**

So Odysseus makes his men swear that they won't touch the
cattle, no matter what happens. He almost doesn't dock at the
island at all, except the men ask to stop for the night, just one
night, before going on. So they do, and then are pinned for a
month by an onshore gale, starving and going mad as they listen
to the lowing of the cattle they can't eat.
Odysseus wakes from a famished dream to the smell of roasting
meat. His men, crazed with hunger, have defied him and
slaughtered the forbidden cattle. But when Odysseus, raging,
comes upon them at their fires, he finds them standing in horror,
looking at the meat on the flames that refuses to die, writhing on
the spits and, headless, footless, lowing still, unkillable. This was
the last test, and they failed it. Now nothing will go right, ever
again.

That night I have a dream. I'm him. I'm standing at a crossroads,
thumb out. Each direction I look, the road gives him a beginner's
course in perspective, parallel lines meeting in a V. The horizon is
merciless, completely flat. A heat wave lies on top of it like the last
taste of gin in a shot glass, like the standing tear in the faded blue
of an old man's eye.

The sun is rummaging through my open head like a boy looking
through a box of mementos. The things boys keep, who knows
why? A shell here, a photograph there, a key to what?
Baby teeth, bits and pieces, bones and bullets picked from the dust
of old battlefields.

Song: Heat Wave

Here's an ugly little something,
Broken bit of who knows what.
Here's a bloody little secret
What I did and what I thought.
Here is what I lost forever
Open hands, a certain laugh.
Here is what I thought I wanted
Some lost smile in a photograph.

Let a wind come
Let a wind come blow it all away.
Let a rainstorm
Let a rainstorm swallow me.
Can't you do that?
Can't you hide me, God?
Can't you sweep me someplace you can't see?

God help me,
Hide me from you.
God have mercy,
Save me from you.

I can't get out of the sight
Of you. Of you.
Please let me out of the sight
Out of the sight
Out of the sight of you.

So this is what I think happened: The semi driver who found him
by the side of the road was a woman. She knew heatstroke when
she saw it, and she had a first-aid kit equipped to a fare-thee-well,
bound in leather, full of vials and powders and old-fashioned

implements you didn't want to think through the uses of. He woke up wearing silk pajamas, smelling of some exotic cologne, traveling feetfirst at about ninety miles an hour directly into the setting sun. He crawled over the slippery sheets to look down on her at the wheel, swiping her thick black hair back from her face, her foot planted on the accelerator. Let's call her Calypso. When he tried to call to her over the roar, she didn't answer, so he crawled back to where she'd left him and didn't wake until he felt her on top of him, her mouth all over him, the pajamas coming off. Weeks went by like this. She didn't like it when he wanted to get out, kept telling him he wasn't ready to leave the semi. Things were further complicated when he found out what she'd done to his clothes when she first took him onboard, just flung them out the window along that first stretch of highway while he was sleeping in the eternal pajamas.

She was considerate of him though; he couldn't complain, it was a kind of kindness, the way she'd thread through the parking lots balancing whatever she'd bought for him to eat that night on her uplifted palm. She kept trying to get it right. Did he like sweet stuff, salty? What about ribs? What about corn bread? He didn't know what he liked anymore, just knew he wanted out, out, out of the goddamn pajamas, and not just at night, not just to have her moving over his body like a storm. But it was easier to do what she wanted, and he liked lying on his belly looking over her head to see the highway forever falling under her singing wheels.

How long did he stay with her? A long time, it seemed like a long time. Until one day when he's sitting in the passenger seat at a truck stop while she's buying the meal and a kid comes up and sees him there. He's a bored kid, but not as bored as he is, he can guarantee that. Kid says he wishes they could just stop and go fishing sometimes, his dad and him, it'd make a nice change, but they just never seem to stop anywhere they could do that. And they keep passing places they could stop—this lake, that river, or even that one back there. Odysseus finds himself feeling some sympathy for the father, whoever he is, it must be tough to be always having to tell the boy no.

"How come you're dressed like that?" the kid says. And it's a simple question, merely curious. "Don't you got no daylight clothes?"

"No, I don't. I wish I did. I lost them."

"Well, my dad's got a lot of them. Want me to fetch you some?" And he does, and they fit. Turns out, it was that easy. The truck driver and his son even give him a ride away from there that very night, before Calypso makes it back to him, his dinner balanced on her palm. I look at him now and I wonder—did he even look back?

SONG: CALYPSO

Didn't he think of her,
Standing in that parking lot,
The stars are out, night drops down on her.
She is alone again, she's alone again.
She holds his cooling dinner in her lifted hand,
Something he just might like
Sweet or salty,
No one will eat it now.

She looks for him in darkness
Stands alone now once again
Tries to see where he might have gone
Where could he go?

She looks for him in darkness
Stands alone now once again
Tries to see where he might have gone
Where could he go?
He might have gone.
Where could he go without her?

(Well, I think of you, Calypso, all the time. Is it because just like
you I've stood in the darkness, looking for him?)

We look for him in darkness
Stand alone now once again
Try to see where he might have gone
Where could he go?

She looks for him in darkness
Stands alone now once again
Tries to see where he might have gone
Where could he go?
He might have gone.
Where could he go without her?

But he was long gone by then, off with the truck driver and his
son to drive all night. And come dawn, they stop and go fishing
before they leave him and head on. He's still wearing the truck
driver's clothes when he gets to me. At least that's what I decide.
He smelled like fish, just a little like fish.

So in the book, Odysseus spends seven years on Calypso's island.
That's how long it takes before the gods finally decide to talk
Calypso into letting Odysseus leave for home on a raft she helps
him make and provisions herself. But Poseidon isn't done with
him yet and throws the sea into chaos around him one more time.
Odysseus, alone on the night sea, trapped in the killing storm,
hangs onto a scrap of his wrecked raft as he careens, helpless, in
the vicious waves. He screams to his fate,

Why should I have lived for this? Why could I not have died with
the best of the Greeks in glory underneath Troy's walls? Why
should I be saved? Saved for this? Choking on salt, forgotten in
the waste of the trackless ocean, lost. Why could I not have died
with my friends?

When I look at him, I can see it, but I can't go in, not this time. This is something between him and the men he led. It's something different from that massacre—the berserking in the village when he got hit. No, this is about leadership and guilt. It's the raw look of a man who has failed the people he loved. Whatever it was that he did, it's what's kept him all alone in there, deep inside that head of his.

Terrible. He did something terrible. That's all I know.

When I come downstairs that night, I hear him whispering and without shame I creep soundlessly behind his chair to eavesdrop. "But, I'm telling you, man, I didn't get away with it. Nobody can get away with that. You can't just walk away, man. Forget it. That just can't happen."
And then he goes silent. He must hear me behind him. I stop breathing. He stops breathing. Now we're both listening to each other not breathing.
I think, for the first time: Maybe everybody who's been warning me is right. Maybe my life is in danger here. This man has killed people. And he's killed them for doing less to him than what I've just done, which is to sneak up behind his back in the dark and listen to him talk to himself.

I turn on the overhead light. We're both blinded by the glare. Still I've come around in front of him now, so he can see me. I say, "It's me, it's me, it's me! Please, just, it's me! Don't! I'm sorry!" But when I can finally see his face, it's not murder I see, just shock, like he hasn't seen me for, well, like he hasn't seen me for twenty years.

But this is the thing: For the first time, *he looks like he knows he once knew me.* A long, long time ago. And though he still doesn't remember my name, for the first time he looks like he thinks he probably *should* remember it.
And that, well, that's something.

Odysseus lies asleep, half dead after his miraculous survival of
the storm that washed him up on this foreign shore. Naked, all he
possesses now is his life.

He wakes in beauty, startled to look upon a girl, a princess.
Nausicaa is what Homer calls her. I've forgotten what the name
of the girl in our story is, but she only lives five blocks away. I see
her all the time. She's a demon at jump rope, plus she's no slouch
at jacks.
Her red sneaker is the first thing he sees when he wakes up. Turns
out he fell asleep on a playground, he rolled himself in the old
popsicle wrappers and autumn leaves in the far corner, up against
the chain-link fence. A dodgeball game has been interrupted—
he wakes to the sound of a big red rubber ball hitting the fence,
then bouncing away. The girl who was chasing it is shock-still,
looking at him now. His eyes travel up from the red sneakers, to
the scabbed brown knees, to the kilt, to the white T-shirt over the
still-flat chest, and then the solemn face on her, curious, uncowed.

It's like a movie, he thinks, I'm in a movie. Her companions are
backing away, hands at their mouths.

He sees it as if adjusting the focus on a telescope—the others slide
backward while this girl stays put, going no place.
Oh, he thinks: it's a monster movie and I am the monster.
So he gets to his feet and he tries to look like a good monster:
blinking, slumped.
He's trying to come up with whatever such a creature should say,
when a strange thing happens. The girl with the red sneakers
speaks to him.

SONG: STRANGER

Don't be afraid, Stranger
I'm not afraid,
I'm not afraid of you.

You look so lost, Stranger
But you're not lost,
'Cause I just found you.

Just take my hand, Stranger
Just take my hand
And I will lead you home.

So she takes him to her own back door, and her mother is
surprised to see this gaunt, grubby man standing gingerly on the
wet linoleum she just finished mopping. She's trying to figure out
why he seems so familiar. And then she remembers. It was a long
time ago, back when she was in high school, but sure, she used to
see him all the time, working on that boat of his in his front yard.

The house is only a few blocks away. They used to talk sometimes.
He was a handsome man, he made it worth your while, woodchips
in his hair. Now he seemed a little lost, dazzled by everything.

Well, she could just run him over there right now. Would he like
that? Save him the walk? Such a quiet, sad old guy. And to think
of her trying to flirt with him all those years ago. What a fool.
But, well, she could still see it. A kind of muted glow, what had
once been his beauty.

She gets him in the station wagon and backs it down the driveway
and out to the street.

And that was the day I met Odysseus.

Odysseus returns to Ithaca at last; but comes disguised as a
beggar to his raucous hall, now the feasting ground of all the
young men who, insatiable for roasted meat, slaughter Odysseus's
herds and swill all his best booze. But you really can't blame them,
they don't know any better. These are the boys left behind by the
fathers Odysseus took with him to Troy and didn't bring home, not

a single one. He eyes the young men with murderous contempt. These too will have to die before his voracious narrative can be satisfied. Which will make it two generations of his island's men, all his male subjects, hundreds of his own people.
That's how many deaths it will take to bring this warrior home.

All this talk of roasted meat, which seems to be the only fare in the ancient world, makes me do something uncharacteristic. I run out and buy us steaks for dinner. I get nice cuts of meat and grill them on the barbecue, the first time I've used it since the summer.

That seems like another lifetime—the long warm days, the house milling with all those men opening wine bottles, checking out the record collection.

I flip the steaks and bounce on my heels, trying to stay warm in the chill air, looking out at the naked trees, thinking about how quiet my days and nights have become.
We don't conduct our lives in complete silence—that would be unbearable. We do talk, usually about the house, the weather, the immediate and tiny concerns of the day-to-day.

But it's a poor substitute for that ineffable thing, conversation. Something the man I once married excelled at. As it happens, that was one of his many gifts.

The steaks turn out nicely, if I do say so, and in celebration, I decide to set the long table instead of feeding him in his chair, as usual. He doesn't seem fazed when I invite him to the table and give him a glass of wine. About halfway through the meal, an odd thing occurs. I notice him picking up a scrap of meat from his plate and holding it under the table. It's a little gesture, and I probably wouldn't have noticed it, except I used to be on the lookout for it, twenty years ago, when we had Alice, the sweet spaniel he used to feed surreptitiously under the table, much to my irritation, since I thought it encouraged her to beg.

I just go ahead and say, "What are you doing?"

He says, "What?"

And, oh my god, I know that face, that composed, bland face,
so very different from the one he's presented to me all this time.

Because this time he's dissembling; it's a *constructed* face.

He's lying.

It's not that unbearable empty plate of a face I've found it so hard
to look at all this time. No, this is *pretended* innocence.

Something like jubilation floods through me. I say, "The meat
you're holding under the table. Who's that for?"

And then there's that other long-lost look, the sly, rueful
concession of a man who's been found out. He actually smiles as
he pops the meat into his mouth.

Then he says, "Well, where is she?"

"Who?"

There is just a flicker of doubt before he says, "Alice."

And then slowly, carefully, I tell him the story of Alice, our dear
old dog, whose heart he broke when he left us all those years ago.
Because she was fond of me, but she adored him.

She waited for him in all weathers, lying at the front door, looking
down the road, a furrow appearing in her speckled face. It was a
furrow I would stroke, trying to smooth it, erase that unending
confusion, but it only deepened with the years as her face went
white. Until there was a morning in the early spring, just as it was
getting warm, when she chose to finally forgo continuing her vigil
for the man who never returned.

He didn't say a word through all of this, the saga of Alice. Until he
asked if I had buried her, and in fact I had. Her ashes are right out
in the back, under the plum tree. I even carved her name into a
round stone from the beach. We went out there and stood in the
spill of light from the house and looked at it.

And then we wept. It took a long time.

And then we came in and sat at the table and began to speak.

It's a bloodbath, the end of the thing—hard to enjoy, really. The merciless slaughter of all those suitors and then the peculiarly horrid hanging of the hapless serving girls the suitors had raped or cajoled or simply enjoyed, the way they enjoyed the household goods of the absent owner over all those long years of lolling about.

The girls are strung up on a sort of pulley system, cleverly devised for efficiency, and they writhe and then hang limp in awful maidenly consort.
There they are, throttled no more ceremonially than one might crank the heads off a bunch of birds. They dangle whitely, swaying together. Their hard hands, chapped from their work, hang in bunches, red as chicken feet.

Then there is the moment the book was built to elucidate—the reunion between man and wife, a night of sex and stories. A night Athena, hardly a romantic, nevertheless goes so far as to make longer for them by stalling the dawn.

Odysseus goes off the next morning to see his wretched father, cruelly and unaccountably toying with the old man by dissembling one last time before revealing himself. The guy spends half the damn book in disguise or nameless—I guess it's a habit it's hard to break.
And then the families of the killed suitors attempt to avenge those deaths. Yet another melee ensues before divinity intervenes and breaks the thing up, sending everyone home to their empty houses and the new regime.

Except that's not where it ends.

Well, that's where the book ends, but not the story. Because the story isn't done with Odysseus yet. We know he has yet one more odyssey to make, the last one, and it's the one he must make alone.

It's a prophesy he heard in the land of the dead, something he must do to bring his long story to an end. He must carry an oar far inland, so far inland that no one knows what the thing he carries is because they've never heard of the sea. And if they've never heard of the sea, perhaps that means he will finally be in a place where no one's ever heard of *him*.

And for the first time he will no longer need to dissemble. He will at last be a stranger. He will have arrived at the place where he can finally make sacrifice and atone for all he did.

And there he will plant his oar and weep.

He's reading now. He's sitting out in the backyard, overlooking the ocean, a baseball cap shading his eyes. He's got the book in his lap.

I've been thinking about death a lot lately. I think he has too.

Of course the Greeks thought that when you die and make your journey down to Hades, you have to drink from and then bathe in the river Lethe, the river of forgetfulness. It washes your mind away, and there goes all the particularity of your own life's joys and sorrows.

You are left clean of personality, clean of history. Until you are interchangeable with every soul that ever was, all of you like so many white eggs, poised along the shore, shining with river water.

But there was a rumor of another river farther on, the river Mnemosyne, which is a river of memory, also in Hades. And in the waters of that, all of your life is restored to you entirely and you remember everything, everything, from the high drama to the tedium, the stupidity, the fretting, the accidental grace, the joy, the hurt we inflicted wherever we went, whether we meant to or not.

It's all there in the water. There's what we managed to understand and what we couldn't fix, the ways we protected ourselves and the way we flung ourselves about, heedless, grasping for that thing, that elusive thing we thought was beneath the surface of it all.

Complete remembrance. That was the rumor anyway. If you could make it to that second river, you could plunge in and spend eternity endlessly rolling in the waters of your one life story. But lately I've been wondering if that's what any of us really wants. And if we do, can it even be achieved?

Well, the Greeks had their doubts. Apparently cults grew up in ancient Greece that attempted to train you for the journey we will all have to make into the landscape of death. You were taught to endure insatiable thirst so that maybe, maybe you could resist the desire to drink from the first river of forgetfulness and actually make it to the last river, the river of remembrance. But it seems well-nigh impossible to pull off, doesn't it? Passing up the comfort of oblivion for that terrible immersion in your own truth. The water is so cold; the river is so deep.

I wonder where he is in the book, but there's no way to tell. He's looked up from it now and he's staring out to sea, his face in shadow. Beneath his gaze, the pages are turning in the sun, turning in the wind.

It moves like a live thing in his hands. Turning its pages, telling itself. Backward and forward like the tide. As he looks out to sea.

END OF PLAY

Mercury's Footpath

For Brian Kulick

Introduction

Brian Kulick has always gotten me into the best kind of trouble as a playwright. Indeed, he can be held responsible for my entire career as an adapter of Greek plays, since it was his commission to write an adaptation of Sophocles's *Electra* for a new version of *The Oresteia* to be produced by The Actors' Gang in LA back in 1994 that started me on the whole business in the first place. So when he approached me in the spring of 2015 and asked me to participate in something he was calling The Fragments project, I listened hard. Brian was then artistic director of Classic Stage Company, where my play *Iphigenia and Other Daughters*—which was what that first adaptation of *Electra* became—premiered. The Fragments project consisted of giving three playwrights—Chuck Mee, Mac Wellman, and me—fragments of lost Greek plays and asking us to write full-length plays in response. Some of the fragments are quite small; mine was about a page of collected broken sentences—all we have—of a Euripides play. But we do know the myth it's based on, which is that of Protesilaus, the first Greek soldier to die in Troy. His wife Laodamia's grief was so outsized and unrelenting that (depending on which version of the myth one favors) the gods uncharacteristically took pity on her and allowed Protesilaus to return from the Underworld, but only briefly, before he was recalled to death forever. In every version of the story, it was the second irrevocable loss that spurred Laodamia to commit suicide.

I was intrigued, but when I heard that it was apparently this myth that inspired Thornton Wilder to write *Our Town*, I was hooked. From our earliest contemplation of that all-too-understandable desire to bring loved ones back from the dead, there has also been something uncanny and worrisome about the thought. The Greeks are always unsettled by the implications of it. One has only to think of Alcestis, mute and veiled, returned but somehow still absent at the end of her play, to know that there is something fundamentally wrong about the attempt, even if it succeeds. It may be that Orpheus turns to lose Eurydice back to the mists of death because he senses this. Perhaps it's not that he doubts she is behind him, but that he has misgivings about whether she *should* be.

I knew I wanted a presiding deity for the play and so thought unsurprisingly of Hermes, or, in this version, Mercury, whose relationship with humans is so much more intimate than any other god's since he is the one who takes us down the path to the Underworld and so has to listen to us—our laments, our complaints, our regrets, our leave-takings—as we make the long passage to our eternal home. It's his familiarity with our mortality, that particular human inexorability, that gives him a more nuanced view of what we are, how we suffer, and how we love. Is it pity, or whim, or just curiosity that leads him to consent to Laodamia's request? Whatever sparks him, I can't think of another god who would have acceded as he does, and accordingly the play belongs to him.

We have so little of the original play that we don't know much of anything about what Euripides did with the myth. So I was free to imagine my own way into the story. I heard that Protesilaus had been revered as a hero, the man who had willingly given his life so that the war could begin. His was a conscious death, a self-sacrifice for the sake of history, or Greece, or . . . again, it depends, like so much of mythology, on who is telling the story. But thinking about the unenviable first soldier to die in a war led me to invent the Greek soldier who had what is to my mind the even greater misfortune of being the last to die. I wanted to hear what those two men might have to say to each other in the gray silence of the twilit world the Greeks thought was in store for us all.

Characters

PROTESILAUS, hero of the Trojan War, thirties to forties

TELEFTEOS, foot soldier of the Trojan War, thirties to forties

MERCURY, God of the Crossroads, Beginnings, and Endings, immortal

LAODAMIA, wife of Protesilaus, thirties to forties

KALLISTO, wife of Telefteos, thirties to forties

Place

The Underworld, Laodamia's place, and a liminal space.

Time

Immediately after the end of the Trojan War, and also all time. The pre-WWI period that Mercury mentions needn't factor into costuming, unless that seems helpful.

Note on the Text

A slash (/) indicates the point at which the next character should begin to speak, overlapping the rest of the first character's line.

Scene 1

The Underworld. Sound of water, perhaps a river nearby. Protesi-
laus alone. Telefteos enters, trailing a gray silk ribbon, which was
tied to his wrist but which, as he walks across the stage, falls off of
it. He is barefoot and his feet are wet.

TELEFTEOS
Are you Protesilaus? The first of the Greeks to die at Troy?

PROTESILAUS
Yes. Who are you?

TELEFTEOS
My name is Telefteos. I was the last.

PROTESILAUS
So it's over.

TELEFTEOS
Yes. I came to tell you.

PROTESILAUS
How long did it take? There is no time here, and the counting in
my head stopped.

TELEFTEOS
Ten years.

PROTESILAUS
That's a long time, isn't it?

TELEFTEOS
It's a long time for a war. And if it wasn't for you, it would never
have happened. I'd be home, tossing seed into furrows, my farm,
my wife. Days and days in the sun ahead of me. Something to look
forward to. But that's all gone forever. Thanks to you.

PROTESILAUS
Some would say it was heroic.

TELEFTEOS
Some would. Not me. Why'd you do it?

PROTESILAUS
If it hadn't been me, it would have been someone else.

TELEFTEOS
But it was you. And I never understood why. You knew that the
first to set foot on Troy would be the first death of the war. We all
heard the prophesy.

PROTESILAUS
Yes, and so had they. So there we were, a thousand ships lined up
along the shore, all of us staring across the water at them, and no
one getting out. It was absurd.

TELEFTEOS
(Nodding) And strange. The silence going on and on, all the armor
creaking, flashing in the heat. I remember thinking, Please, don't
anyone start the damn thing 'cause maybe then we can all go home.

PROTESILAUS

What? You think the might and glory of Greece could just back up in a mess of oars and run away from our greatest story?

TELEFTEOS

I've got a story. Good story. Kid grows up, meets a girl, falls in love, they start a life together, then—here's the best part—they *live* it. And then they die, holding hands.

PROTESILAUS

It was a story that had to happen, that war. It was too big, and too long in the making. And I didn't start it. Not even close. If you wanted to stop that war from happening, you'd have to go a lot further back than me. Like maybe all the way back to a party-planning mistake—what to do about the unpleasant relative. Because if the old hag had just been invited to the wedding then she wouldn't have been stung enough to ruin it by throwing the Apple of Discord into the ceremony in the first place, which started the squabble over which of the goddesses was the prettiest.

TELEFTEOS

(Nodding) —Or if they hadn't chosen Paris, some prick of a playboy, to be the judge.

PROTESILAUS

—Or if Helen hadn't looked like that.

TELEFTEOS

(The best idea yet) —Or if she'd never been born.

PROTESILAUS

(Running with it) —If Helen's mother, Leda, had never been raped by the swan Zeus because she'd never caught his eye in the first place.

TELEFTEOS

—If, say, a scrap of cloud had drifted past and hidden her from
sight when he was looking down.

PROTESILAUS

—Or if Hera had called him and he'd turned away just long
enough for Leda to close her door—

TELEFTEOS

—Just close her door and disappear inside, out of his sight forever.
We wouldn't be here. Either of us.

(Pause.)

PROTESILAUS
How did you die?

TELEFTEOS
I was thinking of my wife. The end of the war was so close we
could taste it as we crawled out of the belly of the hollow horse.
The Trojans were drunk or asleep after all their crazy celebrating,
so sacking the city would be nothing, just the matter of a night,
and then it would be over. Easy. I was the last to leave the horse.
I watched my comrades coursing down the dropped ladder,
heard the little grunts as they landed and ran, landed and ran,
helmets bristling as they streamed off in different paths through
the sleeping streets, swords glistening in the dimness. We'd been
crouching in the dark for so long, all of us sweating together
through the day and night, our fear and boredom, the way you
could smell it, how we'd stunk the place up. So I just hung there
for a while, breathing the cool night air, looking at the open city
below me. I thought about my wife, how I was as good as headed
home to her, and then, it was the weirdest thing, I could smell her
neck, the sweet musk, ten years gone. It hit me like a wave, that
memory, must have dazed me, I guess, 'cause I lost my footing
on the ladder rung. I fell without calling out, feeling like a fool,

knowing my comrades wouldn't look back, their feet slapping away from me as they fanned out into the city to do the final work of slaughter. Broken, I listened to the screams beginning as the city woke up to the end of things. And then I died, the last of the Greeks, a nobody, left behind in a heap and forgotten. There was too much to do that night to remember me.

PROTESILAUS
Does she know?

TELEFTEOS
My wife? I don't know. I hate to think of it. No one to choose from for another husband but the boys who were too young to take with us. Fatherless pipsqueaks, who of them could be worthy of her?

PROTESILAUS
You wouldn't mind if she married someone else?

TELEFTEOS
(Shrugs) Now that I'm gone, what does it matter? But only if it makes her happy.

PROTESILAUS
It brought happiness to us, marriage. Though we didn't have long. Not even time enough to make a baby in her.

TELEFTEOS
Us neither. The war snapped its jaws and that was it for us.

(Pause as they consider this.)

I wish I'd looked at her harder. I'd have more to remember. But we were shy of each other, always glancing away. As if there was time. We thought there would be all the years to know each other. The sweetness of the bed.
It wasn't big, but it was mine, that story, and I'll take my little one over your big one any day.

PROTESILAUS

It's not mine. It's everybody's. And we need the big stories. They give us something more than our own circle of hills to think about. We can lift our eyes and dream of greatness.

TELEFTEOS

It was just a war. And it was only a bigger story because stories live by their endings and that had thousands. Death upon death upon death.

PROTESILAUS

But always a first and a last.

TELEFTEOS

Which is where we came in.

PROTESILAUS

You and me. It was our fate. Who can say which of us was the most unlucky?

TELEFTEOS

I can. I was. It was a long war, and there wasn't a day I didn't want it to be over.

PROTESILAUS

But I died before I got to do anything. You had a chance at glory.

TELEFTEOS

No, the glory was all yours. You died for history, or, I don't know, *something*. You were the first, so your death had meaning. After that, it was all just a bloody blur for most of us. The only person my death will matter to is my wife. You got to be part of the big story, you got heroism. The likes of me just got on with finishing what you started.

PROTESILAUS

It didn't feel particularly heroic. It felt more like impatience. I wanted to get it over with. Whatever it was. Anyway, I couldn't help myself. Before I knew what I was doing, I had put one leg over the side and the other was following it and I found myself sliding down into the shallow waves. That's when I looked up at the sky and saw the arrows arcing toward me. I knew I wouldn't even make the beach. The war would begin and end for me right there, yards from the shore, my own blood circling me in the water as I went down. I thought, look what I have begun, just by getting off a boat: everything. And then I was dead.

TELEFTEOS
And when did you remember her?

PROTESILAUS
Too late. Too late.

(Pause.)

And now it's all I do. Remember her. Everything else has lost its color. She's all I've got, and there's not much—a handful of memories, a few bright days.

TELEFTEOS
All the little stories that never got to happen. That's the thing about the big stories. They always eat the little ones.

(Pause.)

PROTESILAUS
You never get used to it. The dark down here.

(Pause as they look up.)

TELEFTEOS
I wonder.

PROTESILAUS
Yes. Me too.

TELEFTEOS
If they think of us.

PROTESILAUS
And what they remember.

TELEFTEOS
What she's doing right now.

PROTESILAUS
Perhaps it's morning.

TELEFTEOS
Her neck.

PROTESILAUS
Her mouth.

TELEFTEOS
Her eyes opening as she wakes.

PROTESILAUS
Turning her wrist as she stretches toward the ceiling.

TELEFTEOS
A yawn.

PROTESILAUS
Then a smile.

TELEFTEOS
Looking out at the day.

PROTESILAUS
The day that hasn't happened yet.

TELEFTEOS
A day we might have lived out together.

PROTESILAUS
Just an ordinary day.

TELEFTEOS
All of it before us.

PROTESILAUS
A day that can't help but begin.

TELEFTEOS
The light.

PROTESILAUS
The light.

(The scene ends with them both looking up.)

Scene 2

Mercury enters. He is in silver gray, wearing his characteristic winged helmet and sandals. He carries in one hand several long gray silk ribbons, which trail behind him. He is entirely comfortable speaking to the audience. This is, as far as he's concerned, his play.

MERCURY
Yes, I'm that one. The one who takes you down to the Underworld.
It's a good job. Not without interest. I hear a lot of stories.
The long walk down the gray corridor to the shore is almost
never a quiet journey. The compulsion you all have to talk—your
memories, your regrets, pain and joy, babbled childhood rhymes,
snatches of song, last-minute attempts to assemble a theory about
what it all meant, the life you just had, as the pinprick of light at
our backs gets smaller and smaller . . . All the talk. I hear it all
spooling out behind me as we travel deeper and deeper, away
from the sun and down to the damp mist rising up the passage
from the river shore below.
Centuries upon centuries now I've listened to you all—the tiny
knots and snarls and snapped threads of ordinary existence.
Because most human lives, it's just . . . stepping on the rake, losing
that bracelet, the dog wanders off, it rains on the ballgame,

a poorly aimed arrow here, a house burnt down there, oopsie daisy, coughs and bruises, bee stings and cancer, night falls before you're home safely, the dropped match is still lit, someone leaves the cage door open by mistake and . . . death.

Death, death, death. And that's where I come in.

I am the God of Endings.

Scene 3

Laodamia lives in the frozen chaos of her obsession. Perhaps it's a kind of wasp's nest made of newspaper clippings of war news and scraps of letters, along with personal photographs and trinkets. Even if there is no scenic indication, she should seem to be living inside a fixation—an airless, lightless half-life that is part refuge, part open grave. Kallisto enters.

KALLISTO
Are you Laodamia, wife of Protesilaus, first of the Greeks to die?

LAODAMIA
Yes. Who are you?

KALLISTO
Kallisto. Wife of Telefteos, the last. I came to let you know.

LAODAMIA
So it's over.

KALLISTO
Yes. We won.

(Pause as they look at each other.)

232

LAODAMIA
Well, *we* didn't.

KALLISTO
No. Not you and me so much.

LAODAMIA
I lost that war. Seems to me we both did.

KALLISTO
(She looks around) You've spent ten years like this?

LAODAMIA
Is that how long it took? The clocks stopped for me.

KALLISTO
Ten years I never quite let out my breath. So when they tell me
it's over and the boys are coming home, I get drunk and dance
all night. I walk across the wet summer fields the next morning,
carrying my sandals in my hand, and when I get home, there's a
strange boy outside the house looking down the road away from
me, sucking his dirty fingers. I can hear the servants crying inside,
my father banging around yelling for me, but even then I don't
worry. What could happen to me now? I thought I had nothing
to lose. He seemed like just a kid, that messenger, fingers wet
with spit, but then he turned and saw me, and there was this look
of, well, I guess it was pity, and suddenly he didn't look like a kid
anymore, and what he was about to say he didn't have to say,
because I knew.

LAODAMIA
Mine was an old man, wheezing after running up from the ships,
asking for wine before he could speak, as if it was good gossip.
Told it like a story. Took his time to break me.
It doesn't matter how it comes, it's the same.

KALLISTO
No, it isn't. You've had less time to live in fear.

LAODAMIA
And more time to live like this? Which of us can you say is luckier?

KALLISTO
(Sitting down) Oh, I don't know.

LAODAMIA
I don't either. All I know is that I don't know how to live past this.

KALLISTO
You mourn.

LAODAMIA
I can't. I don't believe it.

KALLISTO
Believe what?

LAODAMIA
That he's dead.

KALLISTO
I know what you mean, it just doesn't / seem—

LAODAMIA
No, you don't. I mean that I don't believe it. I won't believe it.

KALLISTO
But he is. Dead.

LAODAMIA
Not as far as I'm concerned. I won't accept it. Until he comes to
me himself to tell me he's dead.

KALLISTO
But his death is exactly what makes his coming to tell you of it
impossible.

LAODAMIA
Until he comes, I won't accept it. He'll have to tell me himself.

(Pause.)

KALLISTO
But that's insane.

LAODAMIA
You can love your husband any way you want. This is the way I love
mine.

KALLISTO
It's not about love. It's about the nature of things. You're being
perverse.

LAODAMIA
Perverse?

KALLISTO
Irrational.

LAODAMIA
Why should I be rational? I won't pretend this makes sense.
It doesn't. To lose him like this. And for what? A war? In some
country I'll never go to, off at the end of things, someplace I can't
even imagine, where he went to kill people he never knew, people
he would never have even met anyway, and for . . . what? Does
that make sense?

KALLISTO
No. But—

LAODAMIA
I refuse it.

KALLISTO
You refuse it. I don't even know what you think that means.
And what does this refusal of yours *do*?

LAODAMIA

I've made my demands. I have reason to hope.

KALLISTO

Why? You have no power. Nothing to bargain with.

LAODAMIA

I have my rights.

KALLISTO

No you don't.

LAODAMIA

It's the force of my despair.

KALLISTO

Women, human beings, *all human beings*, have always suffered like this. And worse. What makes you think you're special?

LAODAMIA

I can feel it; something is happening, a shifting in the basement of things. Little creaks and sighs. Something is giving way.

KALLISTO

(With concern) Oh, honey.

LAODAMIA

He will come to me. I know it.

KALLISTO

I hope you're wrong.
For your sake, God, I hope you're wrong.

(A sound. Both of them look down. Then Laodamia turns to Kallisto and smiles.)

Scene 4

MERCURY

God of Endings, yes. But also God of Beginnings. I have an interest in those too. Or perhaps it would be best to call me, as some do, the God of the Crossroads. Because who's to say at what point history . . . tips? It may be that the fate of thousands upon thousands of souls hangs upon such an inconsequential thing that only a god can see it. Perhaps it all depends on some nearly unnoticeable moment, a tiny gesture, forgotten almost as soon as it's made. There are times when even you can feel it: destiny hanging, breathing in the balance. But whatever it is that will change everything? That is what I know and you never really do. Might a war that would be the death of an entire civilization have been averted? Say that what it all came down to was a small stone thrown or not thrown by a sickly child? For instance, consider one sunny day in the morning of the twentieth century. It's a family picnic in the summer after their dead queen mother left her descendants to rule the world without her. Cousins mill about in white, speaking different languages, but all alike in their watery eyes, delicate skin, and tentative expressions. The fate of the world rests on this frail shell of an afternoon. The girls in white, parasols, lace, and ribbons, the boys in pale tight suits, knickers, and soft hats. The children, not knowing what to say, feed the ducks, their kid-leather boots stepping carefully through the fresh-cut grass. The boys skip stones. Except for the smallest boy, a silent, wide-eyed child, fawned on by his sisters, who flutter about him like so many doves, touching him constantly, straightening his sailor's cap, murmuring warnings. He is not to climb on rocks, lest he scrape his hands, eat too quickly, lest he choke, run too fast, lest he stumble. Danger is everywhere for this pale child, apparently, even at this regal duck pond in the middle of a gentle summer day, the sugar dust of cream puffs still gritty in the corner of his mouth.

He shifts his weight in his clean shoes and watches his cousin, older, dark-eyed, kind, a boy among boys, lofting one flat stone after another out to fly in languorous beats across the lake, one, two, three, four, five, then a blur of disappearance, as it runs in footsteps into the water. He likes the intent sidelong expression on the boy's face as he leans away from the lake, the muscle of his bared forearm flexing as he flicks the stone away in a long, shallow arc. He finds himself wanting, more than he has wanted much in his life, to know something of that in his own body, a physical ease so forgetful of itself. But he knows such things are beyond him and so, with his bodyguard's shadow striping across his feet, he looks down, pretending to search for stones to throw, as if he could. So that when he looks up and sees his cousin approaching him, his body shakes with the alarm of joy. His tall, dark cousin holds out to him a perfect stone, smooth, flat, a roundness that feels like a benediction on his palm. The dark cousin's brown, sure hand encompasses his for a moment, showing him the grip. He imitates the older boy's angled stance as best he can, and then, in a sideways sling he prays will be worthy of the perfect stone, he flicks it out across the shining water. With surprise and gratitude, he sees it hop twice awkwardly, a stone he has transformed into a gray toad of some kind, the first magic trick he has ever performed. It may be, he thinks, his first accomplishment of any kind at all. He stands open-mouthed, watching the ripples fanning out, then turns to his cousin, who nods, smiles, and turns away, as if this is no miracle, only what might be expected of such a boy as he is.

Then they are moving back and forth along the shore, in quest of what they throw, pausing only to admire each stone's stuttering little journey into nothingness. Further gifts are exchanged, stones for stones, but it is a wordless companionship punctuated by small triumphs, muted whoops, or minor failures unremarked upon as they turn back to the search.

It's a long afternoon, but it will end, he knows, the pale boy. The sisters and the mothers and the fathers are all calling for him. The light has changed, the time has come. He stands there holding the last gift of stone, cradling its smoothness in his hand, thinking, Once I throw this, the next thing will happen, and the next and the next, and the moments will skip out and away from this and this most precious moment will be lost to the past, hardly believable, no way to get it back. But also, if I throw this, everything will *start*. He feels the weight of history pressing at his back as he tries to hold the moment in his hand. He can sense it, what will happen. The end of all brightness, the death of everything he has ever loved. He sees everything that is to be lost, all that is at the mercy of this particular second, if they only knew. All the heads of state with their ribbons and medals, all the mothers and nurses, their hats bobbing and whalebones creaking, the sisters and cousins with their giggles and sashes, the fathers and monarchs squinting and pacing, the mute attendants standing like arrows, the bodyguards with their white cuffs and red hands, all the mustaches and hairpins, the whole enormity of this family party which is not a family party—it all depends on this, he thinks, the stone he holds in his hand, given by his cousin. Given to him who might soon be a tsar from him who might soon be a king, their empires now stretching in wild, unfurling vastness away from them, oak and pine forests, pastures and mountains, running with rivers. Their great, fragile countries, vulnerable to each other, held in the teeth of history, just before the jaws meet, just for this moment, if only he could stop it from happening, but no, it's gone from his hand before he can help himself, and he and his dark cousin watch the stone he was given vanish prettily, stepping into nothingness in the pinking water. And he knows, he can feel it, everything to come.

Scene 5

Mercury appears to Laodamia. He carries the gray silk ribbon that trails offstage in one hand.

LAODAMIA
I knew you'd come.

MERCURY
Well, yes.

LAODAMIA
I longed for you. I've been doing nothing but longing for you for years.

MERCURY
And here I am. *(Gestures off)* Shall we?

LAODAMIA
(Confused) Shall we . . . ? Oh, no. That's not what I had in mind.

MERCURY
A little late for that, I'm afraid.

LAODAMIA
I'm not ready.

MERCURY
Yes, they usually say that.

LAODAMIA
I think there's been a mistake.

MERCURY
That too.

LAODAMIA
No, I think you misunderstood me. I didn't want you for myself.

MERCURY
(Looks around, as if for a body) Did you kill someone?

LAODAMIA
No, no, it was for him, my husband. I want him back.

MERCURY
It seemed to me that you only wanted to join him where he is.

LAODAMIA
No, just the opposite. He needs to be back here, with me.

MERCURY
Cannot happen. So sorry.

LAODAMIA
I don't think you understand. He wasn't done.

MERCURY
Done?

LAODAMIA
With his life. We'd just gotten married. We were just starting out.

MERCURY
Yes, yes, and yet . . . *(Snaps his fingers)* Shall we?

(He holds out the loop of ribbon, gesturing for her to give him her wrist.)

LAODAMIA
No, no, I don't want to die. That isn't what I want. I suppose I might have given that impression but—

MERCURY
I really don't have time to discuss this. Either you come with me or you don't, but there is no third alternative.

LAODAMIA
I thought you could make an exception if you wanted to.

MERCURY
Oh, dear. This again.

LAODAMIA
Just this once. And we would be so grateful.

MERCURY
I don't think you would, really.

LAODAMIA
No, but I would be. I would never stop singing hymns to you.

MERCURY
I don't need hymns. *(Looks at her and sighs)* You're so maddening, you people.

LAODAMIA
Me and Protesilaus?

MERCURY
No, people. People, people, people. All the same endless craving and whining and resistance to the inevitable, not to mention the absolute certainty that you are somehow unique, each one of you, that what you ask me for has never been requested, when you have never stopped asking for it from the beginning.

LAODAMIA
Which is . . . ?

MERCURY
"Please, please, let me go back. Just once, even for a moment.
Now I know what I've lost, if I could feel it again, life, if I could
only . . ." Or, "Just give him back to me, it doesn't have to be for
long, just time enough to see his face, tell him one thing, let him
know that I really truly . . ." And so forth.

LAODAMIA
But we *are* unique, each of us. Our stories differ in detail after
detail and each tiny difference determines the people we become.
A chance encounter on the street, a missed train, a dropped glove,
a moth bangs against a window and makes you turn your head
and suddenly the whole course of a life shifts and—oh, if you could
only understand—because each one of us looks back at this long
skein of random incidents but it adds up to something that seems
monumental, as if it couldn't be any other way, and at the same
time wonderfully fragile, and, and, *yours.* For instance, he and I,
how we first met, and the way that we loved each other—

MERCURY
Oh, please, don't. I've heard it, your great human devotion to the
differences between you, how every one of you is *distinct.* When
all I see is how you share the same limitation, time, which is why
you all seem alike to me.
If you could only see yourselves from where I stand. Each one
of you. Only one little fizzle of a candle apiece to light and burn,
and never to the end. It's out before you're even able to pierce
the darkness of the tiny room you've tried to see with it. But as
these long centuries of death have rolled past, I have stood on a
mountain and watched forests burning below me. That is how
much human life I have seen wear out its flames.

LAODAMIA
And yet you have noticed me.

MERCURY

(An admission) There's a kind of keening you can hear sometimes above the roar if you listen for it. I do. And yours has been hard to miss.

LAODAMIA

It's the size of my sorrow.

MERCURY

Human sadness. That's the strangest thing for us. And impossible for us to understand. Because we gods don't lose anything. We aren't built for that. Whereas it's all you people do. From the moment of your birth, you begin scattering your possessions like so much seed—baby teeth, innocence, hopscotch pebbles—right up until the moment of your death, when you abandon pulse, sky, color, music, life, life, life. I can see it coming off you like steam as I take you down the path. So that by the time we are standing together by the river waiting for the ferryman, there's nothing left to distinguish you at all. By then all your little whiffs of exception and idiosyncrasy have danced up into the nothingness and left you mute at last at the water's edge. Your long work of losing is finally done.

LAODAMIA

There are losses that cannot be borne.

MERCURY

And yet they are. Or you decide that they can't be and I take you down a little sooner. That's all.

LAODAMIA

I'm not ready to go down. I demand that he come up.

MERCURY

I know, that's what's so peculiar about you. How unreasonable you have been, and for how long.

LAODAMIA

So I am exceptional after all?

MERCURY
Only in your stubbornness.

LAODAMIA
Well, then. Perhaps that gives me something to bargain with.

MERCURY
Believe me, you have nothing to bargain with.

LAODAMIA
Then why are you still talking to me? I think you're curious.
It must be monotonous for you. All that wheedling and
lamentation. You must have wanted to see what would happen if
you gave in, just once.

MERCURY
For one thing, it's not my place.

LAODAMIA
But you could do it, couldn't you? Say it's an experiment. Just to
satisfy your own curiosity. It could be a secret little transaction
with the darkness. No one would ever have to know. Just us.
The three of us. And then you would have found something out.

MERCURY
What would that be?

LAODAMIA
What happens when you actually give human beings what they
want.

MERCURY
What they think they want.

LAODAMIA
I know what I want. And I will never want anything more.

MERCURY
Oh, I think you will before we are done.

(Pause while he considers her.)

I can do something odd for you.

LAODAMIA

I knew it, I knew you could! You will give him back?

MERCURY

No. That's not in my power.

LAODAMIA

What then?

MERCURY

I can lend him to you.

LAODAMIA

Lend him to me?

MERCURY

For a few minutes, not more than that.

LAODAMIA

That's all?

MERCURY

(Infuriated) That's more than all the countless souls who have ever lived have ever had in the history of humankind.

LAODAMIA

I'll take it, I'll take it! Whatever of him you can give me. Please.

MERCURY

(Looks at her dubiously, already regretting this) Wait.

(He exits. She stands there in absolute stillness, waiting.)

Scene 6

Kallisto comes back to Laodamia's place. Telefteos approaches Protesilaus.

KALLISTO AND TELEFTEOS
Something's happened, hasn't it?

(Both Laodamia and Protesilaus nod.)

LAODAMIA
He told me to wait.

PROTESILAUS
I'm supposed to wait.

KALLISTO AND TELEFTEOS
Wait?

PROTESILAUS
Which is what I've been doing all this time.
But never *for* anything.

KALLISTO AND TELEFTEOS
Wait for what?

LAODAMIA
He's coming up.

PROTESILAUS
I'm going up.

KALLISTO
He what?

TELEFTEOS
To what?

PROTESILAUS
To her.

LAODAMIA
Just for a time.

PROTESILAUS
Not long.

KALLISTO AND TELEFTEOS
What then?

(Sound. Kallisto and Laodamia look down, Telefteos and Protesilaus look up. Laodamia pats the top of her chest, right below her clavicle, three times. It makes a sound. Kallisto turns to her.)

KALLISTO
What's that?

LAODAMIA
It was our signal that we were thinking about the good times. That we remembered. We did it when we could see but couldn't touch each other for some reason. Like when he was on the boat, leaving for the war, and I was standing on the shore. We could see

each other. It's the last thing I saw him do. When I do it now,
I think he can feel it.

KALLISTO
We should have come up with something like that. I'd do it all the
time.

*(Sound. Kallisto and Laodamia look down, Telefteos and
Protesilaus look up.)*

TELEFTEOS
If you see your wife, could you tell her to give my wife a message?
Tell her that when her nose itches that means I'm thinking of her.

PROTESILAUS
Her nose?

TELEFTEOS
I used to make fun of her, the way she'd always have to scratch her
nose when her hands were full, or wet, or . . . and she'd ask me to
do it for her. Tell her that's when I'm thinking about her.

PROTESILAUS
(Distracted) Her nose. Right.

TELEFTEOS
(Resigned) You won't remember.

KALLISTO
So, I've been thinking. Do me a favor? If you see him, I want you
to tell him to give my husband a message. Tell him that when I'm
thinking about him, I always remember the night when we made
love in a field and all the fireflies were out, that when he closes his
eyes and sees them that means I'm thinking of him. Got it?

LAODAMIA
(Distracted) Fireflies. Right.

KALLISTO

(Resigned) You won't remember.

(Suddenly a great shaft of light penetrates into the Underworld. It's like an incredibly intense follow spot, narrow and brilliant white. It searches around the darkness until it finds Protesilaus and then it stops on him, completely still and vertical. A gray ribbon falls down to him from above. It is looped at the bottom. He places it around his wrist. Suddenly his hand is jerked directly up. Blackout.)

Scene 7

*Sound. Laodamia stands, apprehensive. Suddenly, Protesilaus
is there, looking disoriented. The long gray silk ribbon stays
attached to his wrist, limply extending offstage. Laodamia gasps,
then runs to him. Carefully, she puts a hand out to him, touches
him. They are both amazed to find that he is real and that they
can touch. He lifts his hand, looking at it, places it on her face.
She weeps. They kiss carefully.*

LAODAMIA
How long?

PROTESILAUS
I don't know. Not long.

LAODAMIA
You're so pale. So cold.

PROTESILAUS
I'd forgotten. The sun. Your eyes too. Blinding.

(They kiss.)

LAODAMIA
This very body, here, with me.

PROTESILAUS
(Places his hand on the top of her head) This is where I used to
live. *(Places his hand on her hip, her mouth, her breast, saying)*
And here. And here. And here.

LAODAMIA
(Places a hand on his chest) And I. *(Places her hand on his cheek,
his neck)* And I, and I . . .
Look at you. You're still intact.

PROTESILAUS
Intact?

LAODAMIA
Whatever comes, age is something that will never come to you.

PROTESILAUS
"Whatever comes"? Nothing "comes" to me now. Nothing will ever
come to me.

LAODAMIA
I will come.

PROTESILAUS
No, not you, my love. At best an echo. A sort of snapshot.

LAODAMIA
But we will be together.

PROTESILAUS
Not the way you think. Death is . . . it's only made up of what it isn't,
which is life. That's all it is, death—not life.

LAODAMIA
But we will be together.

PROTESILAUS
I don't know what you think that means, but you don't understand.
We'll never be able to touch. Not there. The body . . . it's only here.
Only here.

LAODAMIA
Well then. *(Touches him)*

PROTESILAUS
(Holding her) How much longer? The time, the time, the time, the
time . . .

(They embrace, rolling across the space.
Darkness.
Lights up. They are sitting on the floor, cross-legged. She holds his
wrist.)

PROTESILAUS
Pulse?

LAODAMIA
(Feeling for it) No. *(Pause)* Yes!

PROTESILAUS
That's yours, I can feel yours in your fingers.

LAODAMIA
No, it can't just be mine.

PROTESILAUS
It's not my pulse I feel, it's time passing. I haven't felt it in so long.

LAODAMIA
I haven't felt it since I heard about you. Time. That's when it
stopped. Not until now. It's terrible.

(She places a hand on her chest and pats three times.)

Remember?

(He puts his hand on his chest and does the same, then continues in time to his heartbeat; she does the same. They look at each other, feeling a kind of rising panic.)

Stop!

(They stop.)

Stop.

(They embrace. They try not to pat each other's bodies in the same beat, but finally end up doing just that, holding onto each other and patting each other in time to a heartbeat.
Darkness.
Lights up. They are in the middle of an argument they don't want to be having.)

PROTESILAUS
You talk as if my death were a choice between love and honor, between you and, and, and some abstract, some other, some *them*.

LAODAMIA
But that's what it was!

PROTESILAUS
That's not what it seemed like at the time.

LAODAMIA
But that's what you did. You chose. You left *me* for *that*.

PROTESILAUS
War?

LAODAMIA
For death. You chose death. How do you explain that?

PROTESILAUS
I can't. No.

LAODAMIA
Because you think I can't understand?

PROTESILAUS
Yes. Well, you can probably understand. But it would be intellectual.

LAODAMIA
How could anything I understand about you be intellectual?
Everything I know about you, anything I really know, when it
comes to you—

PROTESILAUS
It wasn't personal.

LAODAMIA
It's personal. Everything about this is personal.

PROTESILAUS
It wasn't at the time.

LAODAMIA
It should have been.

(Pause.)

PROTESILAUS
All right. Let me try to say this. It had meaning for me, that death.
Violence is inevitable. So war is inevitable. And if war is inevitable,
then—

LAODAMIA
To say something is inevitable is to make it just that.

PROTESILAUS
But death is. Inevitable.

LAODAMIA
(A gesture) Apparently not.

PROTESILAUS
Yes. And is this how you want to spend this time?

LAODAMIA
No. *(Touching him, near tears)* No. No. No.

(They embrace.
Darkness.
Lights up. They are in a different physical relationship, perhaps
not touching.)

PROTESILAUS
But it will happen, your death, and then it will be forever. What
isn't forever is this, the ordinary sweetness of ticking time. It's
what I've missed most of all . . . *change*, variation and surprise and
sunlight and shadow, the sense of the world, everything in it, all
things being *in progress* somewhere.

LAODAMIA
Yes, and for me it's been like being on the deck of a ship helplessly
watching the life we once stood in together recede faster and
faster into the distance as I pull away from that beloved shore.

PROTESILAUS
But you should, you can do that: Go on to become an old woman,
live out the span of what you have ahead, years and years of *your*
particular life. All the mornings and evenings, rainstorms and
sunny days that are there, still all there ahead, waiting for you,
untouched.

LAODAMIA

But you will always be this! Don't you understand that I don't
want to get old if you don't? Every step I take into time takes me
further from you.

PROTESILAUS

Do it for the stories. Death is long. It's an endless now. And you
would have more stories to tell me in it.

*(Suddenly, the ribbon attached to his wrist starts to go taut. They
watch. The ribbon pulls him to his feet. She hangs onto him.)*

LAODAMIA

I'm coming with you.

PROTESILAUS

No. Stay. Get old.

*(He is pulled away. She lets him go. For one moment more he
stands across the stage from her, pats his chest three times.
She does the same on hers. He is pulled off. She collapses.)*

Scene 8

Split scene. The Underworld and Laodamia's place. Protesilaus is approached by Telefteos; Kallisto approaches Laodamia.

TELEFTEOS
Did you tell her?

PROTESILAUS
Who?

TELEFTEOS
My wife. About her nose itching when I was thinking of her?

PROTESILAUS
Oh. No. I forgot.

KALLISTO
Did you tell him?

LAODAMIA
Who?

KALLISTO
About the fireflies. That when I was thinking about him, he would see the fireflies?

LAODAMIA
Oh. No. I forgot.

KALLISTO AND TELEFTEOS
It's the only thing I asked you to do.

LAODAMIA
I know. / I'm sorry.

PROTESILAUS
I know. / I'm sorry.

LAODAMIA
I wasn't thinking. / I wasn't thinking of you.

PROTESILAUS
I wasn't thinking. I wasn't thinking of you.

KALLISTO
So? What was it like?

LAODAMIA
It was . . . it was . . .

TELEFTEOS
Was it good?

PROTESILAUS
No. Or, I mean . . .

LAODAMIA
It wasn't what I thought it would be.

TELEFTEOS
Why? You saw her?

PROTESILAUS
Yes.

KALLISTO
What did you think it would be?

TELEFTEOS
So what happened?

LAODAMIA
A . . . correction.

PROTESILAUS
It was too . . .

TELEFTEOS
Too what?

KALLISTO
And instead?

PROTESILAUS
Good. Because now. All I can feel, all I can feel . . .

PROTESILAUS AND LAODAMIA
All I can feel is regret.

TELEFTEOS AND KALLISTO
For what?

PROTESILAUS
What I didn't see, / what I didn't feel, what I didn't do, when I had
the chance.

LAODAMIA
What I didn't see, what I didn't feel, what I didn't do, when I had
the chance.

Scene 9

Mercury enters Laodamia's place.

MERCURY
I think there's been a mistake.

LAODAMIA
No, no mistake.

MERCURY
Some sort of misunderstanding.

LAODAMIA
I'm perfectly clear.

MERCURY
You mean to tell me that after I went to all that trouble, after
I risked all that for you—

LAODAMIA
It didn't work.

MERCURY
What did you expect? What would it "working" have meant?

LAODAMIA

It would have fixed the, the *error*. It would have felt . . . it would have made sense.

MERCURY

I knew this, I told you—

LAODAMIA

I would have been able to live with it. Accept it. That's what I thought, that if I saw him just once, even for an hour . . . but instead it's even worse now, the crush of this sorrow, the sense of living inside a, a *mistake* . . .

MERCURY

A mistake that you think your death can solve?

LAODAMIA

I know it can't be *solved*, but this pain—

MERCURY

The pain will just follow you down. You won't escape it, even there. You just shift it from one pocket to the other.

LAODAMIA

(Final) But at least there will be no more sunlight on it.

(Pause.)

MERCURY

I told you, I said before you went—

LAODAMIA

Please. You were right. *(Lifts her wrist for the ribbon)* Now. No more.

MERCURY

How are you going to do it?

LAODAMIA
I've already done it. Poison.

MERCURY
Ah, well. Shouldn't be long.

LAODAMIA
No. *(Something kicks in, a convulsion, her eyes close)* Cinnamon.

MERCURY
What?

LAODAMIA
(Having difficulty staying conscious) Cinnamon. The taste of it.
I will miss . . .

(But she collapses, dead. A pause. He watches her. Then her eyes open and, serenely, she lifts her wrist to him. He loops the ribbon around her wrist and she stands and follows him off.)

Scene 10

Laodamia is standing in a transitional place.

LAODAMIA

I've seen it in my head so many times. I will hear the ferryman's muttering song down the water, the tuneless tune he sings to himself as he makes his way through the fog. And then he'll be in sight, plunging his long pole into the silt of the river bottom. When he sees me standing there he won't question me. He will know. He's seen it before. The girls with the bruises on their necks from the ropes they trail behind them, the wet tangled hair of the ones who drowned themselves, and then us, the wasted eyes and waxy skin of the self-poisoners. All the sad girls who have waited for him there, as if waiting for their lovers to come out of the mist. He will put a hand out to me without a word, and I will step into the gently rocking boat.

And as he pushes off from the one shore, I will turn my face to the fog and listen to the silence as we make our way across the dim water to the last.

Scene 11

Kallisto is in a sunlit place, kneading bread dough. Protesilaus
and Telefteos are together in the Underworld.
Laodamia walks into the Underworld. Her feet are bare and wet.
The looped gray ribbon of silk falls off her wrist as she enters.
The men look up and see her.

PROTESILAUS
(Apologetic) I can't . . . *(Meaning that he can't touch her)*

LAODAMIA
I know.

(She sits down near them. Pause. Protesilaus pats the top of his
chest three times, looking at her. She pats the top of her chest three
times in response. Then they look out. Telefteos looks up. Kallisto
suddenly looks up and out. She stops kneading the dough. She
rubs her nose with the back of her hand. It's awkward because she
has dough on her hands. Telefteos closes his eyes. Kallisto laughs
to herself. Telefteos smiles.)

TELEFTEOS
Huh. Fireflies.

(Protesilaus and Laodamia look out and then up. Protesilaus pats the top of his chest three times. Laodamia pats the top of her chest three times. A pause. They are all three looking up now. Kallisto continues to knead her dough, smiling. Protesilaus pats the top of his chest three times. Laodamia pats the top of her chest three times. Pause. Lights begin to fade. Protesilaus pats the top of his chest three times. Laodamia pats the top of her chest three times. Darkness, in which we hear Protesilaus pat the top of his chest three times. A pause, then Laodamia pats the top of her chest three times.)

END OF PLAY

The Oresteia

For Michael Kahn

Introduction

Michael Kahn, then artistic director of the Shakespeare Theatre Company in Washington, D.C., approached me in the
spring of 2016 with the commission for this adaptation of *The
Oresteia*, the trilogy of plays by Aeschylus that are among the most
difficult, mysterious, and powerful in all of theatrical literature. He
told me to trust my instincts and to feel free to step as far from the
source material as I needed to make a new version of these ancient
plays for our times. He gave me only four conditions: One, I had
to combine the action of the three plays into one play that could
be performed by a single company of actors in under three hours.
Two, the chorus, unlike Aeschylus's, should remain the same set of
characters for all three plays. Three, Michael felt that in order for
a contemporary audience to understand Clytemnestra's motive for
murdering her husband Agamemnon on his return from the Trojan
War, we needed to incorporate the story that precedes the war and
initiates it—Agamemnon's sacrifice of their daughter Iphigenia.
And four, I had to deal somehow with the Furies, who appear in the
final and most problematic play. These vengeful figures of appalling horror for the ancients can easily devolve into mere actors in
monster costumes in modern productions. Michael's request?
"They need to be "f*cking terrifying."

Michael spoke about why a new version of the trilogy seemed
right for his final directing project at the theater. They are, after
all, among the oldest plays we have, the only complete trilogy; and

271

the story of the House of Atreus is one of our most ancient myths, one that's been disinterred and retold again and again—durable, dramatic stuff. It seemed right to him that the last thing he did in the classic theater he had long loved and nurtured would be, as far as "classics" go, the epitome of the form. But he also said that what had engaged him from the first time he read *The Oresteia* as a young man was the supreme issue of the trilogy: What do we do about the human compulsion toward violence? How do we transcend the cycles of blood that have created so much of the misery of human existence since our very beginnings?

Aeschylus considers this problem most deeply and coolly in the third play, his *Eumenides*, which is my third act. In it, he presents us with the trial of Orestes, the matricide, which Aeschylus depicts as the first trial in history. He gives us a happy ending in which the bloody cycle is finally brought to a close with the establishment of order and the triumph of the sky gods over the older, brutal forces of blood vengeance, the Furies.

I began writing my version of *The Oresteia* in the summer of 2016, in what seems another world, and got a draft of the first two acts together fairly quickly, turning them in by late October. I was puzzling over how I might approach the third act, the one everyone agrees is the hardest because it can become a kind of tedious civics lesson, when the unthinkable happened with the election of that American president. I came to a dead stop and could see no way forward, not only in the play but in my life.

While commiserating with my friend, Katrin MacMillian, who works in human rights, mostly in Africa, I said, "This is not the first time people have felt this way. Indeed, *The Oresteia* is about how a people moves on after having seen the worst that human beings are capable of. What do we do once we have become morally unrecognizable? How did people in the past recover the best of human nature, even when they thought it had been lost forever? There must have been times in human history when, even after the worst has happened, people have done the right thing." She mentioned the Truth and Reconciliation Commission in South Africa, without which, she maintains, that country would be in a state of perpetual civil war, embroiled in a bitter past it could never escape. The principle at work is that both the perpetrators and the victims of violence have been exiled by those experiences from their community and that something must be done to reinstate them into the circle of the human. She spoke about what was borne out time and again when the glorious simplicity of the concept was honored. It's not about absolution, it's not about forgiveness, though those can sometimes happen. It is simply about gathering in a public space open to all. Everyone concerned, both the victims and the perpetrators of the violence, is present. Nothing is promised. But all will be heard and have the chance to speak their truth. And in so doing, we, all of us, recognize one another. It's an ancient concept, a Greek one in fact, that notion that in recognizing one another in all our confusion, pain, and jagged moments of violence and cruelty, bravery and kindness, we draw ourselves back to the circle of what we share, what gives us a stake in one another, our happiness, and our enlightenment. It's born of the belief that only by bringing us all into the same place, and hearing the truth if we can speak it, can we heal. *Which is of course the basic principle at work in theater.* I thought, if I can manage to evoke that essential grace in the third act of my play, I might be able to write my way to something like hope in these dark times. So that's what I tried to do. We don't offer judgment at the end so much as the mystery of mercy, born of the act of listening and recognition.

Athens in her ancient glory may have fallen, as her playwrights and poets always warned she might, but the scent of her lingers all these centuries hence with the handful of plays we are still marveling at. The world has kept some of that beauty and the memory of her best dreams. They survive in us, and they can serve us as we serve them in our own bad times, knowing that something of us too will last, even if the worst happens, even so.

Production History

The Oresteia had its world premiere at Shakespeare Theatre Company (Michael Kahn, Artistic Director; Chris Jennings, Executive Director) in Washington, DC, on April 30, 2019. It was directed by Michael Kahn. The scenic and costume designs were by Susan Hilferty, the lighting design was by Jennifer Tipton, the sound design was by Cricket S. Myers, the original compositions were by Kamala Sankaram, the movement direction was by Jennifer Archibald; the dramaturg was Drew Lichtenberg, the production stage manager was Joseph Smelser. The cast was:

CLYTEMNESTRA	Kelley Curran
IPHIGENIA	Simone Warren
AGAMEMNON	Kelcey Watson
CASSANDRA	Zoë Sophia Garcia
ELECTRA	Rad Pereira
ORESTES	Josiah Bania
CHORUS	Corey Allen, Kati Brazda, Helen Carey, Jonathan Louis Dent, Franchelle Stewart Dorn, Alvin Keith, Patrena Murray, Sophia Skiles

The Oresteia had its New York premiere digitally, as part of the Artists and Community Series presented by Theatre for a New Audience (Jeffrey Horowitz, Founding Artistic Director; Dorothy Ryan, Managing Director), on June 25, 2021. It was directed by Andrew Watkins. The sound design was by Joanna Lynne Staub, the original compositions were by Kamala Sankaram; the production stage manager was Ralph Stan Lee. The cast was:

CLYTEMNESTRA	Kelley Curran
IPHIGENIA	Simone Warren
AGAMEMNON	Obi Abili
CASSANDRA	Ismenia Mendes
ELECTRA	Rad Pereira
ORESTES	Reynaldo Piniella
NARRATOR	Kathleen Chalfant
CHORUS	Corey Allen, Helen Carey, Franchelle Stewart Dorn, Rinde Eckert, Robin Galloway, Sophia Skiles

The Oresteia was made possible with generous support from the Roy Cockrum Foundation.

Characters

CLYTEMNESTRA, a queen, thirties to forties

IPHIGENIA, a princess, perhaps ten years old

AGAMEMNON, a king, perhaps a bit older than Clytemnestra

ORESTES, a prince, twenties

CASSANDRA, a former princess of Troy who is still an unwilling priestess of Apollo and a prophetess, twenties to thirties

Chorus

An androgynous and diverse group. Their general identity should be along the lines of "the household help," and one should sense that, if not actually onstage, they are always about, engaged in various obscure minor tasks, doing the work of keeping the place going in some mysterious way. It should be easy to lose track of them since they are unremarkable, but, except for the bulk of Act II, they are onstage, if only as witnesses. Indeed, they are mostly understood as figures on the margins of the action, since what they are up to seems so commonplace by comparison to the grand business of the rest of the play. But this is their power.

Watchman and Nurse emerge from the chorus and return to it. Electra doesn't appear in Act I but emerges from the chorus in Act II. She remains dressed as a chorus member throughout. Clytemnestra will join the chorus briefly after her death.

CHORUS A/WATCHMAN, earthy, folk wise

CHORUS B, cool, pious, otherworldly

CHORUS C, reasoned, questioning, just

CHORUS D, fierce, frightening, decisive

CHORUS E/ELECTRA, creature energy, watching, wary, sly

CHORUS F, older, ironic, cool; formerly the nurse of Orestes

CHORUS G, motherly, capable, experienced; formerly the nurse of Electra

CHORUS H, unpredictable, ancient soul, powerful

CHORUS I, young, questioning, fair

Place

The House of Atreus.

The house is a terrible place, stark and ancient, isolated in a barren landscape. The facade need only have three openings in it: a massive central double door below and two large windows above, shuttered or curtained so that we might occasionally see a figure moving behind them.
The roof, where Watchman is perched, should be high enough to give him prominence.
When Agamemnon arrives, he must be elevated above the stage such that he has to step down onto the cloth laid out for him by Clytemnestra. This can be achieved by bringing him in on a wheeled conveyance like a chariot, or, as was the case in the original set, designed by Susan Hilferty for the production at Shakespeare Theatre Company in D.C., having him appear on a platform that hinges down from the wings and which he then steps out onto, followed in time by Cassandra.

Note on the Text

A slash (/) indicates the point at which the next character should begin to speak, overlapping the rest of the first character's line.

Note on Production and Cast Size

This published version of the play was written for a cast of fourteen: eight chorus members and six principals. (Chorus E/Electra only begins as a member of the chorus.) There is an alternative version of this play, meant for easier producing, which uses twelve actors: a smaller chorus of six in Act I, with the two actors playing Cassandra and Iphigenia shifting into the chorus for Act II and Act III. (Chorus E/Electra doesn't appear in Act I.)

Twelve is the minimum number for the cast.

If you are interested in the smaller cast size for your production, please contact the author at her website: www.ellenmmclaughlin.com.

Act I

The ancient house. Night and stars above. Sound of crickets, night creatures. A watchman is on the roof alone, looking up. A cry from within. A nightmare cry, female.

CHORUS A/WATCHMAN
Happens every night. Her. Bad dreams. Years I've been up here
listening to her. Waiting like a dog, propped up into the sky,
watching, just like she told me to, for the beacon. The light in the
dark that says that Troy is fallen. She thinks she's set up some kind
of system. The flare off the first mountain above Troy signaling
the guy on the next mountain down the line to light his stack
of greased wood. And then that mountain signals the next and
the next and the next, crossing languages, entire peoples, and
countries as it runs. And it's supposed to happen all in one night.
She says news can do that—pass from a battlefield at the end of
the world all the way to this palace here, fast as thought. So she's
put me up here every night now for years. I watch the majesty
of the sky drift over me and wait for this new man-made star
to bloom on the horizon there. Like that could happen. Seems
crazy to me. As if she could make a star. They're even older than
the gods, the real stars. They've all got stories, and I tell them
to myself all night to keep from closing my eyes. The skies are
full of blood and jealousy. Long, tricky narratives, constellations
elbowing one another up there, fizzing away and telling

themselves. All that glory just for sleepless, lonely me. Up on the roof of this terrible house where nothing good happens. I ride it like an animal as it twitches through its dreams.

(Clytemnestra enters in her dressing gown, which is elegant. She speaks, apparently to us, but there may be chorus members visible now as well.)

CLYTEMNESTRA
I had the strangest dream.
I was cleaning the house, which God knows could use it. It's always been too much house for me. It's packed like a . . . what? . . . a reliquary, a museum, a brain? . . . so old and honeycombed you can't find your way through it sometimes, crammed with all these artifacts and relics and so much *history* . . . Don't get me started. The rooms—too many rooms—you can get lost in it. You start in one century and you find yourself in another and then you're suddenly someplace else entirely, a room drifted with dust but also a sense that someone was just here, even though that's impossible, ages must have passed since anyone . . . But it's the strangest thing, like the carbon fizz of a match just blown out, just there, just . . .
Why does everything seem as if it just happened in this house?
Anyway. I was cleaning the house.
Which felt good at first . . . I was really getting the job done, swiping away cobwebs and the soot of centuries. My house. Walls, ceilings, and hallways gleaming with this liquid I was swabbing everything down with. Gleaming pink. Because it was blood. That's what I . . .
I looked in the bucket, the bucket of miraculous cleaning fluid.
It was a bucket of blood. Whose? I don't know. Mine? His? But here's the thing: It worked. The house. It was clean.
So it was a good dream. Wasn't it?

(The chorus speaks. They may have been listening all along and the audience is only now aware of their presence.)

CHORUS B
I think you need to leave the cleaning to us.

CLYTEMNESTRA
Do I?

CHORUS C
We know where everything is.

CLYTEMNESTRA
I know a thing or two.

CHORUS D
Of course you do, dear.

CLYTEMNESTRA
You haven't seen everything.

CHORUS B
Enough. I think you'll find.

CLYTEMNESTRA
You mean, the walls have ears?

CHORUS F
(Nods, then taps her head with a finger) A mother knows.

CLYTEMNESTRA
You're a mother?

CHORUS F
My children are . . . dispersed.

CLYTEMNESTRA
Mine are here.

CHORUS G
Yes dear, the ones you have left.

CLYTEMNESTRA
What did you say?

CHORUS H
The ones you've kept hold of.

CLYTEMNESTRA
My children are all here.

CHORUS I
They are all *present*, yes . . .

CLYTEMNESTRA
Every single one.

CHORUS F
Of course. It's just that they aren't all exactly . . .

CLYTEMNESTRA
Exactly?

CHORUS F
Alive.

(Iphigenia is heard offstage.)

IPHIGENIA
Mama?

CLYTEMNESTRA
(Confused) I . . .

CHORUS F
You're thinking of ten years ago.

CHORUS G
She's thinking of ten years ago.

IPHIGENIA
Mama?

CLYTEMNESTRA
But I, she's . . .

IPHIGENIA
I can't sleep.

CHORUS D
She's going back.

CLYTEMNESTRA
Iphigenia?

CHORUS H
She can't help it.

CHORUS F
Go ahead.

CLYTEMNESTRA
Coming! I'm coming.

(It's ten years earlier. The chorus backs away to let Clytemnestra shift back into memory.)

IPHIGENIA
(Still offstage) Stay, Mama. I'll come to you.

(Iphigenia enters from the house. She has a stuffed animal, wears a nightgown.)

It was about a war.

CLYTEMNESTRA
Bad dream?

(They embrace and Clytemnestra leads Iphigenia to sit somewhere.)

IPHIGENIA
There were two big eagles.

CLYTEMNESTRA
Oh, that one.

IPHIGENIA
They, they *swoop* down on this fat bunny rabbit. And she's fat
because she has babies inside her and they *swoop* down—

CLYTEMNESTRA
How is that about a war?

IPHIGENIA
Because Daddy's in it.

CLYTEMNESTRA
Daddy?

IPHIGENIA
He's there with Uncle Menelaus.

CLYTEMNESTRA
Watching the eagles?

IPHIGENIA
He's got blood on him.

CLYTEMNESTRA
From the mother bunny?

IPHIGENIA
She was going to have babies, but they eat them instead. They eat them in the sky.

CLYTEMNESTRA
Goodness.

IPHIGENIA
Daddy says that's what has to happen.

CLYTEMNESTRA
The eagles have to eat the rabbits?

IPHIGENIA
So they can win the war.

CLYTEMNESTRA
The eagles?

IPHIGENIA
That's what Daddy says.

CLYTEMNESTRA
I see.

IPHIGENIA
I think he's wrong.

CLYTEMNESTRA
Do you tell him that?

IPHIGENIA
I can't.

CLYTEMNESTRA
Why not?

IPHIGENIA
I can't talk.

CLYTEMNESTRA
Yes you can. You're talking to me right now.

IPHIGENIA
In the dream. I can't talk.

CLYTEMNESTRA
Why not?

IPHIGENIA
'Cause I don't speak. He makes sure of that.

CLYTEMNESTRA
Daddy does?

IPHIGENIA
Maybe I really was a bunny, all along. Maybe he's right.

CLYTEMNESTRA
Daddy?

IPHIGENIA
He said.

CLYTEMNESTRA
In the dream?

IPHIGENIA
That's why I can't sleep. I mean speak. I mean . . . *(She is asleep)*

(Agamemnon comes in.)

AGAMEMNON
Bad dream?

CLYTEMNESTRA
The same dream. The eagles, the pregnant hare. Did you tell her
something that would make her come up / with . . . ?

AGAMEMNON
Why would I tell her anything like that?

CLYTEMNESTRA
It just sounds so much like the kinds of things that are making the
rounds. Why the wind won't pick up. Why the fleet can't sail. All
that mumbo jumbo.

AGAMEMNON
(Correcting her) It's not . . . There is a mystery here, something
larger than . . . It's a matter of finding a way to *talk about* these
things, and ordinary language is not going to work . . . it's not
enough. So, yes, dreams are significant. If we are to try to
understand what is most important, we have to use metaphor.
That's how they speak to us.

CLYTEMNESTRA
The gods?

AGAMEMNON
Yes. What they reveal to us they reveal in symbols.

(She settles the sleeping Iphigenia and steps away from her.)

CLYTEMNESTRA
So you really think that the gods take some sort of personal
interest / in—

AGAMEMNON
It's not personal, it's—

CLYTEMNESTRA
That they invest themselves individually in the matters of human
beings, as if—

AGAMEMNON

I don't know how it works! But I know what's in the balance . . .
Don't you see what a disaster this is? I am the general of an army
I can't command because we can't get to the battlefield. We can't
sail. Weeks now. And every day that goes by . . .

CLYTEMNESTRA

Why is that *your* fault?

AGAMEMNON

Because someone has to take the blame.

CLYTEMNESTRA

Why? Isn't it just . . . what has happened? There is no wind.
Why does it have to *make sense*?

AGAMEMNON

Something is wrong. Something *big* is wrong. And if that's my
fault, if there's something I've done . . .

CLYTEMNESTRA

Why should it have anything to do with *you*?—

AGAMEMNON

(Losing patience) If there is any action I can take to make this
better, to put my army into the right *alignment with the universe,*
then I will do that. Why wouldn't I?

CLYTEMNESTRA

I just . . . I don't understand why you're suddenly lost in all this
cryptic superstitious nonsense. When did you become so . . .
religious?

AGAMEMNON

You have no idea what my spiritual life entails.

CLYTEMNESTRA
What spiritual life? You are a military commander, you order troops around. You organize death.

AGAMEMNON
Exactly. Which makes me all the more aware of how much is at stake in everything I do. I can't afford not to *get this right*.

(He stands looking at Iphigenia.)

I don't like that dream.

CLYTEMNESTRA
She has it every night now.

AGAMEMNON
I don't like it.

CLYTEMNESTRA
Isn't it just a matter of how you interpret it? The story you tell about it?

AGAMEMNON
The *story* I tell?

CLYTEMNESTRA
Yes, whatever you come up with to calm her down? So she isn't so scared?

AGAMEMNON
There's more to it than that. She might be capable of *sensing* something we can't, a clear vessel for the truth.

CLYTEMNESTRA
So you think our daughter is a prophet?

AGAMEMNON

It's not about her, it's about the dream. It's something that must
be understood.

CLYTEMNESTRA

Well then, why can't it be a *good* dream? Maybe the hare, the
babies, maybe that's just Troy sacked, the generations of the enemy
snuffed out.

AGAMEMNON

No, it's . . . bloody in the wrong way. If that's me, if that's my
brother, then what have we become?

(She goes to him. He is still standing over the sleeping Iphigenia.)

CLYTEMNESTRA

That's not you. You aren't like that.

(She embraces him. He looks up.)

I see the way you look at her.

AGAMEMNON

Anything, I would do anything—

CLYTEMNESTRA

I know you'd do anything for her.
You are capable of anything.

AGAMEMNON

I have to . . . I'll be back.

*(Agamemnon exits, leaving Clytemnestra alone with the sleeping
Iphigenia, who turns suddenly, in the grip of a nightmare.)*

IPHIGENIA

(Still asleep) Daddy?

CLYTEMNESTRA
Mama's here.

IPHIGENIA
She can't help me.

CLYTEMNESTRA
Sweetie?

(She tries to wake her.)

IPHIGENIA
Only Daddy and he won't.

(Iphigenia opens her eyes.)

CLYTEMNESTRA
You're awake now. See? Everything's fine.

(Iphigenia is indeed awake, but still terrified.)

See? You're home. Safe and sound. All is well.

(Iphigenia just shakes her head. Mute with panic.)

Sweetie? What are you looking at? It's just the house. Everything you know. Nothing different. The way it's always been.

(She takes Iphigenia by the hand and begins to lead her into the house. But we can see that Iphigenia is still open-eyed in terror. She balks at entering the house. Clytemnestra croons a bit, as if it's a kind of lullaby.)

And always, and always, and always will be.

(Clytemnestra gently leads her into the house.)

And always, and always, and always will be.

(They have exited.
The chorus speaks to one another.)

CHORUS C
Almost impossible, ten years later, to remember that there was ever
a time before the war. Ever a time when it didn't seem inevitable.

CHORUS D
When it was still a matter of little girls waking, frightened by
nightmares.

CHORUS H
Parents arguing over portents and prophecies.

CHORUS F
When no one had died for anything yet.

CHORUS G
And for a moment it seemed like no one ever would.

CHORUS C
Helen had been abducted, yes, her husband and his brother had
called up an army to get her back. But still.

CHORUS I
But still.

CHORUS D
But still.

CHORUS G
But still.

CHORUS B
But still nothing had happened yet.

CHORUS C
There they all were, standing outside the door of history.

CHORUS B
The coastline filled with the might of Greece.

CHORUS G
Jostling, teeming, bristling with spears.

CHORUS D
Splayed for miles and miles down the shore.

CHORUS H
All in readiness for the long sail across the ocean to their waiting
fates.

CHORUS I
But then.

CHORUS D
But then.

CHORUS G
But then.

CHORUS B
But then the breath of the world dies, and nothing is possible.

CHORUS F
Rumors flare in the tinderbox of the camps.

CHORUS H
Someone somewhere has somehow put everyone on the wrong
side of the divine.

CHORUS B
Who is the / sinner?

CHORUS I
Who is the sinner and what is / the sin?

CHORUS B
What is the sin?

CHORUS F
Nothing is revealed, so everyone is guilty.

CHORUS C
And then the starving begins.

CHORUS I
And the stealing.

CHORUS G
And the fights.

CHORUS H
And no one is safe from the knives and rancor.

CHORUS D
The army without an enemy can only turn on itself,
Like a famished wolf who begins to chew off his own paws.

CHORUS C
And at the center, the general,
The little god of the great army.

CHORUS B
Pity him.

CHORUS F
No longer the single inhabitant of a single fate,

CHORUS C
He paces the cage of his responsibility,

CHORUS G
The gathered strength of the known world,
Amassed in its roaring might,

CHORUS C
All for him.

CHORUS B
All for him to lead to glory.

CHORUS F
All for him to botch.

CHORUS C
Every day, he stalks the shoreline of the sea
he cannot get his ships out on.
Every day, under the shadeless eye of the sun
on that windless beach,
He sees all that he is in charge of tip further toward ruin.

CHORUS I
Until at last the cry goes up.

CHORUS B
The seer has seen.
The message received.
The gods have been offended and must be appeased.

CHORUS G
They will never let the wind blow,

CHORUS F
Nothing can happen ever again,

CHORUS B
Unless a sacrifice is made.

*(Agamemnon bursts onto the stage, panting, distraught. He leans
over, catching his breath, as if he has run a long way.)*

CHORUS C
A sacrifice.
Just one.

CHORUS I
One.

CHORUS G
A child.

CHORUS F
One child.

CHORUS H
One particular child.

CHORUS D
One child.

CHORUS B
And only that one particular child.

CHORUS F
And the sacrifice must be made by one person.

CHORUS I
And only one person.

CHORUS B
He must do it himself,
And he must do it tonight.

IPHIGENIA
(Offstage) Daddy?

(Agamemnon looks up, frightened. Iphigenia comes in, once again in her nightgown. She stands across the stage. They look at each other.)

I know. I saw it.

AGAMEMNON
Saw what?

IPHIGENIA
My death.

(Agamemnon begins to cry. Iphigenia goes to him, climbs up onto him. He holds her but turns his face away. She takes his face and turns it to hers. He looks at her.)

Daddy?

(He turns away.)

Daddy?

(She takes his face again and turns it to her.)

CHORUS D
Nothing teaches us,

CHORUS C
Nothing tells us the truth,

CHORUS H
Except pain.

IPHIGENIA
I lo—

(Agamemnon covers her mouth with his hand. They stare at each other.)

CHORUS F
We learn nothing except through suffering.

(She slides down him, his hand still clamped over her mouth. He hugs her to him.)

CHORUS B
This is how the gods convey their love.

(In a sudden moment of decision, Agamemnon scoops Iphigenia up in his arms and runs off, carrying her. A moment of stillness. Then, shutters open and two long red silk streamers fall from the highest windows of the house. Offstage, Clytemnestra screams. Clytemnestra comes out of the house to see Agamemnon enter, covered in blood, carrying a knife. They stare at each other across the stage, shaking. Suddenly, the wind buffets the stage and the streamers fill like sails. Agamemnon exits.
The streamers blow out the windows and drop to the ground, where chorus members gather them up quickly and carry them off. Lights change.
We are back at the beginning of the play: the watchman on the rooftop, Clytemnestra in the yard, having just recalled her dream. The watchman sees the beacon.)

CHORUS A/WATCHMAN
VICTORY! VICTORY!
It's over, it's over! The end of all our waiting. All will be well. All will finally be well.

(Dancing, he exits the rooftop.)

CLYTEMNESTRA
It's over. *(Looks off to where Agamemnon exited)* At last. Ten years waiting.

CHORUS C
It's over.

CHORUS F
It's over.

CLYTEMNESTRA
But he lived through it. And he will return, victorious. I always
knew he would.
I can see him now, this night of nights, standing in the rubble that
was Troy,
Lit by fire, bathed in blood and smoke.
That city, once the glory of the world, is now a hunting ground,
Where all night long the Greeks pick off their prey.
Through empty marketplaces and abandoned schoolyards,
House to house, they pursue them,
Slaughtering Trojans in their kitchens and on their beds.
Tonight, the Greeks, ten years in exile,
Ten years camped in sand and rain, lice and flies, sleep,
Their bloody bodies wrapped in fine linens and silk,
In the houses, in the beds, of dead men.
Free of fear at last.

CHORUS G
Free of fear.

(The chorus repeats this under their breath like a prayer.)

They sleep.

(The chorus repeats this under their breath like a prayer.)

CLYTEMNESTRA
Gorged on their enemy's raided larders.

CHORUS G AND F
They sleep.

(The chorus repeats this under their breath like a prayer.)

CLYTEMNESTRA
Deaf to the wailing of women over bodies.

ALL CHORUS
They sleep.

CHORUS G
Surely nothing / can harm them now.

ALL CHORUS
Surely nothing can harm them now.

CHORUS G
Our dear ones will return at last.

(Pause.)

CLYTEMNESTRA
The men who left us will not be coming home. It has warped
and buckled them, that war.
They know what they did, what they sacrificed from the start.
No darkness can hide them from themselves. Justice is patient,
and time means nothing to the truth. The Greeks may leave Troy
behind them, but they pull sorrow in the wake of their ships along
with all their loot.

CHORUS B
Ten years of war. And all for what?
For the sake of a woman with too many husbands.
Helen,

(The chorus echoes "Helen" with contempt.)

for whom two nations sank to their knees in blood.

CLYTEMNESTRA
You cannot blame my sister for this war.
As if her little affair with a foreign prince—some sordid grappling
behind a palace door—could have brought down such destruction.

It was the brother generals, her husband and mine,
Who rounded up the might of Greece and drove it through ten
years of shouting blackness to punish one adulterating boy.

CHORUS B
She knew what she was. She knew nothing she did could ever be
unremarkable.
Hell on ships,

(The chorus echoes "Helen.")

Hell on men,

(The chorus echoes "Helen.")

Hell on cities,

(The chorus echoes "Helen.")

The bride of fury for whom
Thousands on thousands died.
Dreadful power, too much beauty.

CLYTEMNESTRA
(Contemptuous) That's not power. She did nothing. Helen. She
might as well have been a statue bundled from one court to
another.
Never made a decision, never had to reckon the consequences of
a single act. Let her run a country for ten years while her husband
is off at war. Then she'd know something about power and what
it takes.
But I don't have time for this.
I must prepare to greet my returning hero.

*(She exits. Chorus A enters around the side of the house to find the
rest of the chorus in silence.)*

CHORUS A
Why is no one rejoicing? The war is finished.

CHORUS C
Hard to believe . . .

CHORUS I
But it's true, the war—

CHORUS B
The war is finished—

CHORUS C
Hard to believe that war is finally finished with us.

CHORUS I
And we are finished—

CHORUS H
And we are finished with / war.

CHORUS F
And we are finished with war.

CHORUS G
War has finally taken all it can take.

CHORUS C
Enough.

CHORUS H AND D
Too much.

CHORUS B
We gave what was asked and we gave it willingly. Didn't we?

CHORUS G
It was not asked of us,

CHORUS H
It was demanded,

CHORUS D
And by our king.

CHORUS C
Our / king.

CHORUS I
Our / king.

CHORUS A
Our king.

CHORUS G
A man of fears / and rages.

CHORUS H
A man of fears / and rages.

CHORUS C
A man of fears and rages.

CHORUS B
We thought he was a man who could / do anything.

CHORUS I
We thought he was a man who could do anything.

CHORUS A
Anything.

CHORUS H
And then we / knew.

CHORUS G
And then we knew.

CHORUS D
We knew.

CHORUS F
He was.

CHORUS G
He was indeed a man who could do anything—

CHORUS C
He could and would do anything—

CHORUS D
He was a man who would do anything.

CHORUS F
Any terrible thing.

(Pause.)

CHORUS A
But what choice / did we have?

CHORUS I
What choice did we have?

CHORUS B
He was our king.

CHORUS A
He was our king. We gave him / what he wanted.

CHORUS B
We gave him what he wanted. He was our king.

CHORUS F
I gave him my children. And he marched them into the maw of death. We sent them / out—

CHORUS G
We sent them out, our hopes circling their heads like butterflies,

CHORUS F
Only to have him deliver them home to us, our dear ones, as tin urns filled with dust.
Ash and / bone—

CHORUS C
Ash and bone, the coinage of war.

CHORUS F
No. We who mourn our dead can never speak the name of the man who took them from us without horror. And at the scent—

CHORUS G
And at the scent of so much slaughter and swagger,

CHORUS A
Foreboding / wakes.

CHORUS B
Foreboding / wakes.

CHORUS I
Foreboding wakes.

CHORUS G
Foreboding wakes.

(Agamemnon enters on some conveyance that glorifies his arrival and gives him some distance and height from which he can address his people.)

CHORUS A
Great King!

(Chorus B and I echo "Great King!" with less conviction.)

Welcome home!

(Slight hesitation.)

We have not prepared a way to address you.

(A moment of awkwardness. The chorus looks at one another.)

CHORUS F
You are, after all, the man who took our boys from us to fling
them against the walls of a city at the end of the earth, and all to
bring back one errant wife.
We couldn't help but think that you were dangerous, a madman.
And when you made the sacrifice, we won't name it,
Your bargain with the wind,
We thought, well, we can't say . . .

CHORUS C
But it seems it has worked.

CHORUS F
And here you are . . . Well done.

(Uneasy pause as Agamemnon realizes that's all he's going to hear from them.)

AGAMEMNON
First, I must thank the gods who have guided me home. It was
a great victory. Total. So it must have been their will. It must

have been . . . *right.* Troy stole from us and now Troy has been punished, punished to the ground. The perfumes of its orchards turned to stinking smoke. All her quaint buildings and splendid palaces, just winking embers now. That was the price. As for her people: Rest assured, there was no mercy. The lion of Argos leapt from the belly of the wooden horse onto the sleeping city, then left his bloody paw prints down every street and lapped the blood of kings. He gorged himself. Gods be praised. Look what they can do if they are angry enough. It's beyond anything. Exhilarating stuff.

(The chorus can't quite muster the necessary enthusiasm.)

I appreciate your honesty by the way, I can always see through flatterers. You can't trust anyone. I left that city all alone, betrayed by all of them, the bastards. But that's all over now. I'm home, home by the grace of the gods.

(Clytemnestra appears in the doorway, formally dressed, impressive.)

CLYTEMNESTRA

Happy, happy day! My conqueror has returned.
Oh, what a woman goes through when her husband is off at war. Shattered by rumors, shivering with dread. His face always burning before her. Every one of her dreams, night after night, is of her husband's death. His blood spatters her, his screams wake her. She thinks she hears him call her name across the oceans. And years go by. I must confess it now. I tried, I did, to kill myself. To end the jolting misery of it all. Cut down twice, no, three times, but you see I couldn't believe I would ever live to see this day. This fine day. When you have come back to me, my husband.

(Pause.)

Ah. You noticed. A child is missing. You're right. A child should be here to welcome you. At least one of your two . . . remaining children. There is Electra, of course, but I'm sure the one you

want is the one you left in my belly when you sailed off all those
years ago. A son, Orestes. I promise you will meet him soon. I just
wanted you all to myself for these first few hours. These tender
hours. Your son will see you later. Everyone will. After this.
Come, my king, you have reached your journey's end.
But first, indulge me. It's a ceremony I devised myself.

*(She gestures and the chorus unfurls onto the ground a piece of red
fabric that stretches from the threshold of the house to Agamemnon,
making a path of red for him to walk up to the door.)*

Let not the foot that trampled Troy touch earth again. No, he shall
only walk on finery from now on. May the man who felled a nation
stride in glory through the door of the home he never hoped to see
again!

AGAMEMNON
Daughter of Leda, I cannot help but feel sheepish, a bit . . .
overpraised. I am not some woman who lives on flattery, or
some peacock of a potentate who needs to strut about, trampling
luxuries. I am a man, not a god; I feel a sort of dread at this.

CLYTEMNESTRA
You don't think that you have earned the right to swagger? The
great should be allowed to luxuriate in their bounty. If they
inspire jealousy that is only their due. The price of glory. You are
the envy of the world. Exult in it.

AGAMEMNON
It's . . . unseemly, an offense to the gods.

CLYTEMNESTRA
And haven't the gods been good to you? Crowned you with
victory, rained down blessings on your house? Your wealth is
as inexhaustible as the sea. *(Gestures to the fabric)* Look at the
abundance of what you own, what you can afford to destroy.

AGAMEMNON
This is too fine to wreck.

CLYTEMNESTRA
We can always get more.

AGAMEMNON
It matters so much to you to win this?

CLYTEMNESTRA
Give me this. It is gracious to yield when it costs you nothing.

AGAMEMNON
I don't know why it's so important to you.

CLYTEMNESTRA
I can't explain it. I have seen it in the eye of my desire since
I watched your ship sail away ten years ago. Your return to our
house across this carpet of red.

AGAMEMNON
Well.

(Pause. He gives in.)

Just let me take off my boots, these old soldiers of mine, filthy
with the dust of Troy. And when I crush the delicate splendor of
my house under my unwashed feet, let no one look down and
condemn me.

*(He steps down on the fabric. A pause as he looks at his foot
uneasily.)*

It is done.

*(A moment of suspension. All hold. Iphigenia appears. She is
wearing the nightgown, as before, but now bloody at the neck.
A red strip of fabric, the same that Agamemnon is standing on,*

*gags her mouth, the knot of it on her neck, the length of it reaching
the ground like a stream of blood. No one sees her. She slowly
walks around Agamemnon, looking at him where he stands. Then
she turns and looks across the stage at her mother. She starts back
around. As she passes in front of Agamemnon, he looks up from
his foot to Clytemnestra and they stare at each other. Iphigenia
walks off. As she passes Cassandra, whom we may not have
noticed before, Cassandra puts a hand out to her. Cassandra
makes an involuntary noise. Iphigenia exits. At the sound of
Cassandra, Agamemnon turns and looks at her.)*

There is one more thing.

(He gestures. Cassandra emerges.)

This royal creature, now our slave: Cassandra. Be kind to her. She
was given to me by the army, the most priceless of gifts—the spoils
of battle, but something more than plunder. She has . . . touched me.

CLYTEMNESTRA
She is precious to you. Say no more.

AGAMEMNON
The life she once had, a princess, a priestess of Apollo, is utterly
lost. Now she belongs to me.

CLYTEMNESTRA
She will be treated with the respect that would be shown to any of
your things, Great King.

AGAMEMNON
And now it seems, to please you, I will walk into my father's house,
trampling beauty.

CLYTEMNESTRA
Rejoice in the plenty of this moment. This day of days. May all our
hopes be accomplished like this.

(Agamemnon exits. She looks up.)

And now, justice, perfect me.

(She quickly and easily pulls the red fabric up from the ground and follows Agamemnon into the house, trailing the fabric behind her. The door closes. A moment of stillness. The chorus is now alone onstage with Cassandra. Silence.)

CHORUS A
This terror that has ruled me for so long, why won't you release me?

CHORUS B
Our fleet is restored, our long desires realized,

CHORUS A
And yet

CHORUS I
And yet

CHORUS A
And yet

CHORUS F
And yet

CHORUS B
Our king has returned, clanging victory and its spoils.
And yet

CHORUS C
And yet

CHORUS B
And yet

CHORUS D
And yet

CHORUS A
Today is exultant,

CHORUS B
All our prayers answered,

CHORUS A AND B
And yet

CHORUS C AND I
And yet

CHORUS A AND B
And yet

CHORUS F AND D
And yet

CHORUS I
Why do these black wings rustle in my chest?

CHORUS A
Deep in the darkness of my fisted heart a match is struck to light the bright little fire of dread.

(Clytemnestra comes out of the house. She addresses Cassandra.)

CLYTEMNESTRA
You. Come in. It's time. Everything is waiting on you. You don't have any choice in this, so just . . . Look, I'm sure it must be very hard to be a slave. But this is your fate, so you better get used to it. There are worse masters. We will treat you as you deserve.

(Pause.)

You. You have "touched" him, have you? I bet you did.

(Silence. They stare at each other.)

What is it? Why are you looking at me like that? She's like a sparrow in a snare. Can you not understand me? *(Overarticulating)* Is this not your language? Do you speak some exotic barbarian bird language?

CHORUS G
She's wild-caught, it's true. But I think she understands. *(To Cassandra)* Don't you? *(To Clytemnestra)* She must.

CLYTEMNESTRA
It doesn't take much imagination really. I mean, how stupid could she be? You're not stupid, are you, Birdie?

CHORUS F
Can you hear her? Your new mistress is speaking to you.

CLYTEMNESTRA
Why are you looking at me that way? What are you so afraid of?

CHORUS I
This is your house now. You're home.

CHORUS D
She'll never be home again. Just captive.

CHORUS H
What will it matter to her now? One cage or another, one house or the next.

CHORUS B
You'll have to make the best of it. You must obey.

CLYTEMNESTRA
She knows what she's doing. Don't you? You're trying to unnerve me with this stubborn silence. Are you pouting, Birdie? Too proud to sing for your new mistress, is that it?
Well? Go ahead. *(An order)* Sing!

(Silence.)

CHORUS C
Maybe she's beyond speech, beyond all of this. Just think of what she's—

CLYTEMNESTRA
Oh, I don't have time for this. She's just crazy or something. Her brain's been choked by the stinking smoke of Troy and she's come undone. But I can't stand here all day waiting for her to come to her senses. *(Shouts)* You'll have to come in eventually, like it or not. *(To the chorus)* Any wild horse can be broken. She can bloody her mouth, but she'll have to take the bit in time.

(Clytemnestra exits back into the house.)

CHORUS A
(Beckoning, as to an animal) Come on now, it's time. Come. Just get it over with, submit.

CHORUS I
Maybe she doesn't know what's happening.

CHORUS H
She knows enough. Look at her.

CHORUS I
Whose fault is she?

CHORUS C
That's not the question. The question is whose problem is she?

CHORUS H
His?

CHORUS B
Hers?

CHORUS F
Ours. Of course. Along with everything else he brought home with
him from his war.

CHORUS H
Broken things and ruined lives.

CHORUS A
Things to fix,

CHORUS B
Or sweep into corners,

CHORUS G
And try to forget.

CHORUS D
Is this what we do now? Take care of things like this?

CHORUS F
What else have we ever done?

CASSANDRA
(In Greek) Apóllon! Apóllon! *("Apollo! Apollo!")* O katastroféas
mou! *("My destroyer!")*

CHORUS I
What is she saying?

CHORUS D
Who is she talking to?

CASSANDRA
(In Greek) Apóllon! Poú me éferes? *("Apollo! Where have you
brought me?")*

CHORUS F
Did she just call on Apollo?

CHORUS G
Did you say Apollo?

CASSANDRA
(In English) You, god of my destruction, where have you brought
me?
You, my ruin, you brought me across the face of the world. For this?
(To the chorus) What is this house?

CHORUS B
The House of Atreus.

(Cassandra is seized by a prophetic vision.)

CASSANDRA
House of spite. House where family eat family.
This is the killing floor of innocents.

CHORUS A
(Horrified) That ancient story, the dog has caught the scent,
tracked the blood—

CASSANDRA
(Sees an invisible child and addresses it) Yes, child, I see you. *(And
another)* And you, dead beauty.

CHORUS G
Terrible.

CASSANDRA
Yes, I can hear you.

CHORUS C
That a stranger should know our worst history . . .

CASSANDRA

Is that your father? What is he eating? What? Your uncle was your butcher and your father . . . *(She makes an involuntary sound)* Yours, is it?

CHORUS C

It's too shameful. Make her stop.

CASSANDRA

Yours? Toe, cheek, finger bone, cut at the knuckle, tender joints, chopped, skewered, and roasted. Yours?

CHORUS F

She sees the vile feast that was eaten in this house: the children killed by their own uncle and then served as food to their unwitting father. The feast that cursed this place forever.

(Cassandra has been crawling, gagging, and now looks up as another vision takes her.)

CASSANDRA

But what is happening? Up the stairs, out of sight. The sound of the water? The wife welcoming her beloved, no, despised, bully, no, victim, no . . .

CHORUS A

This makes no sense.

CASSANDRA

Apollo, please, why must I see this?

CHORUS I

What is she talking about?

CASSANDRA

Home to bathe in . . . to bathe in . . . He reaches out for her but she pulls him into nothingness . . .

CHORUS G
(Attempting to calm everyone) Birdsong, that's all. Just a frightened bird twittering.

CASSANDRA
Her great fish flipping in her net, glistening, naked, caught, caught, caught . . .

(She crumples, the prophecy ebbing away. She recovers a bit.)

What have I been saying?

CHORUS D
Words, just words. Useless, empty . . .

CASSANDRA
Useless, yes, no use at all. For all my sight, my great city toppled to ruin and my prophecies rolled over it as the river over her stones. All my people, deaf to my warnings, dying the deaths I prophesied for them. Useless, hateful gift, to see it all and have to live it twice. What good has this hammer of truth ever been to anyone?

CHORUS I
Who did this to you?

CASSANDRA
Apollo. This is his love. I stared into his great blank eyes, shaking with awe, and still, I would not submit to him.

CHORUS I
You refused the god?

CASSANDRA
I heaved him off. So he cursed me.

CHORUS B
Well, what could you expect?

CASSANDRA

I have never been believed since then. I speak in the dark like a
nightingale to nothing and no one.

CHORUS C

We hear you, but we do not want to.

CASSANDRA

(Thrown once more into a vision) That sound again, do you hear
it? The sound of the water filling the bath? The knife like a biting
fish flashing . . . the water going pink . . .
(Fighting to escape the sight) Apollo, please! Release me from
your visions. Leave me, go plague some other jabbering girl. Let
her wear your awful prophet's hat.

CHORUS H

This can't be believed. Just another person babbling nightmares.

CASSANDRA

(Out of the vision) What does it matter if you believe me? Idiots!
The future is plummeting down on us all. You can hear me now
or remember me with pity later, but we will all be crushed.
Blind fools.

CHORUS I

Why is she so bitter with us? We didn't do this to her.

CHORUS A

It's her nightmare, that's all.

CHORUS H

Nothing to do with us.

CHORUS D

She brought this misery upon herself.

CASSANDRA

(Back inside the vision) Oh, Apollo, I see it. That flashing thing there in the water pink with blood, the knife that does the work and then, yes, it's coming, knife sharpened in one body and then, oh . . . yes, it is for me. *(To the god)* Was that the last thing you have to show me? Was that your final gift? That I should die, not at my father's altar with the rest of my people, but here? Just another throat-cut girl for this cursed house?

CHORUS G
Such a sad girl.

CASSANDRA
Let it be one clean stroke; then I'll be home.

CHORUS F
Such a brave girl.

CASSANDRA
People never say that to the lucky, do they?

CHORUS B
It is something to go out with grace.

CASSANDRA
Oh, my dear "graceful" slaughtered father, and all his "graceful" slaughtered children, splayed in blood. And now me. So graceful and so damned.

(She starts toward the door, then hesitates.)

Just one moment more. Dear sun, I will miss you. I give thanks to you, and to the last seconds, like a string of beads, that are left to me here, the shine on the things of the world, breath in my chest, heat on my face, this life.
This sunlit life. Thank you.

(To the chorus) Oh, humans. A flicker of happiness and it is over. It's you I pity now.

(She exits into the house. Now the sound of running water is audible.)

CHORUS D
Why are people always telling us their nightmares?

CHORUS H
Is it because they want to scare us, tug us into their panicked houses to keep them company?

CHORUS C
Or because they think they *can't* scare us—because our minds are so unlike theirs, our imaginations just bland white rooms with nothing in the corners?

CHORUS G
Perhaps they think we will comfort them, pat their hands and escort them back out into the shadowless ordinary world.

CHORUS F
Because that's where they think we live.

CHORUS I
So we listen to them, and the fear rises and we tell ourselves, "But that's just someone else's nightmare."

CHORUS C
But then we know it's too late. Because we have already imagined it.

CHORUS B
To fear something is to create it.

CHORUS A
Their visions climb into our heads and make themselves at home.

CHORUS D
Elbow into our jumbled pantries to make new concoctions out of
what we have on hand.

CHORUS F
Which is the past.

CHORUS B
Oh, the past.

CHORUS C
The past. Which we are always tinkering with, twisting and
remaking it, asking it back so that we might . . . what?

CHORUS I
Know what it was?

CHORUS D
Try to get it right this time?

CHORUS F
Bury it better?

CHORUS B
So we can forget it for good?

CHORUS A
The past. Which is not past.

CHORUS G
We dust the mud off graves to let it blink at us again, reborn and
familiar.

CHORUS H
We are peopled, this household. And no one ever dies.

(Iphigenia comes on, as before, but this time ungagged. And this time, everyone sees her.)

IPHIGENIA
I used to sing to them, the men who killed me.
Late in the evening, when they were in their cups
I would enter
My hair braided back
My square brow and girl's direct gaze
My pure voice spooling up to cool the smoky room.
An admonishment, I suppose.
So when the last moment came to me
I lay there on the block
My bare neck spiced by the morning air,
And I thought
Perhaps I am to die for my own excellence.
Perhaps if I had just
Sung less well
Looked more ordinary
I might have been spared this.

(She exits.)

CHORUS G
There are dreams and there are memories. And sometimes—

CHORUS I
—sometimes—

CHORUS G
—they are both.

(A sound, hard to distinguish, from inside the house.)

CHORUS I
So when the fear rises up in us, we think, is this / the truth?

CHORUS H
Is this / the truth?

CHORUS D
Is this the truth?

CHORUS I
Or am I just dreaming?

(Another sound.)

CHORUS D
Is this something I know?

CHORUS F
Or something I know I don't know?

(Another sound.)

CHORUS A
Do I remember this?

CHORUS C
Do I remember / this?

CHORUS B
Do I remember this? Or is this what's about to / happen?

CHORUS H
What's about to / happen?

CHORUS C
What's about to / happen?

CHORUS I
What's about to happen?

(A cry, muffled, from inside the house.)

CHORUS G
And when it happens, when it / actually happens,

CHORUS B
when it actually happens.

CHORUS G
Why is it, despite all the fear and foreboding,

(A cry, still muffled, but louder, from inside the house.)

CHORUS D
—why is it? —

CHORUS G
—when we finally realize this is no dream, no vision—

CHORUS A
—this is no / dream—

CHORUS H
—this is no / dream—

CHORUS B
—this is no dream, no vision—

CHORUS G
—this is not in my head, this is the truth—

CHORUS C AND F
—this is the truth—

CHORUS D
—this is the truth—

(The doors begin to open.)

CHORUS G
Why are we never, ever—

CHORUS A AND I
—never, ever—

CHORUS G
Why are we never, ever prepared for it?

(Clytemnestra is revealed standing over the bodies of Agamemnon and Cassandra, both of them wrapped in bloody bundles of the red streamers.)

CLYTEMNESTRA
I have never spoken the truth until now. I have never done
anything until this moment. Just this. This is all I have ever done.
He killed my daughter—the treasure I made inside my body and
gave to the world—he killed her. Set *this* in motion, the years of
nights, nights of years, through the war he chose, the war that
killing my daughter allowed him to fight. I could wait. I had to.
To make this justice.
It felt, it felt like a mighty birth. The same yawning pain, the size
of me stretched out, aching wide to bring it bloody and sprawling
into the light.
I had to be made wide enough to match the size of my great idea.
And then the knife, sliding in, meeting his center, locking into him
sweetly, locking in his fate, his fate, his fate, with every blow.
He chose this long ago. He came back here for it, bringing his
foreign slut by the hand, all the way home, to me. He knew me.
He had to return to me. So that this could happen. And I did.

I did it. I bathed in his blood like a summer rain, flowers opening after a drought of years.
It is done. Oh, the glory of it. The rightness. My arm is heavy with justice.

CHORUS A
Oh, my king. Where do we live now? A place where this can happen?

CHORUS B
How will we mourn you? Who will do your rites?

CLYTEMNESTRA
Don't you worry about that. I will. Who better? Family does as family must.

(A grave opens up, center.)

First we take out our garbage, what doesn't belong.

(She kicks the body of Cassandra, which rolls into the grave.)

And then we take care of our own. He has achieved his just end and nothing can happen to him anymore. He is fine now.

(She kicks the body of Agamemnon, which rolls into the grave.)

Rejoice!
It's finally over. The curse is lifted from this place.
It is done. All is finally well.
I have cleaned the house.

Act II

Ten years later. Predawn. An unmarked grave before the sleeping house. Chorus E tends it. The chorus is onstage, doing their various obscure tasks.

CHORUS B
Ten years gone by and yet every day we wake into disbelief.

CHORUS F
It's always a bad surprise, the lurch into now.

CHORUS E
This house built of tricks and slaughter. Where we are the subjects of such a queen.

CHORUS G
So this is where we live now. This present tense.

CHORUS I
Yes, we wake, and yet we can't seem to wake.

CHORUS C
We dread a future we can't imagine, even as we sleepwalk toward it.

CHORUS D
So we wait.

CHORUS H
We circle our little cares

CHORUS B
Winding the clocks

CHORUS C
Peeling the carrots

CHORUS D
Snapping the sheets

CHORUS F
Wiping the counters

CHORUS G
Making the beds

CHORUS I
Shining the silver

CHORUS E
Tending the grave.

CHORUS B
Trying to ignore the creaking of the rafters and the rumbles from beneath the floorboards.
Sounds of the household's two sovereign deities biding their time.

CHORUS A
In the basement, the ancient lion spirit of household memory circles, then settles onto his haunches and looks up.

CHORUS H
While on the roof, we hear the tick, tick, tick of her talons as Vengeance paces, weighing her demands.

CHORUS D

We know she's up there, our bird of prey, shuffling her leather
wings and sharpening her beak.

CHORUS G

Considering what she might exact from us.

CHORUS C

What she might make us become.

CHORUS A

Can we ever be released from the past?

CHORUS H

What mercy can we hope for from the future?

CHORUS A

The corrupting blood of the old stories never dries.

CHORUS H

Yet the future draws us, implacable.

CHORUS E

Held fast in the jaws of the present,
This is what we know:

CHORUS C

The past does not forget us; and Vengeance will make its claims.

CHORUS I

The waiting will end; the future / will come.

CHORUS G

The future will / come.

CHORUS H

The future will come.

CHORUS B
They will see to / that.

CHORUS A
They will see to / that.

CHORUS H
They will see to that.

CHORUS B
The one above, and the one below.

(The sound of a female voice within, someone in the throes of a nightmare. The chorus looks up. Clytemnestra appears at the threshold, then moves about the yard, disturbed.)

CHORUS G
What was it tonight?

CLYTEMNESTRA
The worst one yet.

CHORUS G
Yes?

CLYTEMNESTRA
It's never been a snake before. But it dropped out of me and wanted to be loved. So I swaddled it and sang to it and told it all the stories. It twined itself up my body, then curled around the back of my neck to kiss me. Its flame of a tongue felt like a fluttering eyelash on my mouth. And I thought, well, this is just another remarkable thing that I'm supposed to deal with alone. Something else that is being asked of me. So I gave it my breast. And it opened its sharp pink mouth, then closed on me like a jewelry clasp and suckled there. Its pointed tail made lazy figure eights as it drank, thinking. It was all so silent, this . . .

transaction. Its green eyes blinking as it stared at me. My blood and milk streamed out of me into it, coursing into its smooth, breathing coils. I could feel my life drain out of me. I didn't make a noise. Until it occurred to me that I might call out for help. But to whom? This was my child. What god presided over such a situation? Who could come to my aid? And if I were released from this what would happen to this child? Who could love it?

CHORUS E
That is the question. Who could love such a child?

CLYTEMNESTRA
I tried, I really did, not to make a sound. But it wouldn't stop sucking.

CHORUS E
It must have hurt.

CLYTEMNESTRA
Fangs like needles, drawing me out.

CHORUS E
So who did you call to? What did you do?

CLYTEMNESTRA
I woke up. *(Shudders)* Why would I come up with something like that?

CHORUS E
Well, you always were an . . . idiosyncratic mother . . . Mother.

(Clytemnestra looks around, startled.)

CLYTEMNESTRA
Who said that?

CHORUS E
Me.

(Clytemnestra looks around to see Chorus E, who is now identified as Electra.)

CLYTEMNESTRA
Electra? I thought you were the, the help.

(Sensing a brewing quarrel, the chorus begins to drift off, leaving Clytemnestra and Electra alone.)

ELECTRA
Well, that's what I am. I am the help. That's what you've done with me. Made me a skivvy in my own house.

CLYTEMNESTRA
How much did you hear of what I . . . ? How long have you been here?

ELECTRA
I've never been anywhere else. You don't let me.

CLYTEMNESTRA
You're perfectly free to leave. I certainly don't care either way.

ELECTRA
Where would I go?

CLYTEMNESTRA
Well, you're not needed here. It's not like you're any *use* to me.

ELECTRA
Who could you talk to otherwise? Who could you tell your dreams to?

CLYTEMNESTRA
I don't *need* to talk to anyone.

ELECTRA
And yet you are always talking. I hear you at it all night long
sometimes. Alone in your room or muttering down the halls. Who
are you talking to? I lie there and think: Is that Mother *praying?*—

CLYTEMNESTRA
(Incredulous) Praying?

ELECTRA
—but then I think, of course not. Because, I mean, what deity would
listen to you? After what you did?

CLYTEMNESTRA
What would you know about the gods?

ELECTRA
What I know I sure didn't learn from you. You raised me to be as
godless as a donkey.
But with every year, I know them better, the gods. And even you
can't stop me loving them, their beautiful certainty, the hope I feel
when their truth floods in. There is meaning to my suffering. Even
this life will be made whole. No crime goes unpunished. I will be
avenged.

CLYTEMNESTRA
Oh, you are your father's daughter.

ELECTRA
Am I? I'd like to think that.

CLYTEMNESTRA
Just as sanctimonious. Just as frightened. Just as ruthless.

ELECTRA

Oh, to think he might have given me something in spite of you.
We didn't have much time, my father and me. You took care of
that, silenced him—

CLYTEMNESTRA

It was the war that took your father from you, the war he chose,
the war he killed your sister for—

ELECTRA

—the war he survived, the war he triumphed in, to come home to
me. But you kept me from even seeing him again, shut us away in
our separate rooms to wait, Orestes and me, so that you could lure
him in and kill him alone, without us clinging to your stabbing
arm to ruin your aim.

CLYTEMNESTRA

Yes, I spared you that.

ELECTRA

When I think of how patient I was—my dress in sharp creases, my
hard, new shoes hanging above the floor—waiting to meet him,
my unknown beloved father, home at last. I sat so still all through
that long afternoon, not knowing that what you were doing was—

CLYTEMNESTRA

Serving justice.

ELECTRA

—killing my father in my own / house.

CLYTEMNESTRA

Doing what needed to be / done.

ELECTRA

Making sure that I would never know a loving parent's / touch
again—

CLYTEMNESTRA
Loving? He never loved you, he barely knew you.

ELECTRA
You don't know—

CLYTEMNESTRA
There was one child he loved, only one, and he killed her with his own hands—

ELECTRA
You don't know what he felt / for me!

CLYTEMNESTRA
—sliced his knife deep into her / perfect throat—

ELECTRA
He kissed the top of my head, carried me / on his shoulders—

CLYTEMNESTRA
—even as she stared at him, her lights flickering out—

ELECTRA
He loved me—

CLYTEMNESTRA
He gave her no mercy, that father of yours.

ELECTRA
He loved me!—

CLYTEMNESTRA
That's how he loved his best little girl.

(Pause.)

ELECTRA

There are gods, Mother, and they have been watching you all this time. You know that. You can feel their gaze heavy on you. Their great eyes blinking. They have been patient. But they won't wait forever. They gather and ferment like storm clouds above this house now. They are leaning so low you can hear them breathing. I know you can hear it, Mother—and yes, that's the in-and-out breath of immortal insistence.

CLYTEMNESTRA

So these gods you talk about. Do they have hands and knives?

ELECTRA

They don't need them. They act through us.

CLYTEMNESTRA

Through you? You and your dustpan? You and your mop? What have you ever done?

ELECTRA

Yes, through me.

CLYTEMNESTRA

You're a no one, I can't even see you.

ELECTRA

Through me. Through my brother.

CLYTEMNESTRA

Orestes? What could you possibly know about him?

ELECTRA

Only that after you killed our father, you sent him away. Someplace out of your sight. But he's never out of your mind.

CLYTEMNESTRA

You know nothing. You never will.

ELECTRA

Because what is the plan, Mother? That you will live forever? What
is the future of this house?

CLYTEMNESTRA

So you think you're qualified to run this kingdom? With the
skills you've accumulated in all these years of—what? Emptying
mousetraps?

ELECTRA

No, I'm waiting for my brother. Just like you. We both know he's
bound to come home sometime, don't we?

(Clytemnestra turns away from her. Electra pursues her.)

It's him you're talking to at night, isn't it?

CLYTEMNESTRA

I don't know what you think you hear. Or what you think you see.

ELECTRA

I know all about you, Mother. Just because you never see me
doesn't mean that I don't see you. I am always here.

CLYTEMNESTRA

I wish you would, you know, just *go.*
I don't want you skulking around all the time. It's, it's unnerving.

ELECTRA

You won't know I'm here. Forget you even saw me.

(She retreats to someplace distant on the stage.)

Just call out if you need me.

CLYTEMNESTRA

I won't. I won't ever need you.

(But she gives up on it, exhausted.)

Oh, what a night.

(She finds herself standing on the grave.)

Ten years in the ground. But even so, maybe it's you doing this to me. Casting visions.

(She kneels and jabs her hands into the grave, then takes a fistful of dirt up and sifts it through her fingers.)

I thought I was done with you. Thought I settled you in silence, where you belong. You still want something from me? Even now? What right do you have to anything more?
Leave me alone. Let me sleep.

(She wipes her hands on her robe and exits into the house. Electra goes over to the grave and smooths it with her hands. Chorus G has entered and is watching.)

ELECTRA
Father? Daddy? Papa? *(To Chorus G)* What did I call him? Do you remember? I was so little when he left. I remember waving, we were all lined up at the door. He put his hand on my head, called me, what did he call me? Honey, sweetheart, angel? . . .

CHORUS G
Electra. He called you Electra.

ELECTRA
Well, you probably wouldn't have known. This was personal, just ours. Like whatever it was that I called him. Why can't I remember these things? Every day I forget him differently. How can I mourn him if I can't remember him?

CHORUS G

If you really couldn't remember him, you wouldn't be so unhappy.

ELECTRA

Well, of course I'm unhappy! There are two truths: My mother is alive and my father's not. Two truths and they're both killing me. She's alive! Which means nothing makes sense.
The horror of what she did, and nothing has changed for her, she is *fine*, untouched. She got away with it.

CHORUS G

She has bad dreams.

ELECTRA

(With pride) I do that. I stand over her bed and watch her sleep, listen to her little mouth sounds. Watch her face when she can't guard it. Oh, I know her to her depths, I've thrust my hands into her guts, fingered her blue entrails and held her organs throbbing in my palms. And when she is open to me like that, splayed in the moonlight, that's when I conjure. That's when I make the dreams. Concocted with garish shards of everything she fears wrapped up tight in packages spattered with blood. I lift the top of her head open and I drop them into her. And then I close her up again and walk away. Night after night.
They are my great accomplishment, her nightmares. They are my art.
I know why I stay here. I have a job to do, hating her. But why do you stay?

CHORUS G

Oh, we're not so different from you. We're all rumbling around in the same house, circling her, our own blistering star. She draws us to her, gives us a center.

ELECTRA

A common hatred.

342 / ELLEN MCLAUGHLIN

CHORUS G

Well, she's an interesting woman, your mother. We can't take our eyes off her. And she keeps the story going. We can't leave because we want to find out. What will become of such a woman?

ELECTRA

I am aching for the end of this story; it's kept me up and walking for a thousand nights. Waiting, waiting for some kind of resolve to awaken in me. The ability to do this thing.

CHORUS G

You mean kill her?

ELECTRA

I seem to have to. No one else will. And she can't live. Someone has to, to, *correct* this thing. My brother.

CHORUS G

Orestes?

ELECTRA

Yes.

CHORUS G

Do you know where he is?

ELECTRA

I don't. But I don't think she does either. Wherever she once sent him, I don't think he's there anymore. So he's lost to both of us now.

CHORUS G

Maybe he's dead.

ELECTRA

He can't be. She's too afraid. She knows that if he's living, he will be coming home for her. And when he does, her time is up.

CHORUS G
So it's just a matter of time? He will be here?

ELECTRA
Unless he won't. Unless he is dead.

CHORUS G
(Confused) But you just said . . .

ELECTRA
What do I know? After all these years, I can't even remember what he looks like. At least with my father I know he's *there. (The grave)* My brother's been gone so long, he might as well not exist for all the good he's done me. I am so tired of waiting for him to return to *do what has to be done.*

CHORUS G
Maybe you should conjure *him.* Orestes.

ELECTRA
Orestes. Maybe I should.

CHORUS G
At least he might still be alive.

ELECTRA
Which would be useful. *(She stretches out on the grave)* Or I could just sleep here. Dream him up.

CHORUS G
Yes, you must be exhausted.

ELECTRA
I can't sleep. All the nightmares loose in the house, flapping around, looking for a head to nest in. I know it's my fault, I called them in, but now that they're here . . .

(She falls asleep.)

CHORUS G
Well, that will hold her for a while.

(Chorus G exits. A moment when the stage is empty except for the sleeping Electra. Orestes enters.)

ORESTES
On the day my father came back from the wars and stood where
I stand, what did he see? A place where he could finally close his
scorched eyes in peace, safe at last?
Oh, my father.
Did he think he had come home? Home.
What a word for such a house.
Or did he know, like me, that hell swung wide behind that door?
(To the voice, which has reawakened in his head) I hear you,
Apollo, my god. Yes, Shining One, your flame licks high in me.
You have delivered me, as you promised, to this.
You show me that I have no choice. How could I have ever thought
I did? Still glistening with the salt seas of my mother,
I was dropped, writhing,
falling through the sharp air,
into the open net of fate.

(The voice exits him.)

It never had anything to do with me.
But I'm the only one who can act now. And anything I do will be
wrong.

(He sees Electra.)

Who is this sleeping scrap of sorrow? Oh, my sister. Is this what
has become of you?

(Electra murmurs in her sleep, a nightmare brewing. He goes to her, kneels, and takes her, sleeping, into his arms, a sort of pietà.)

ELECTRA
(Still asleep) Daddy?

ORESTES
He's not here.

ELECTRA
Then no one can help me.

ORESTES
Electra?

ELECTRA
Only Daddy and he won't.

(She wakes. She realizes that she's in someone's arms but can't see who it is because he holds her from behind. Thinking that she's in a dream, she carefully puts her own hands over Orestes's hands.)

The same hands. You have the same hands . . . as . . .

ORESTES
Yes.

ELECTRA
Am I dreaming this?

ORESTES
If you are, then I am too.

ELECTRA
Am I making you up?

ORESTES
If you are, then I'm making you up.

ELECTRA
It can't be you. Orestes.

ORESTES
Orestes.

ELECTRA
Home?

ORESTES
(With some irony) Home.

ELECTRA
At last!

(She turns to look at him. They embrace.)

When I last saw you, you were only ten. Just a green shoot of a boy.
And now . . . now you're my avenging stranger.
I couldn't have invented anyone better.

ORESTES
I am just what happens when the ticking stops.

ELECTRA
You are perfect.

ORESTES
I am only on time.

ELECTRA
No, you are Justice, long lost, walking home at last. My little
brother. Look at you.

ORESTES
That boy you remember is dead. I am just a ghost here.

ELECTRA
A ghost with a knife. That's what you came back for, isn't it?

ORESTES
(Uneasily) Oh, Electra.

ELECTRA
You were sent here, weren't you?

(He nods.)

Who sent you?

ORESTES
(Reluctantly) Apollo.

ELECTRA
I knew it! The gods have always been at work in you. They never forgot us. Apollo sent you?

(Orestes nods warily.)

How?

ORESTES
He . . . he spoke to me.

ELECTRA
You met him?

ORESTES
(With difficulty) It's not . . . he's . . . his voice is . . . he's . . . I hear him.

ELECTRA
In your head?

ORESTES
Yes . . . it's . . . yes.

ELECTRA
Is he speaking to you now?

(Orestes shakes his head, looks at her, and then slowly nods.)

ORESTES
Never-ending.

ELECTRA
Can I hear?

ORESTES
(Confused) Can you . . . ?

ELECTRA
Tell me. Tell me what he's saying.

ORESTES
I don't think it can be, should be . . . spoken, the sound of . . .

(He looks up, as if to ask permission, but then is suddenly in the throes of a different voice. The god speaks through him.)

"Black knot . . . It is for you, son of the mother-monster, she who, steeped in . . . Cut it—now!—the black knot . . . It is for you to, you and only—now! now!—It is for you and only you, it is for you to, you and only, you and only *you to* . . . *do.*"

(During this, as the god takes violent hold, Electra skitters away from him, out of danger. As Orestes returns to himself, she approaches him slowly, her hand out, as if to flames.)

ELECTRA
(Awed and quiet) Yes!

ORESTES
(Coming out of it, with dread for both of them) Oh, Electra, I need
a chance—

ELECTRA
Yes, we must!

ORESTES
Wait, Electra! Please wait, I need—

ELECTRA
—I'm done with waiting! Every minute that goes by, every minute
she's alive—

ORESTES
—I need a chance, I need a chance to mourn him—

ELECTRA
I'm sick of mourning! It's all so . . . decorous and defeated. It doesn't,
it doesn't *meet* this, what she did to him, to us, she must be—

ORESTES
I *know*, Electra. The god has raged in me for years, driven me
through my life with his certainty. But for myself alone and as
myself I came to mourn my father.

ELECTRA
And then?

ORESTES
Yes. I . . . I am bound. But first . . . please, just let me . . . Is this . . . ?

(He gestures to the grave. She nods. He kneels.)

Father.

(He doesn't know how to do this. He looks up at Electra.)

I never even met him. And now . . .

ELECTRA
Yes, now you must act for him. It must be done.

ORESTES
Please, I just . . . if I could just talk to him somehow, it would . . . I could . . .

ELECTRA
It's all I do—talk to him. It's a lot like praying, I guess. And about as effective.

ORESTES
You must have prayed for me and here I am.

ELECTRA
(Newly hopeful) I did. I did. It worked.

(They kneel, side by side, at the grave.)

ORESTES
How is it done?

(They begin to improvise a ritual together.)

ELECTRA
Oh, Father.

ORESTES
Oh, Father.

ELECTRA
Look up with your hollow eyes through the heavy dirt and see us, your miserable children.

ORESTES
We cannot do this without you.

ELECTRA
Help us make her suffer as you suffered—

ORESTES
Help us teach her the price of what she did to you.

ELECTRA
Let us light up your house again with the glory of justice.

ORESTES
We will kill her for you, God, Father, God.

ELECTRA
We will do this for you, God, Father, God.

ORESTES
We will, we, we must, we know it. We are sorry it's taken so long.

ELECTRA
Oh, Father, we are sorry. We will do what's right.

ORESTES
Oh, Father, we don't know how to do this—

ELECTRA
Forgive us, Father.

ORESTES
Oh, Father, hero of Troy, look up at your unheroic children.

ELECTRA
Take pity and come to us.

ORESTES
Help us to do this terrible thing. In your name.

ELECTRA
In your name, whatever that name is, or should be, forever more.

*(Finally, in some despair, they are just pounding the grave
with their palms. Unseen by Orestes and Electra, Agamemnon
appears, covered in dirt. He walks over to stand behind them and
then drops a knife down on the ground between them. He walks
off. Orestes and Electra look at the knife, then at each other.
Something, perhaps a bell, sounds. Orestes stows the knife and
stands up. He goes to the door of the house and bangs on it.
A member of the chorus answers.)*

CHORUS F/NURSE
Why are you pounding like that? Are you trying to wake the dead?

ORESTES
Yes. Wake the house. I have news.

CHORUS F/NURSE
And who should I say is here?

ORESTES
Doesn't matter. She wouldn't know me.

CHORUS F/NURSE
Some stranger then, is that it?

ORESTES
A stranger to her, yes.

CHORUS F/NURSE
Wait.

(She retreats into the house. Silence as they wait. Lights go on inside. Clytemnestra comes to the door, followed by Chorus F.)

CLYTEMNESTRA
Have we met?

ORESTES
No, I'm a stranger to you. And I am far from home. But I have come with news for this house. Who, who should I speak to? Who is the . . . that is, who is in charge here?

CLYTEMNESTRA
I am. I am the mother of the house.

ORESTES
Then it is your . . . I have a message about your . . .

CLYTEMNESTRA
I have a son. / Orestes.

ORESTES
Orestes, yes.

(Silence. He can't speak.)

CLYTEMNESTRA
Yes?

ORESTES
It's hard to say.

CLYTEMNESTRA
And yet you've come so far to tell me.

ORESTES
He's dead. Your son.

(Clytemnestra doesn't react. Odd moment.)

I'm sorry.

CLYTEMNESTRA
I'm sorry. Say that again?

ORESTES
I'm sorry?

CLYTEMNESTRA
What did you say? Something about my son?

ORESTES
Orestes.

CLYTEMNESTRA
Orestes, yes.

ORESTES
He's dead.

CLYTEMNESTRA
It's funny. I thought you might have said that. But it didn't make sense. Because, you see, he can't be dead. He's all this family has left. If he's gone, the line is snuffed out. So what's it all been for? All this struggle and terror and long, bad nights? If he's gone it's all been for nothing.
The only way it works, all this, is that he's always off somewhere, safe. That's the point. That he not be here, but that he be alive.

ORESTES
I don't, I don't know . . . what to . . .

CLYTEMNESTRA
Well, it's not *your* problem. Him.

ORESTES
There is, there is a question.

CLYTEMNESTRA
A question?

ORESTES
Where should his ashes be buried? Where he died or here, where
he was from?

CLYTEMNESTRA
What does it matter? When we are dirt, who cares where we are
heaped? *(She suddenly leans over, gasping, as if knifed in the gut)*
Sorry, sorry. It's nothing.

ORESTES
It was not my choice. I wish it didn't have to be me who had to . . .
It was given to me to do.

CLYTEMNESTRA
(Recovering a bit) Well, if it hadn't been you, it would have been
someone else. What has to happen does. Will you come inside?
We have everything a traveler breaking a journey could want . . .
hot baths, hot food, hot knives and forks and . . . excuse me . . .
(To Chorus F) See to him, make sure he's . . .

(She goes off abruptly, as if to vomit. Chorus F watches her go.)

CHORUS F/NURSE
What on earth? *(Looks at Orestes)* I'll never be able to read her.
Was that real, what she said? Does she even remember that boy?
It was me who raised him. She wasn't ever around. Too busy
running things, her. Nursed him a bit and handed him off when
she got bored. Because it's mostly boring, children, let's face it,
mostly a matter of trying to figure out what they're crying about
now. And just when you think you've cracked the code and do

something about it, the crying starts all over again and you've got another mystery to solve . . . Of course, he was lovely too. Good company, for a baby.

She's right about one thing though. It doesn't make sense. Him being dead. He was just here, really. That's what it seems like.

(Pause.)

Just here.

(She looks hard at him.)

ORESTES
Go and get her. Bring her back.

CHORUS F/NURSE
It's odd that you think you can just—

ORESTES
—I don't have *time.*

CHORUS F/NURSE
But then you always were like that. Babies. Men.

ORESTES
What? Please—

CHORUS F/NURSE
It's all now, now, now, me, me, me—

ORESTES
Get her! Bring her out!

CHORUS F/NURSE
Ah. I knew it. It didn't make sense otherwise.

ORESTES
I don't have time!

CHORUS F/NURSE
Well. Welcome home.

(She exits into the house. A moment of complete stillness. The sense of time ticking. Clytemnestra comes back on, then stops, looking at Orestes.)

CLYTEMNESTRA
(Dawning panic) I think there's been a mistake.

ORESTES
You did what you should never have done and now you must suffer what you should never have to suffer.

CLYTEMNESTRA
I think that you have misinterpreted the . . . *logic* here. What you *don't* want, what you *don't* want is to become what, what your father became, some cursed killer who takes the life of—

ORESTES
I don't have any choice in this. It's being done through me—

CLYTEMNESTRA
But look what happened to him—

ORESTES
You. You were what happened to him. You chose, you decided, and then you killed him. There was no god at your back, prodding you into it, you came up with it, all by yourself—

CLYTEMNESTRA
He did it! He killed your sister! That's what he *did*.

ORESTES

You tricked him, lured him into the house, made him helpless and then / you—

CLYTEMNESTRA

He knew it was wrong. He came back to me because he knew I'd do it. He knew he had to die for it. I just held the knife he fell on.

ORESTES

I have a knife now, Mother. I will hold it for you.

CLYTEMNESTRA

No! You are not going to kill your mother. This is completely different. I killed some man I married, some stranger who walked into my life and ruined it. He slaughtered our daughter, slit her throat like some backyard goat. What father, human or animal, could do that? It was an abomination, against nature, and he knew it, knew it as he drew the knife across her neck. She was his favorite and still he did it. Gagged her so that she couldn't curse him, the man she thought was her father, her protection against the world, now just the man with the knife.

ORESTES

I am the man with the knife. That's all I have ever been allowed to be.

CLYTEMNESTRA

No, you are my child. *(She goes to him, touches him)* The child who took my breast. Blood of my blood. You will never do this. It would destroy you. Any wound you make in me would open in you and never heal.

(She holds his head to her breast in a kind of embrace; he relaxes into her and then pulls abruptly away, looking up.)

ORESTES

(To the god) What am I to do?

CLYTEMNESTRA
Not that. Not that.

ORESTES
(Still to the god) Tell me! What am I to do?

CLYTEMNESTRA
Listen to your mother. What do gods have to do with this?

ORESTES
The god is inside me, has been since the moment you did it. You began him in me, the river of his speech.

CLYTEMNESTRA
But we know each other, you and I.

ORESTES
I don't know you, I don't know anything.

CLYTEMNESTRA
I'm your mother. You *lived in me*. You *are* me.

ORESTES
Then I'm also my father. He gave me this.

(He draws the knife.)

CLYTEMNESTRA
How did you get that? That's the knife, the same knife . . .

ORESTES
You killed him with?

CLYTEMNESTRA
That he killed her with. Iphigenia.

ORESTES
(Disturbed) Iphigenia.

CLYTEMNESTRA
You see, my love, you see it now, don't you?

(Orestes is desperately looking up, searching the sky for some kind of help.)

You're not a man who would do that. *You don't want to be him.*

(No help at hand, he looks back at his mother.)

ORESTES
He was my father and you killed him.

CLYTEMNESTRA
It won't be undone. Killing me won't bring your father back.

ORESTES
I can't hear you.

CLYTEMNESTRA
You will be cursed. You will run for the rest of your life under a twisting, biting cloud. *You can't kill your mother!*

ORESTES
I have no choice!

(He lets out a howl and runs at her. She runs toward the house. Electra runs to block her at the door. Clytemnestra turns back to Orestes. A standoff.)

CLYTEMNESTRA
You are my snake. It was you.

ORESTES
Yes, I am yours.

CLYTEMNESTRA
I let you live, sent you away from here so you wouldn't have to do this. I could have, after he was dead, I could have killed you. Don't you see? But I let you go. Out into the world where you could be free of this, this hateful house. You are the shape of my mercy. I couldn't do it.
You were my sweet boy. I couldn't do what he did. I couldn't kill my own child. Even to save myself. I let you happen. Because I loved—

(She has gone to him, heading into an embrace, when he stabs her simply. She looks at him as she dies.)

ORESTES
Oh, Mother. Why did you let me loose in the world? I've always been your death.

CLYTEMNESTRA
And I will be yours. You will never be free of me now.

ORESTES
It is done. That's the end of it at last.

CLYTEMNESTRA
Listen. Listen. They are coming for you.

(She gestures up to the sky, then, dying, slides down his body. The sound of wet wings, quiet at first and then growing louder, as if hundreds and hundreds of great birds were landing and settling on the stage. The chorus enters, each holding a bucket. Once Clytemnestra is dead on the ground, Orestes, staring at her, backs up onto the grave and is suddenly aware of the chorus around him. The chorus throws the contents of the buckets, blood, at

*Orestes. He falls to his knees on the grave, drenched. Electra picks
up her own bucket.)*

ELECTRA
Rejoice! It's finally over.

(She pours the bucket of blood over herself.)

The curse is lifted from this place. It is done.

*(As the sound of the birds settles, the chorus turns slowly from
putting down their buckets and begins to rise, looking at Orestes.
We see them as he sees them, and they are the Furies now. Still
kneeling, Orestes pleads with them, and then with us.)*

ORESTES
I just . . . justly . . . killed . . . just . . . justly murdered . . . just . . .
blood . . . just blood . . . just so much . . . so much . . . just blood.

Act III

Days later but the blood is still fresh. Electra sits on the ground next to Orestes, who is curled, sleeping on Agamemnon's grave. He is having a nightmare and occasionally twitches and makes sounds. Both siblings are blood-spattered, their hands in particular still red. The knife used for the murder lies, bloody, beside them. The chorus is onstage, some of them sleeping, but one or two are up, watching Electra. Electra speaks to them, but also to us.

ELECTRA
In the emergency . . . which has been my life . . . In the emergency, there has been no . . . What would be the word? I have heard, for instance, of the blue of the sky. It is something one hears about. But I haven't been able to . . . through the blinding smoke of all this . . . hatred I have been tending . . . the crackling furnace I have known so well . . . the blue of the sky has been . . . unseeable. I have spent my time doing errands for the inferno. A long, sweaty job, keeping hatred alight. There hasn't been much time for anything else. Years spent stoking that roaring, endlessly hungry mouth. No birdsong in the morning, bell song at night, no. I've heard nothing above the snap and heave of the fire. The smell of bread, of grass, the nape of a baby's neck? That was not for me with my soot-clogged head, scorched by flame.

I have not danced, not once, with the bare-armed girls in the
summer, their green world blurring as they spin. I could almost
hear the laughter, the pipes, but no.
It was not for me. The world. I have been too busy for that.
I tended the furnace.
And so now. This is what I thought I wanted.
He held the knife, it's true, but only because I handed it to him.
I made that knife in the furnace, the one I've been tending.
Until finally, finally . . . my furnace blew up.
So we sit here, my brother and I, on the cooling ash of its ruins,
deafened and blinking in this new, raw silence. And we have bad
dreams. Well, he does. I don't sleep.
There are so many hours in every night it turns out. And not
much to do. So I watch his nightmares.

(A small moan of fear from Orestes.)

He thinks he'll wake up from them. But he won't.

(Orestes tenses.)

There he goes. And now you watch the rabbit run.

*(Orestes twitches, dreaming of panicked flight. A chorus member
steps toward him.)*

No, let him sleep. It's only when he's dreaming that he ever gets
away from them.

CHORUS D
Who?

ELECTRA
You know who they are. He's terrified of them.

CHORUS G
You mean the Furies?

ELECTRA
(Nods) They work for my mother.

CHORUS G
Ah. The help.

ELECTRA
(Uncertainly) Yes.

CHORUS D
Like us.

ELECTRA
Well, not like *you* . . . He says they're judging him. He thinks he
sees them.

CHORUS H
And you think he doesn't?

*(Electra looks around, confused. The chorus is awake now, looking
at her.)*

ORESTES
(Beginning to wake) Oh!

ELECTRA
Wake gently, Brother.

(Orestes opens his eyes.)

All is well. See?

(Orestes sees the chorus and cringes.)

ORESTES
You standing snakes! Your eyes are gleaming spite.
Leave me alone! I have nothing left to give you.

(He scrambles on all fours. Electra embraces him from behind and tries to calm him. It is the same position he first held her in, reversed now, and he is terrified, staring at the chorus. He suddenly becomes aware of Electra and looks down at her arms.)

Who is this?

ELECTRA
Your sister.

ORESTES
She can't help me. Where is my father?

ELECTRA
He's not here.

ORESTES
Then no one can help me.

ELECTRA
Orestes?

ORESTES
Only Daddy and he won't.

(He begins to cry, closing his eyes and relaxing back into Electra's arms.)

I'm alone with them, inside this madness, all alone. It's so cold with them.

ELECTRA
I'm here with you. I will always be here with you.

ORESTES
The same hands. You have the same hands as . . . Did you say sister?

ELECTRA
Yes. Electra.

ORESTES
I have two sisters. *(Uncertain)* Don't I?

ELECTRA
There were once two. But only one now. Just me.

(He turns so that he can see her face.)

ORESTES
Am I dreaming this?

ELECTRA
If you are, then I am too.

ORESTES
Do you hear him too?
Whoever that flapping, jerking stickman is, raving away? He won't
shut up.

ELECTRA
(Reluctantly, delicately) Yes. Sometimes.

ORESTES
Are you mad too then?

ELECTRA
(A slight hesitation, and then) Yes. *(Beat)* No. Just you.

(He touches her face.)

ORESTES
Then this must be very hard on you.

ELECTRA

I would do anything for you. You are all I have now.

ORESTES

So you've heard him, the stickman? Yammering away. Something about his mother?

ELECTRA

(Carefully) Yes, it's upsetting.

ORESTES

What did he do to her?

(Electra hesitates.)

CHORUS H

(Impatiently) He killed her.

ORESTES

(Shocked) He . . . ? No.

CHORUS H

In fact, he killed *your* mother.

ORESTES

My mother is dead?

CHORUS D

Yes. And the person who killed her—

ORESTES

There's a knife here.

(Silence. Everyone waits.)

It's bloody. Who left this blood on this knife? I've seen this knife before.

(He looks around.)

Is this a test?
Because it looks like . . . Is this *my* blood?
(Sudden horror) No, wait.

*(Silently, one after another, chorus members fall to the ground
in the same way that Clytemnestra fell as she died. Orestes spins
around, horrified, as they fall around him.)*

WAIT!

*(He runs to the last of the chorus members to fall and rolls her
over. It is the actor who played Clytemnestra. Her eyes snap open.
He recoils, terrified.)*

CLYTEMNESTRA
Did you think you could just get away with it?

ORESTES
No!

CLYTEMNESTRA
As if killing your mother was something a son could just do?

ORESTES
The god, the god, I was told . . . he said I had to, to . . .

CLYTEMNESTRA
This god of yours? Where is he now?

ORESTES
He's . . . *(He looks up desperately)* He's . . .

CLYTEMNESTRA
Funny how that happens. The gods you think you are serving,
when you've done whatever it is you thought they wanted you
to do . . . where are they?

ORESTES
He said . . . he said . . .

CLYTEMNESTRA
Yes, well, that's why I've always worked for myself.

*(She gets up and brushes herself off. She puts a hand out to
Orestes, who is still on his knees. He takes it gingerly, afraid of her,
and gets up with her aid. Suddenly, violently, she pulls him to her.
She holds his face in her hand.)*

Yes, you're right. You see her face. She's everywhere. Get used to it.

*(She drops him. Orestes scrambles to get away from her, but she
pursues him.)*

It's true. Something is wrong.
Something is loose.
You can hear it, the stalking weight of it, breaking the small
breakables of the forest floor,
Shattering all that you thought you knew.
What is this thing unleashed?
What are you?
You are unmothered.
Bathe yourself eye-deep in the waters of the shrine,
Plead your prayers by the hour,
Crawl up the holy mountain on your raw knees in the blind,
cold night, seeking forgiveness—
will you ever find it for what you've done?
You have unmothered yourself.
She who brought your body through her own.
Without her there would be no world.
Without her what are you?
Something to be paid.
The currency of a crime.
And pain is how you are tendered.

(He collapses, cowering, as she turns from him to the rest of the chorus.)

And as for you: You have no queen, you have no gods.
Your work is before you. Begin.

(Clytemnestra exits.)

CHORUS I
Begin what?

CHORUS H
Our work? What does she mean?

CHORUS D
What work have we ever done?

CHORUS C
Cleaning? She can't mean—

CHORUS G
Does she want us to *clean?*

CHORUS B
Clean *this* house?

CHORUS H
Now?

CHORUS F
Can it even be done?

CHORUS I
All the blood.

CHORUS C
Blood on blood.

CHORUS A
Crime on crime.

CHORUS D
Until this. This crime.

CHORUS F
This last crime.

CHORUS G
Can we clean this house?

CHORUS C
What happens if we can't?

CHORUS F
That's the question.

CHORUS A
No. Something else is being demanded of us. Something—

CHORUS I
Something like—

CHORUS C
Something, a problem must be—

CHORUS A
(About Orestes) Him. This man here. The question is: What will
we do with him?

CHORUS B
That is too great a problem for us to solve. We must wait for the
gods to—

CHORUS F
The gods have nothing to do with this. He concerns us.

CHORUS B
It is for the gods to judge—

CHORUS C
If there is a judgment to be made, it seems . . . we are the ones to
do it.

CHORUS A
Yes. This is a human problem and it demands a human solution.

CHORUS B
We are to judge him?

CHORUS G
We are all they have.

ELECTRA
Then he must be allowed to defend himself.

CHORUS D
Can he defend himself?

CHORUS H
Do you deny that you killed her?

ORESTES
(Terrified) —I . . . I . . . —

CHORUS H
(Impatiently) He killed her, that's all that matters.

ELECTRA
No one is denying—

CHORUS H
He's covered in blood, you both are—

ELECTRA
You have to listen to him!

CHORUS H
(Taken aback) Why?

ELECTRA
Because if he never speaks, he will be locked inside his crime forever.

CHORUS D
But he is—

CHORUS H
But he *is* locked inside it. It's a box made of tin and nails and no light will ever shine into it. That's where he lives now.

CHORUS D
He is only his crime now.

ELECTRA
He's my brother! I won't abandon him to some box of torment forever! He can't be left alone!

CHORUS H
Oh, but he isn't alone. You live there too.

ELECTRA
But I didn't, I didn't—

CHORUS D
Or you could leave him there. It's up to you.

CHORUS H
But neither of you are welcome *here* anymore.

CHORUS I
Wait! This isn't right, this isn't—

CHORUS A
Something more has been asked of us than to just—

CHORUS C
Before we can decide what to do about him, we have to try to
understand this, to know the truth—

CHORUS D
We know the truth! It happened in front of us.
And my judgment here is guilty. Done.

CHORUS I
It can't be so simple.

CHORUS C
No matter what they did, they deserve something from us,
something / like—

CHORUS A
What they deserve is justice.

CHORUS F
Well, "justice," that's the question, isn't it? Because in *this* family—?

CHORUS G
We have seen what justice looks like here.

CHORUS F
—in *this* house? Justice would mean vengeance at the hands of his
own child.
(To Orestes) Isn't that right?

ORESTES
I—

ELECTRA
We have no children.

CHORUS F
Exactly. There's no one left to hand the family knife to.

(Pause.)

ORESTES
Who are you?

CHORUS D
Don't you recognize us?

ORESTES
You do seem . . . familiar.

CHORUS F
That is precisely what we are. We have known you all your life.

ORESTES
I thought you were the Furies.

CHORUS G
We are the servants of this house. We have always been here.
You know us.

CHORUS H
As much as you've ever known anyone.

CHORUS F
And so it falls to us to judge you.
You want to be judged. Don't you?

ORESTES
(A slight hesitation, then) Yes.

CHORUS C
Then we are the only ones left to do it.

(Expectant pause.)

ORESTES
Wait! There must be someone who can see things whole, without passion, without—

CHORUS B
The gods perhaps?

ORESTES
No. They can't imagine what it is like to do what they make us do.

ELECTRA
It was Apollo who made this happen. You can't *choose* whether to obey a *god*.

CHORUS D
We saw it all but we never saw Apollo. We only saw you and your brother and what you did.

ELECTRA
It's not our fault.

CHORUS H
Then whose fault is it?

CHORUS D
Who held the knife?

ELECTRA
Who watched and did nothing?

CHORUS H

You think *we* could have stopped this?

CHORUS D

There is no blood on us.

ELECTRA

No? You, who watched my father walk across this yard to his death
as I did not, as my brother did not? You, who heard his cries for
help as he slid into the bloody water under her killing arm? You
have no place in this? What if you had stopped her? What if you
had come inside and *done something*? You with all your smug
certainty and clarity, where were you when my father was dying
in this house? Your house. Would we be here if you had done what
surely could have been done, should have been done, when he was
calling for your help? And when you saw the murderer exulting
over her fresh kill, the man who had been your only king, did you
ask yourself how you could have let that happen in your house?
No? Then where were you all the ten years we waited for our
future to return? And what did you do on the day he did? Did you
warn my mother? Did you try to stay my brother's hand? No? You
are of this house, you share in our fate, our glory, and our guilt.

CHORUS C

We do. We have a part in these crimes. But after the catastrophe
has done its worst, someone must judge. That falls to us. Because
something like justice must be done.

CHORUS A

But justice for who? His father? His mother? How can it be for both?

CHORUS I

How can it not be?

CHORUS G

Justice for him. He is a child to both.

CHORUS D
But acted only for his father.

CHORUS F
The dead are always killing the living here. The dead are to blame
for this.

CHORUS C
Only the living are before us now. And a decision must be made.

CHORUS D
The crime demands retribution.

CHORUS G
But the cycle of vengeance has gone on long enough. The wheel
must spin to a stop.

CHORUS D
Retribution in kind is the only way, the only means to satisfaction.

CHORUS A
Aren't we better than our worst crimes? Are we just going to go on
trading blood endlessly back and forth? What is the sense of that?
Aren't we tired?

CHORUS D
If we let his crime stand without penalty, he wins an unearned
victory because, of all the crimes of this house, his crime alone
goes unpunished. What is the sense of *that*? Is that just?

CHORUS H
Harm must be answered with equal harm.

CHORUS B
But it's absurd! What are you saying?
As the last of the house, must he kill *himself* to avenge the murder
he himself committed?

CHORUS H

Perhaps. That makes sense to me.

CHORUS C

But it has to make sense to all of us. We will all have to submit to whatever we decide.

CHORUS A

How can we? Any judgment will only serve one side.

CHORUS I

Kill him or free him, someone will object.

CHORUS D

If he goes free, what's to prevent anyone from doing anything at all?

CHORUS H

Our obligation is to the victim.

CHORUS I

Don't we also owe something to the guilty? Isn't justice also for him?

CHORUS A

But he is both. Isn't he? Look at him. He is a victim of his own crime.

CHORUS H

You're saying he deserves pity but his mother does not?

CHORUS B

He was acting for a higher truth, for a god. His mother was not.

CHORUS H

Her husband had killed their child. What truth is higher than the bond between a parent and a child? He deserved to die. She did not.

CHORUS B

If anyone deserved to die, it was the one killer who acted only for herself.

CHORUS I

But justice must serve *him* now. Him and his sister. They're the only ones left.

CHORUS F

Justice must serve *us*. We have to find a way forward after what happened here—

CHORUS H

Yes! *We* need satisfaction after what he did.

CHORUS C

He did it, yes, but he is of us. We can't abandon him without abandoning ourselves. And there is no justice without him at the center of it.

CHORUS A

If we can't figure out how to forgive him, / then we can't—

CHORUS D

Forgive him? What / are you . . . ?

CHORUS H

Impossible!

CHORUS I

Whether we forgive him or not, he deserves our help—

CHORUS D

He *deserves* to die, anything else / would be—

CHORUS A

This is not some / clear-cut—

CHORUS G

You can't mean that you actually / want to—

CHORUS H
We are only asking for justice, that he get what he deserves—

CHORUS F
But that . . . that's just *spite*—

CHORUS I
You really think *death* is what is / needed here?—

CHORUS A
More death?

CHORUS D
What he deserves is to be brought down exactly the way / his—

CHORUS B
(To Chorus D) What *you* deserve is to be silenced forever, what *you* deserve is—

CHORUS D
And you? What gives you the right to sit in / judgment on—?

CHORUS B
Because I know what you are, and / I know—

CHORUS I
(To Chorus B) But that isn't any more just than what they / are saying—

CHORUS D
Justice! What we deserve / is—

CHORUS G
—Oh, this is insanity—

CHORUS I
(To Chorus H) But that isn't justice, is it? It isn't even . . .

(Silence. No one knows how to proceed at this point.)

CHORUS C
(A quiet struggle) Justice? I don't know. Maybe that's too great
an idea for the likes of us to grasp. I mean, look at us. But . . . but
still, one part of it might be simple. It could be that it's a matter
of everyone being in the same place. A place where each truth is
spoken if it can be spoken. And at the end, if we are lucky, perhaps
something like meaning can be drawn clean out of this chaos of
blood and its claims on us. Is that what you want?

ELECTRA
Yes.

CHORUS C
Will you submit to whatever of justice we can come up with for
you together?

ORESTES
Yes.

CHORUS C
(To Electra) You're right. We are none of us innocent here. We are
flawed; each of us is limited by our own needs and fears. And we
don't have much power. But we have the power to let you speak
and we have the power to listen.
So.

(All turn expectantly to Orestes.)

ORESTES
I, I, I don't know where to . . . it never felt like something I *chose*
(who would choose this?) or something I could be held accountable
for. It seemed like I was born for it, compelled before I ever knew
who I was. I was . . . I was a child.

CHORUS H

We were all children. Once.
And we were born bloody.
But none of us did what you have done.

CHORUS B

Let him speak!

ORESTES

There must have been a time before the god spilled down into me,
before he settled like some barbed star in my chest, heavy and
shrieking. But I can't remember it. I was so young when she did
it, killed my father. I was bent over some game on the floor in my
room, something I had made myself, but I can't . . . *(Remembering
suddenly)* —Oh, yes!—it was, it was a tower of sticks, trembling,
balanced carefully, a perfect thing. I was marveling at it, feeling
a sort of . . . pride. Wanting to show someone, bring my sister in
to admire it, but I didn't want to leave it, thinking that if I left the
room, even turned my head away, the tower wouldn't feel the
need to exist—it was there just for me, you see—and it would fall
and leave me forever. But the problem was that if nobody else saw
it, no one would ever believe that I could do such a thing.
A conundrum. And that's when I heard the screaming, I guess you
could call it screaming, coming from above me, animal sounds,
thumps, also water splashing, overflowing, and hitting the tiled
floor up there.
I didn't know what it was. It didn't occur to me that that sound
could be coming from anything like a human being, certainly
not my father. The man I had only really just glimpsed that day,
someone on his way up the stairs to . . . Not for a second did I
think a sound like that could come out of such a man. No, mostly
what concerned me was . . . the shaking, I didn't like the way the
thumping was making the house quiver, because the tower, of
course, I was afraid for the tower . . . but it just wouldn't stop,
you see, the thumping, like a beast on a chain stomping, and that
sound that came out of something's mouth, whatever it was, it just

would not stop . . . until I just, I looked away from my tower,
I *betrayed* it. I looked up at the plaster falling, and where the
water was making a kind of widening sore in the ceiling, a blister
that dripped . . . It was then, it must have been, just as
I understood that the sounds were father-dying sounds, mother-
killing-father-dying sounds, that I looked back at the tower I had
made, that improbable, delicate thing that no one would ever
believe . . . including me. Not now. *(He doesn't realize that he is
weeping)* Just splayed, meaningless sticks scattered around like
trash. No trace of it. Nothing like that could ever happen again.
(He recovers) That's when I felt the god's descent, his bright, hot
shout splitting the crown of my head and roaring down into me
like molten metal. From then on, my life, my body, has belonged
to him. He gave me a terrible thirst that never went away, it
burned me up from the inside, wouldn't let me be still. And my
hand never stopped aching. I'd put things in it, a spoon, a pen,
nothing ever felt right. I couldn't ease the ache, the emptiness
yearning. *Years* that went on. Until my hand . . . until it found the
knife, my hand, and curled around it like a snake, a tight coil of
certainty at last.
And then, well, then . . . you know what happened.

(Silence.)

CHORUS D
Is that . . . is that your *defense*?

(Orestes looks around, confused, as if just coming to.)

ORESTES
This dream. I can't wake up from it. I can't . . . I can't . . . I can't
wake up.

CHORUS H
On the basis of this, we are to pass judgment?

386 / ELLEN MCLAUGHLIN

ELECTRA
No, wait . . .

ORESTES
Electra, it doesn't matter. What do you think you can protect me
from now? The worst has happened and I have done it. Look at us.
We are covered in our own mother's blood. What can we expect
from anyone? What do we deserve?

CHORUS A
Justice. But not by blood this time. No more. There has to be
another way.

CHORUS D
If we let him go, we sanction barbarity.

CHORUS B
If we kill him, we participate in barbarity.

CHORUS F
This crime taints us no matter how we respond to it.

CHORUS C
We never wanted to know this, what we learn here.

CHORUS H
What we are capable of.

CHORUS B
Unspeakable things.

(Pause.)

CHORUS I
Is this a test?

(Pause.)

CHORUS G
This knife, this blood, we want no part of it, any of it.

CHORUS H
And yet.

CHORUS B
And yet.

CHORUS D
And yet.

CHORUS C
We know this dream.

CHORUS F AND G
Terrible, terrible.

CHORUS C
We have heard this dream before.

CHORUS A AND I
Terrible, terrible.

CHORUS C
This dream is our dream.

*(By now, all the chorus is standing, looking at Orestes and
Electra. Chorus G picks up a bucket of water and brings it near
where Electra is. She takes a rag from her pocket and dunks it
in the water and wrings it out. She silently gestures to Electra
to come to her. At the bucket, Chorus G helps Electra to join her
on her knees. Chorus G dips a cloth in the water and then simply*

takes Electra's hands and begins to clean them, one hand and then the other. It's done without drama; it's the sense of a preoccupied mother tending to a child in an ordinary way. Chorus F takes her bucket and places it near Orestes, who, like Electra, goes to his knees next to the bucket. Chorus F takes his hand and starts calmly cleaning it. The rest of the chorus continues to stand, watching. Orestes quietly begins to weep.)

ORESTES
I'm sorry . . . I'm sorry . . .

(Chorus F doesn't look up, just continues her work.)

Forgive me, I'm sorry.

(The only sound is the cloths dipping into the buckets, the quiet weeping.)

END OF PLAY

Runaways

Introduction

Written in 2010 as a commission for the University of Maryland, *Runaways* is a response to Aeschylus's *Danaids*, a trilogy of which only one play, *The Suppliant Maidens*, has survived complete. The story begins with the image of fifty women in flight from fifty men, their cousins, who pursue them in an attempt to force them into marriage. The first play concerns the women's search for sanctuary, and the story continues in the rest of the plays, though the plot is mostly conjecture since what we have are mere fragments, some tantalizingly beautiful.

I was introduced to the myth and what remains of Aeschylus's trilogy when I saw the Romanian director Silviu Purcărete's *Les Danaides* at Lincoln Center in the summer of 1997. It was a mighty spectacle involving one hundred twenty actors in which the fifty suppliant maidens hurtled onstage in identical burqas, all carrying suitcases, calling out their lines in chorus as they ran in circles like seabirds skittering across a shore. It was such a striking theatrical image that it seems I have been thinking about it in my work ever since.

There is an old idea, a Greek one, but familiar to many cultures, that the suppliant is holy. To do wrong to the suppliant—the beggar, the sick, the wounded, the child—is particularly hateful to God, and Zeus himself is known as the protector of suppliants. Which may explain the draw of this myth—that image of the refugee and our deep, inchoate sense of kinship with those who are in flight. Perhaps we sense that to be human is, to some extent, to be on the run. The Christian version of the human story, after all, begins with perpetual exile. But then there's something about the idea of the runaway that we understand, however obliquely. There is a longing for release in us, a desire to light out, like Huck Finn, into the territory and away from everything that oppresses us. So when we hear a tale of someone who successfully flees an impossible situation of any kind and makes an escape, some unarticulated part in all of us exults.

Characters

THE WAITRESS, could be in her forties to fifties, could be immortal. She is old enough in any case to be the mother of all the young women in her diner.

THE RUNAWAYS, all are in their teens through their twenties, none of them much older. All are from different eras. All are American, except Molly, who is from Ireland. Actors can be any ethnicity, but Lizzie must be Black.

JENNY, 1930s, a runaway wife

LIZZIE, 1850s, a runaway slave

MOLLY, 1750s, Irish, a runaway indentured servant

LIL, 1900s, a runaway sharpshooter

EMILY, 1690s, a runaway Puritan

Place and Time

An American diner, should feel vintage, perhaps 1930s–1940s. Winter, late afternoon.

Note on the Text

A slash (/) indicates the point at which the next character should begin to speak, overlapping the rest of the first character's line.

A diner in winter. Fogged glass. An earlier time, 1930s? 1940s?
Chrome. Jukebox? The waitress, wearing an apron over a checked
dress, is at the counter. Coffee is brewing. Four young women
sit in the diner, all of them with identical small pink cardboard
suitcases. The women are all from different eras.
Lizzie is wearing a ragged shawl over the dress of a runaway slave
of the 1850s.
Lil is in Western dress from the early 1900s, complete with gun belt.
Molly is in boy's clothing from the 1750s. Her hair is cropped. She
should look enough like a boy that she might actually pass as one.
She speaks with an Irish accent.
Emily is in a plain Puritan dress from the 1690s.
All of the women should look the worse for wear. They have been
fugitives for some time.
Jenny enters with her pink suitcase, snow in her hair, wearing
a 1930s dress and an unbuttoned coat. She is not dressed for the
weather, no gloves, her hands cold and red. The other women turn
to look at her but she's too dazed from exhaustion and cold to take
them in. She sits at the counter and takes a small roll of bills out of
her bra and looks through it. She decides she doesn't want to break
into that. She begins searching in her pockets for change and digs
out various oddments, which she puts on the counter: a pebble,
some saltines still in their wrapper, etc., then finds some coins.
She counts them in her palm.

WAITRESS
(Coming over to Jenny at the counter) It's just a matter of what you're running from.

JENNY
What? I'm not running, I'm just . . .

WAITRESS
What? You're just what?

JENNY
Thinking.

WAITRESS
Uh-huh. You usually pack a suitcase for that?

JENNY
There's no "usually" in my life right now.

WAITRESS
Except the hitting.

JENNY
What?

WAITRESS
Coffee's still brewing. Hot chocolate? Tea?

JENNY
How much?

WAITRESS
Oh, I'll take that lucky pebble there.

JENNY
How'd you know it was lucky?

WAITRESS

Well, you wouldn't be carrying it if it wasn't, would you? Not when you've got so little else. Not even mittens. Or buttons for your coat.

JENNY

I can't give you the pebble.

WAITRESS

No, I suppose not. Not when it's the only thing you have from that beach.

JENNY

Do you know that beach?

WAITRESS

We all do. Or someplace like. We all had home shores once. We've been tracking the sand of them across the world ever since. Everywhere we went.

JENNY

(Holding the pebble) I saw it in the moonlight.

WAITRESS

Lying on the dresser there.

JENNY

I'd forgotten it. I saw it while I stood there in the dark.

WAITRESS

Holding your suitcase.

JENNY

Holding my breath.

WAITRESS

Listening for his sleeping to slow and deepen.

JENNY

Waiting for it to dive deep enough so I could sneak away.

WAITRESS

That stray scrap of you, nearly forgotten with the dust and the hairpins and the pennies and lint.

JENNY

Everything I left behind.

WAITRESS

All that you've cast off, shed, to come here.

JENNY

This one thing.

WAITRESS

That tiny thing, unremarkable to anyone else.

JENNY

But mine.

WAITRESS

Yours.

JENNY

Who are you?

WAITRESS

Oh, that's not important.

JENNY

How do you know so much about me?

WAITRESS

Because you're all alike.

JENNY
Who?

WAITRESS
The runaways.

(She gestures to the other women and Jenny takes them in for the first time.)

JENNY
I haven't run, not really, not yet.

WAITRESS
You. All of you. It's an old story. Maybe the oldest.
Women running away.
Women fleeing together, so many, they were like a lifting, swirling
cloud of mayflies, like a flock of birds wheeling up from that
pebble shore, so many of them they were impossible to count,
all one, in sorrow, in panic, a kinship of flight, so many,
Shall we say fifty?
Fifty daughters
Fifty fugitives
Fifty sisters on the run from
Fifty sons
Fifty pursuers
Fifty brothers on the hunt for
All the women
All the running women.

LIZZIE
(To all of them) How long you been running?

MOLLY
Centuries and centuries

LIL
Walking those highways

EMILY
The long rains slanting

MOLLY
Falling on our shoulders

LIZZIE
Mud heavy on our skirt hems

LIL
Caking our boots

LIZZIE
The baying of the hounds

EMILY
The flash of the lanterns

MOLLY
The sound of us / panting

LIL
panting

LIZZIE
my ragged, / chugging breath

EMILY
chugging breath

LIZZIE
as I run / and run, and run

MOLLY
as I run / and run

EMILY
and run, and run

LIL
I hid in the alley

MOLLY
I hid in the dead leaves

LIL
In the graveyard

EMILY
In the night forest

LIZZIE
Standing still as a tree as the dogs went by, noses to the ground, their ears swinging

MOLLY
I jumped from the window ledge

LIZZIE
I walked in the creek bed to lose my own scent

LIL
I held onto the side of the boxcar all the way to Tulsa.

EMILY
And then I ran

MOLLY
I ran

LIZZIE
I ran

LIL
I ran.

EMILY
The sound of it still in my head

MOLLY
The singing of it in my head

LIZZIE
The crying of my own baby

LIL
The shot I fired

LIZZIE
my milk drying on her mouth

LIL
the one I killed him with

EMILY
before I ran

LIZZIE
before I ran

EMILY
The curses they shouted at me

MOLLY
The burning of it still on my skin

EMILY
The last time they pelted me

MOLLY
There from when she jabbed me with the poker

EMILY
The stones they threw at me

MOLLY
the one she took out of the fire

EMILY
cracking across my back as I went past the courthouse

LIZZIE
even now

LIL
even now

EMILY
even now

MOLLY
as we run

LIZZIE
and run

LIL
and run

LIL, MOLLY, EMILY, AND LIZZIE
We remember.

WAITRESS
It's the first story.
And because it's a human story, it's the story of exile.
Fifty sisters running
from marriages to their cousins.
Fifty brothers

Loveless marriages
Fifty women fleeing.

LIL
From rape

LIZZIE
From the whips

MOLLY
From the hatred

EMILY
From the injustice

LIL
From prison

MOLLY
From the slapping hands

LIZZIE
From the shackles

EMILY
From the curses

LIL, MOLLY, EMILY, AND LIZZIE
From a living death.

WAITRESS
Fifty sisters running hard

LIL, MOLLY, EMILY, AND LIZZIE
for their lives.

MOLLY

I was a small thing then in the boat across, all of us, the bodies
stacked like herring in the dark hold, the bugs swimming in the
buckets of the swaying black water we were to drink, the smell
of the place, and the noise, the misery of sound, day after day,
me ma, me da, lying there, can't get up, the sickness takes them
both, her head rolling with the waves, her dry mouth open. Me
brother Brendan taking me by the hand, he says, they're never
going to rise again, Molly, it's us who's for it now. We'll have to
work our passage and theirs too now. Saw her face covered by her
own petticoat, her body falling like a loaf of bread into the water
there, then me da after her, two splashes and they are gone. It's a
world of water, the tears falling down out of me, I can't speak for
crying, crying, crying, until I stop for good and all and never again.
For there's Brendan, smallest of the indentured boys, waving
goodbye to me as he's taken off to the farm he's sold to. And I get
sent to the wolves. She-wolf her, hands like knives in that stone
house they sent me to. Couldn't do a thing right, me, slapped and
slapped at, black and blue. I run first when I'm only six, took my
dolly made secret from a flour sack with me, that's how young
I was. Only got a day away down the road before they found me
and nearly killed me in the sunset back at the stone house, that
stone on a stone of a place where even the chickens stopped
clucking for fright of her. Tried again at eight and then again at
twelve, but the whole countryside is afraid of her and there is no
place to hide from her. And all the time I'm thinking about the
only person I have in the world at all, Brendan, my brother,
who might as well be on the moon for all the hope I have of seeing
him again I begin to think. Off in that farm working our passage
and theirs, all the years stolen from his life. Until the day comes
I'm on my way to the market, her three coins in my hand, and
I think to steal a boy's clothes from the line and climb the back
of the wagon headed south, buried deep in the hay. When I reach
a new town they ask me my name and I say, Brendan, that's my
name, Brendan, and I keep moving.

MOLLY AND LIZZIE
Prickle on my back

MOLLY
Right between my shoulder blades

MOLLY AND EMILY
Where I fear the hunter's eyes falling

MOLLY
The searching eyes

MOLLY AND LIL
Hot prickle on my back

MOLLY
Cooling with every mile I get away from them.

MOLLY AND EMILY
But still I wake gasping

EMILY, LIL, AND MOLLY
Every night

MOLLY
The hard hand swiping through the smoke of dreams

LIZZIE
The fingers cold and sure

LIL AND EMILY
At the back of my neck

LIZZIE AND MOLLY
And I am caught again

LIL
Taken back

MOLLY

Twitching in her grasp,
hanging like a bucking rabbit
Taken back to that slab of stone to die.
That house, that whetstone of a house
Where knives were sharpened to make hands.
So I wake, blink in the darkness

LIL, MOLLY, EMILY, AND LIZZIE
And I run.

MOLLY

I am Brendan, not Molly anymore
That girl is dead.
I left her on the stone.
I am Brendan, searching for Brendan,
searching for me, the boy I became so that I could find me,
Brendan.

LIL

I won it fair and square, twenty-five shots and every one a beauty,
twenty-five quarters tossed in the air and a hole in every one.
Him, he missed his twenty-fourth for all his grinning, for all his
slick hair and silver spurs. They held the last quarter up—his—
without a nick in it. Every single one of mine bit through. Like
so much confetti on the ground, mangled coins. Everybody saw it.
No questions. Him shaking his head and grinning there. He makes
a pistol with his hand and crooks the trigger, the muzzle of his
finger pointing right at me. And then he's laughing. But
I knew better. 'Cause sure enough when I leave the bar that night,
he's waiting for me, grabbing to catch me, his hand across my
mouth, and I'm biting now, tasting his blood, while he's bending
me over a fence and all I'm doing is figuring out how I'm going to
get to my gun and the moon is a perfect coin in the sky like the
quarters I shot through all day, and I'm seeing it all happen again,
quarter after quarter going up like fireworks in the dark as I take

aim and shoot, quarter after quarter, spinning in the air, and as
I watch I realize I can make them turn slowly, slowly, like moons,
and I wait for the profile shining there and I aim for the eyes,
I aim for the eyes in the dark, the profile of the man who's looking
the wrong way. And when the sound of it is over and he's lying at
my feet, I holster my gun in his little town where the dirt is bright
with my bullet-bitten quarters, I holster my gun and I begin to run.

EMILY

I knew that girl would lay a bitterness on my head, somehow she
would. Because I stopped her from hurting that dog when
I found her in the barn with it, poor thing, digging at it with that
knife. I took the broken creature from her then, spoke harsh to
the vile child, and carried it from there to safety with me. I used
the little skills I'd learned as a girl from Ibby Evers when she lived
by us in the woods, before the black bile took my family and my
brothers and so many and her. With my herbs and my kindness
I brought it back from death, the dog, until the creature followed
me everywhere except back to the place I'd taken her from; there
she wouldn't go. But I knew what the cost might be. It was in the
look of that girl when she saw me. As if she would make blisters
on me with her eyes if she could. Until I heard she was taken with
the same fits as the other girls, the ones who started the trouble.
And they called me to her, asked me to come with my little bags of
herbs, in use for her, that girl. But I stayed away. Told them
I had no art to heal her, no matter what anyone had said, and soon
I heard that she was cursing me in her fits, saying that it was me
who was putting them on her, and sure, sure I was that oh, soon it
would fall on me too, the hand of the time. The hand that swiped
the pieces from the table of the world. Girls and women hanged
by their own neighbors, the screaming in the churches, in the
courtrooms. The fear, you could smell it, moving like smoke down
streets and through fields into the little places in your nighttime
self so your heart beats you awake, drumming, "run, run, run."
But where? Step away from the town and it's a black world
without roads, without fields. The mountains are full of bears

and how can God find me in a night as dark as that when the cold
falls down? Still I saw the bodies in their black dresses hanging on
Tuesday, the day they hung eight together, I knew all their names,
Cassie and Laura and oh, Sara Teale, Sara Teale who suffered me
to take the walnuts from her walnut tree when I was a girl, Sara
Teale, so tiny, so old, her bonnet fallen off her and that white mist
of hair on the broken blossom of her head. And as I stood there,
tears falling to look at them, I see the child at her window, and
I could feel the heat of her eyes on my face and so I knew. Soon
the stones were falling on me, and the yelling my name in the
night. And so I went, out into the cold blackness of the world
without end. And so it has been. So it has been. Alone.

LIZZIE

She was good, the baby, the first full night we were out, sleeping
with the root I had crushed up and put in her mouth. I suckled her
in the morning once we were out far enough to stop underneath
the creek cliffs where we finally thought we might wait for a time
to breathe, our sweat cooling on our backs, my sister Dorrie and
me, couldn't talk we were panting so much, just looking at each
other, so scared all night, but we didn't have to talk, we were like
that, always had been, we just sniff it out, the way through the
woods, even in the dark, we can feel where the other is and run
silent, and sometimes she's the one ahead and sometimes I am,
the baby in the sling against my breast, banging against me, all
night long, like deer we were so quiet. And we're thinking, I can
see it in Dorrie's eyes, we're thinking, well now, well now, we
might just, we might just have done it, could it be? 'Cause there's
no sound behind us, we might just have made it away enough
to find ourselves a place to wait through the daylight until the
night comes again and we can keep at it, up through the woods,
following the North Star, that drinking gourd in the sky, 'til we get
to the depot, outside Atlanta, red-painted house with a white cross
above the door and three goats in a pen, where the conductor told
us we'd be safe. We were thinking we could make it, Dorrie and
me, we were smart girls, we, the smartest girls and the most quiet,

we. Twin girls. No one could tell us apart, except our mother, but she was sold in the spring from us, gone when we come back from the fields, her broom thrown down on the floor in the empty cabin from where they took her off, so it's only us, Dorrie and me, and then the word comes from up at the house, they heard it in the kitchen, that they were going to sell us too away from each other, and well now, well now, that we weren't going to live for, not us, so we ran. And we're dug in next to the creek bed, waiting for the sun to set, and the baby starts to fussing, and that's when we hear the dogs. So we can't wait, we start out without a word, and I'm behind her, and now the baby is crying, and there's nothing I can do for her because we're running, and all we can hope is that the sun goes down fast and hides us and it is, it's falling, but not fast enough, and the dogs are coming nearer, baby banging on me and I'm right behind Dorrie when we get to that cliff, and she spins and turns to look at me and she slips, I see her hand go up, and she's over and there's just a little sound out of her as she goes, and I hear the crack, it's her leg down there where she's fallen when I get to her, she's put a rag in her mouth to keep from screaming, but her leg is broke like a twig there, and now the baby is bawling, I can't stop her and the night is full dark but we can't stop the sounds and she can't run no more and the lights are streaming through the trees above us as they run along the ridge up there, and she takes the baby from me and she takes the gag from her mouth and she speaks, it's the first time I've heard her voice in days, and all she says, all she says, is RUN.

MOLLY, LIL, AND EMILY
Run, run, run.

JENNY
The way he looks around the house at night when he comes in to find it, the thing I haven't done, the thing I got wrong, the thing he'll hit me for this time.

MOLLY
Run.

JENNY
It doesn't matter what I do, he'll find it.

LIL
Run.

JENNY
Maybe it's the song the radio is playing when he comes in

LIZZIE
Run

JENNY
Maybe it's the smoke from the toast I burned that morning

EMILY
Run

JENNY
Maybe it's the corner of the carpet flipped up

MOLLY
Run

JENNY
Maybe it's just the look out of the eye he blacked on me the night before

MOLLY, LIL, EMILY, AND LIZZIE
RUN!

JENNY
I don't know how. That's my life, that is, back there, even with him in it, that's all I got.

LIL
Run from it

EMILY

Place it at your back

LIZZIE

Point your body like an arrow into the world and run

MOLLY

From the beating hot heart of the life you knew

EMILY

Into the chill silence of the unprinted snow of where you've never been.

LIZZIE

Lose it all.

LIL

Trade it all away.

JENNY

For what? For this? What is this?

LIZZIE

It's just a depot.

MOLLY

It's just a stop on the way.

EMILY

It's the place where you haven't made a mistake yet.

LIL

It's the place where you can take out the map, place a finger, and—

JENNY

(Turning to the waitress) But that's not the end of the story.
The fifty sisters running away from the fifty brothers who wanted
to marry them, it's just the beginning, right? There's an ending.

WAITRESS
Yes. But no one wrote it down. Or if they did, it was lost.

JENNY
But there are stories, yes?

WAITRESS
Yes. Lots of stories. There always are when women run.

JENNY
They didn't get away with it, did they?

WAITRESS
Depends on who you talk to.

JENNY
(To the others) That's what she doesn't want you to know. *(To the waitress)* They didn't make it, right? They never do.

WAITRESS
Stories are mostly circles.

JENNY
Meaning what? They couldn't get away. The brothers caught up with them, didn't they, in the end?

WAITRESS
Yes, so the story goes.

JENNY
(To the others) See? I told you. Fifty marriages.

WAITRESS
Yes. So they say. There were fifty marriages.
And fifty women took fifty knives with them to their marriage
beds and drew fifty blades across fifty brothers' throats.
Or that was the plan anyway.

JENNY
But what happened?

WAITRESS
Forty-nine sisters did it, every single one of the forty-nine of them killed that stranger in her bed, but there was one—

JENNY
—the fiftieth—

WAITRESS
—who couldn't do it. Not when he was naked there beside her. Not when he looked at her like that, that stranger with his black curls and the moons on his fingernails as he brought his hand up to her cheek. So she saved him. Told him what she was supposed to do to him and he ran.

JENNY
He ran?

WAITRESS
He got away. And that's the last anyone ever saw of him.

JENNY
And her?

WAITRESS
What do you think?

MOLLY
I say she ran too.

LIL
Not with him. But away.

EMILY
Away from everything.

LIZZIE
Even from her running sisters.

JENNY
One got away? One really got away?

WAITRESS
Like I say, depends on who you talk to.

JENNY
And where's she now?

WAITRESS
Some people think she ran so far and so long that she saw the
length and breadth of the known world.

LIL
Saw it all.

MOLLY
Met everybody who was anybody

EMILY
Changed her name a thousand times

LIZZIE
Learned a thousand trades

WAITRESS
Gave birth to a thousand children, all of them girls.

LIL
Raised them by herself.

MOLLY
Told them all her stories about the places she saw.

EMILY
Taught them everything she knew.

LIZZIE
Watched her babies as they staggered

LIL
Then they're walking and then

MOLLY
And then

EMILY
They run.

WAITRESS
Sometimes she meets them in their travels, pours them coffee, listens to their stories, and then

LIZZIE
She flings them out into the world

WAITRESS
To run.

(Molly, Lizzie, Emily, and Lil stand, take their suitcases, and leave. A silence as Jenny and the waitress look at each other. Jenny stands and gives the pebble to the waitress in payment for the coffee. The waitress looks at it, tosses it in her hand twice, and then lobs it back to Jenny, who smiles, takes it, picks up her suitcase, and leaves.)

END OF PLAY

Conversations at
the Return of Spring

Introduction

In 2012, Madeleine Oldham, literary manager for Berkeley Repertory Theatre at the time, commissioned me and nineteen other playwrights to write short plays for a prospective festival the theater was calling the Food Project. In her words: "The idea is to commission twenty writers to each write a short play (about twenty minutes long) portraying a segment of the story of how food in California is planted, harvested, packaged, transported, distributed, sold, prepared, and served . . . The narrative line might 'follow the food,' so to speak, from the moment it goes into the ground to when it shows up on a dinner table at Chez Panisse and/or Taco Bell. We want to see how wildly different perspectives from different writers can illuminate this most essential process."

The theater provided a marvelous opportunity for all the writers to spend a week together in Berkeley, learning through lectures and interviews with people involved with the food industry or versed in agriculture and its implications. We visited farms, both industrial and organic, all while enjoying meals together in that giddily food-conscious and food-loving city. I also did a lot of research on my own on the history of agriculture—its mixed blessings and the tragedies that have accompanied our species' use of the earth. The plays we created were as varied as we were, and a fascinating spread of responses to the information we had taken in together.

As has been true so often in the past, I turned to the Greeks as a means of understanding the subject at hand. In early childhood, I learned to read by poring over the vividly evocative illustrations in *D'Aulaires' Book of Greek Myths* until, in what still seems a defining moment of my life, the text that up to that instant had been incomprehensible black marks cohered into language. The words became sentences that soared off the page and into sudden meaning. The story I was staring at when the miracle occurred was the myth of Demeter, Goddess of the Harvest, and her daughter Persephone, who is abducted by Hades, the King of the Dead, to be his bride in the Underworld. He takes her by surprise, bursting out of a chasm in his black chariot with its four black horses to snatch her from a field where she is picking spring flowers, then plunging back below with her, sealing up the earth above them as he goes. The abduction is the subject of one of the best illustrations in the book. We see Hades in his black helmet standing at the front of his chariot as it begins its fall back down to the Underworld. The chariot is suspended in air, just passing the arc of its highest point, the horses already beginning their plummet, staring straight into the darkness below. Hades in profile holds their reins in one hand, his other arm crooked around the waist of Persephone who alone is still upright, dropping her flowers, her weeping eyes dark slits on her shocked face.

No one sees the abduction happen, so Demeter courses across the face of the Earth in search of Persephone and can find her nowhere. In her bewildered misery, Demeter neglects her divine duties and the Earth is plunged into the first of all winters. Down below in Hades, Persephone, now the involuntary queen of the dead, wanders through her dim and silent kingdom, wretchedly longing for the daylight world of the living, now irrevocably lost to her. Finally, just as Demeter's apocalypse of grief is snuffing out all life on Earth, she discovers the truth of Hades's crime, but when confronted, he refuses to give his new bride up to her mother.

Lest all nature perish forever in the thrall of an eternal winter, a painful compromise is reached with the introduction into what had been a timeless, abundant paradise of the odd, tricky notion of seasons. Demeter allows Persephone to descend to Hades for several months of the year, during which time, in homage to that loss, the world suffers the death and deprivation of winter. Persephone then escapes back to the surface of the Earth and Demeter celebrates her return with a spring, a summer, and a following harvest before she must relinquish her to a living death once more. The seasons are experienced as a perpetual cycle of mourning and renewal. The agony of loss is mitigated by the promise of return, the joy of return made bittersweet by the certainty of loss. Thus we find ourselves in a world that is the product of compromise, and also of love.

Agriculture is Demeter's gift to humanity and is our necessity once the eternal cycle of seasons comes into being. If we as a species are to continue, we need to survive the terrible trial of winter with the promise of spring and a sustaining, storable harvest. But as we playwrights discovered during our weeklong intensive in Berkeley, along with its gifts to us, agriculture has also always brought humanity its share of misery and, depending on how it's practiced, can be a blight on the natural world as well. It occurred to me that I could write about the history of agriculture by listening in on a few conversations from the thousands had by Demeter and Persephone when they are reunited at the beginning of spring every year. It seems to me that Persephone as the Queen of the Dead has more to do with human beings than any other figure in the pantheon. She hears our stories and knows our regrets and woes as none of the rest of the deities do. I thought that she might be haunted by those stories and trail them up with her as she returns to her mother to discuss what has become of the gift Demeter gave us back at the beginning of seasonal time. Demeter speaks for the natural world, which is her realm, and Persephone speaks for us.

One experience that marked the majority of the plays inspired by that week in Berkeley was a visit to an industrial farm on which strawberries were harvested. We spent some time with the field-workers and their families and heard stories of the sacrifice and suffering that that kind of work entails. A woman of indeterminate age spoke of the many health problems she had dealt with as a consequence of working with the kinds of pesticides that were in use—her back was in constant pain, her hands were crippled, and she was perpetually struggling with intestinal difficulties. One of the playwrights asked if she ever ate the strawberries she picked and her hand went reflexively to her belly as a wave of nausea hit her. "Oh, no. No, no, no, never." She had no need to continue. The history of the human abuse of the gift of agriculture was in her face and prematurely bowed body. None of us who saw that will ever forget it.

Characters

DEMETER, Goddess of the Harvest, mother, immortal

PERSEPHONE, Queen of the Dead, her daughter, also immortal, yet younger

Place

Somewhere on Earth.

Time

The moment when winter gives way to spring.
Starting in early human time and ending in the present.

*Sound of wind, perhaps birds. Demeter stands in the lifting
darkness, shivering. She is dressed true to the statuary and images
on vases—a long pleated dress, perhaps a head wreath made of
wheat. She is waiting expectantly for Persephone's return.*

SUPERTITLES: PERSEPHONE, DAUGHTER OF THE EARTH
GODDESS, DEMETER, MUST SPEND SIX MONTHS OF THE
YEAR IN THE LAND OF THE DEAD WITH HER HUSBAND,
HADES, GOD OF THE UNDERWORLD.
BUT EVERY YEAR HER EXILE COMES TO AN END
WHEN SHE RETURNS FROM BELOW TO HER MOTHER.
AND WITH THAT REUNION THE SPRING BEGINS.
8000 B.C.

*Sound of footsteps, running. Persephone, wearing a crudely woven
hooded robe over her own pleated Greek dress, enters, breathless.
They embrace. Persephone is just perceptibly aloof, looking at
her mother.*

DEMETER
Oh, my darling girl. Look at you.
(About Persephone's robe, dubiously) What on earth is this thing?

PERSEPHONE

It was lent to me. I was cold. It's what the dead are wearing now.

DEMETER

Well, it's an improvement on those stinking animal skins, I suppose,
but you'd think they could get the grit out by now. I don't know
how many times I've shown them how to card wool properly.
Is it ineptitude or just stupidity?

PERSEPHONE

It's exhaustion, Mother, you don't know how hard you've made
their lives.

DEMETER

Me?

PERSEPHONE

Yes, you. Your so-called "gift" to them?

DEMETER

Agriculture? It's their salvation.

PERSEPHONE

Salvation? You have no idea. They were so much happier without it.

DEMETER

They would have died without it! Don't kid yourself. Without
agriculture, they were going fast, it was just a matter of time
before the whole lot of them went extinct. You'll see. They'll
thank me for it. I showed them green places between the rivers
where they can settle and sow their seeds, fall in love with their
fields, raise their children, stay put. The farmlands can thrive as
everything they hunted dies off. It was time. I have high hopes for
them as a species. Finally they might be able to *make* something
of themselves. At least they can feed themselves now.

PERSEPHONE

They fed themselves before, and a lot more easily. There were plenty of plants they could snatch up as they passed and a single antelope taken down would feed them for weeks. Now they're all stuck slaving away on their little patches of land. They can never leave.

DEMETER

Oh, you always sentimentalized that nomadic to-ing and fro-ing. It was a pointless, skittering life, in flight or on the hunt. They were smothering the babies they couldn't carry, you know, it was nasty, brutal stuff. Nothing could . . . accrue. All that running from weather, running from predators, running after bison—so repetitive, such a bore—it made me tired to watch them. Until at least *some* of them can stop having to chase things all the time, they won't have anything to say for themselves. My crops have made them sit still.

PERSEPHONE

It's all just grass, Mother. That's all you gave them. Elaborate grass. It doesn't even feed them properly. They're getting shorter and their teeth keep falling out. Not to mention that your crops are so delicate and tricky to grow that they have to be guarded from, well, everything. Stupid stuff, no thorns to protect it, no defenses at all, it tastes good to everything that tries it and falls down if you blow on it too hard. The people can never leave their fields alone. Who has time to hunt anymore? They spend their whole existence stooped over your rows of fancy grass. They never look up to see the sky without fearing what will come down from it or *not* come down from it. Water—not enough or too much. You've made them a people who can never stop worrying.

DEMETER

But I gave them wine! Now on a feast day they get to hop around in circles—

PERSEPHONE

—It's called dancing—

DEMETER
—while they bang on things and holler—

PERSEPHONE
—It's called music—

DEMETER
You're very sweet about them, aren't you? Their little efforts.
I expect more from them. But that will come, now that I've given
them a foothold. Art! It'll be interesting. But the key is farming,
some *stability*, without that—

PERSEPHONE
Stability? But, Mother, they're terrified. Even if their own crops
don't fail, they're still not safe because the neighbors' crops might,
which means next thing you know you've got a band of hungry
men with painted faces and spears descending on you just when
you thought you could finally relax. You know, don't you, that
that's your real gift to them? War.

DEMETER
They fought each other before.

PERSEPHONE
Not like this. In the old days, whenever they went at each other,
there weren't enough of them in any little group of wanderers to
do much damage, and besides, why stick around to risk getting
killed in a brawl when you can just go to the next valley and find
another herd of antelope? Why couldn't you leave them alone?
Their lives are so dreary now! By the time they get to me they're
bent in two—runty and cowed. The ones who don't spend their
lives stooped double in the fields are eye-deep in mud, digging the
irrigation canals for the thirsty, thirsty grass. The misery of it, all
that incessant shoveling. Did you know they've started believing
they were *made* from mud?

DEMETER
What? People? What do you mean?

PERSEPHONE
Yes! It's in every creation story there is. The first man and woman, they're always made from mud.

DEMETER
Well? See? That's adorable, they know that everything good comes from mud.

PERSEPHONE
I figure it's just that they think they've been standing in mud forever, holding their eternal shovels. Because of course to get all that digging done you need a whole lot of people who spend their lives doing nothing else. Somebody's always going to be controlling the food, getting rich off of it and cracking the whip while everybody else is dying in the mud. So don't expect them to thank you, most of them, because along with war, your other great gift to them is slavery.

DEMETER
Oh, don't be ridiculous. I had nothing to do with that. I never told them that one class of people should do all the work while a handful of people lord it over them and eat everything themselves. The land is generous. There is plenty, enough to feed everyone. It's not my fault that some people hoard the surplus and make everyone else their slaves. That has nothing to do with me, that's your beloved human character for you. Selfish, cruel, power-mad . . . I love them as a *species*, but as *people* they are hard to like.

PERSEPHONE
If you could hear what I hear, you wouldn't be able to talk about them that way . . . All winter long, I listen to them. They all tell me their stories when they come down. If you could hear one of them speak . . . This one *(She indicates her robe)* she says, she says . . .

DEMETER
She says what? Let her speak.

(Demeter reaches out and touches the sleeve of the robe. A sound, something to indicate Persephone's entrance into a different character.)

PERSEPHONE
(Speaking as the woman whose robe she wears) I remember berries, the berries we found one morning when we were still standing up, looking out of ourselves.
Before King.
Back before the fields and the crawling, before the mud and the shoveling.
Before we lost the mountains and the running and became His.
Because now there is King and we belong to Him.
Our backs to the sky, bent to the ground, our hands in the mud.
We bow to Him.
Never see His face because He stands above us with His back to the sun.
What He is is a great darkness with an arm and a whip.
And we give our curled backs to Him as we tend His fields.
But I died dreaming of the berries.
So long ago, I was only new.
I can see my hands still just small and soft,
and I remember standing straight like a flame in still weather.
And it is a morning, cool but the sun is falling between the leaves as we walk through
We are carrying our heads like flowers.
And our eyes are high, looking out of them
and we laugh to watch the shadows moving across us as we walk, all of us, we are walking
and we make the songs the birds make
and we follow them to where they are singing most and they are right,

because the berries, they are right, the berries are shining there
for all of us
and so we move through them with the birds
eating them and singing,
just together like that,
We are all the same with the juice staining our mouths wide.
And when we can't eat them anymore we sleep with the sun in our
eyes, and listen to the birds until we wake to eat them again, the
berries that are just there for us.

*(A sound. The trance breaks. Persephone returns to her own voice.
They look at each other.)*

DEMETER
Well, yes. I can see that the fields have cost them something.
I can see that. They've lost a kind of . . . joy. But it's an animal's
joy, my darling, what they had, and they would have lost it
anyway, because they would have died, all of them, just died out
with all the other animals they were so dependent on. I've saved
them from that. I gave them the chance to be human beings.
You have to understand. I did it for love. Now there is some
hope, if not for these, for the ones who will come after them.
Civilization? It's possible now. Not before. They've had no *time.*
It's been so frustrating to watch them. They're so . . . *short-lived.*

PERSEPHONE
Yes, that's what I'm saying! They have such little lives, Mother,
these people, just a fistful of years and then it's over. But with your
fields to tend, how many times can they be happy before they're
dead now? They're—

(Birdsong, beautiful, sudden. They look up, reminded of the spring.)

DEMETER
Oh, my darling child. *(She touches Persephone's cheek)* Now that
you're here, your people can rejoice. Last night I could tell you

were coming because I could hear the ice cracking in the northern mountains and the rivers being loosed. Can you feel it? Now that you've come back to us, the air is warming, the mist is on the fields. All will be well, the green is returning at last.

PERSEPHONE
The air! It's so good to breathe in the light again!

(She sheds the human robe, revealing her goddess gown.)

DEMETER
Welcome.

PERSEPHONE
Oh, Mother, the world, the sun on it. Beautiful.

DEMETER
Now you've come it is, my darling, it is. How I've missed you. Come, let's walk in the spring you brought us.

(They exit.)

Supertitle: 1851

Demeter waits in the darkness again. Smoke, a baby crying in the distance, perhaps. Persephone enters, walking unsteadily, clutching a tattered, filthy blanket around her goddess dress. Her hands are dirty. They embrace.

DEMETER
It's not my fault.

PERSEPHONE
Well, it's not theirs either.

DEMETER
I don't understand it. Why they are all dying? Only the potato keeps taking the blight, everything else has thrived. There is abundance. It's so strange. I look down and see the fields in harvest, bounty, but the thousands—

PERSEPHONE
—Thousands on thousands—

DEMETER
—going hungry, driven from their farms, walking the roads, dying in the midst of plenty.
Why?

433

PERSEPHONE

(Referring to the blanket) The potato is the only one that belongs
to them. They live on it. That, and milk, when they can get it.

DEMETER

Well, it's a wonderful crop, the potato, I'm very proud of it—

PERSEPHONE

Yes, and they believed in it, thought they could depend / on it—

DEMETER

But you can't live on only one crop.

PERSEPHONE

You can, well, *almost*. Anyway they *have*, for a long time now.

DEMETER

But it doesn't make sense. There is everything else, the plenty of
the world. They're standing in it.

PERSEPHONE

Yes, but it isn't for them, that plenty. They harvest all that for
others, it goes for rent, for the owners, it's not *theirs*, the potato is
the only thing they can grow for themselves.
All of what they could be eating, corn, wheat, barley, livestock—
cart after cart, ship after ship of it—keeps going across the water,
out of their sight. They stand and starve as they watch the laden
ships take their food away from them.

DEMETER

And you blame *me* for this? From the beginning I kept telling them,
diversity, diversity, don't rely on only one crop. This is craziness.

PERSEPHONE

But then why give them a crop that fools them into this kind of
dependence? Why give them a crop that can be destroyed by
a single fungus in one bad night?

DEMETER

How could I have known they could be this stupid and reckless?
They should never have risked everything on one crop. Blights will
come. How many times have I said that? That's the only thing you
can rely on. If they can die like this it just proves that there are too
many of them. It might knock some sense into them. They'll be
more careful in the future.

PERSEPHONE

Oh, Mother, you sound just like the ones who are letting them die.
(Referring to the blanket) If you could hear this woman.

DEMETER

All right. Who was she?

*(She touches the blanket. The sound, as before, of Persephone's
entrance into a different character.)*

PERSEPHONE

(Irish girl) All of August during the hungry months before the first
lifting with the days dank and harsh was the rains and the rains
till the chickens was drowning in the yards. Then the night
before the first lifting of the new potatoes me da had a dream.
He said the fairies came to him with their purple fingers, and they
was feeling his skull as if it was a potato, his skull, but he could
do nothing because they held him tight and as they felt his head
like that he could see the others of them, the fairies, scuttling
like beetles along beside the children where we lay sleeping,
and they were feeling our heads too as if we were potatoes, and
their fingers the same color, he said, that purple, he said, it was
the purple of the blossoms on the potatoes then out in the fields,
and the smell he said, it was terrible, a rotting, wet spitefulness.
And what he could hear was the chuckling-like, the laughing of
them as they cursed the crop. And then they were dancing, he
said, dancing and singing, "Black potatoes, black potatoes, we'll
have them all." And you know when we stood out in the field that

morning after he'd dreamt it, the smell coming off the dirt, it was just like that, the dream of his, and we didn't have to lift them to know that they were black, they were all black. And that was all for us, all we had to eat for the year. Dead and rotting in the field there. The little wheat crop wasn't ours, you see, it was for the rent only. And didn't the landlord when the crop was cut send his keepers to guard it, men with guns, until it could be taken to be sold and then they follow me da from the mill to the agent when me da had to give him all the money of the crop for the rent and then home he comes to us without no money, not a coin at all, and nothing but the stinking empty field and all the year to come with nothing to eat and all his children, eyes in our potato heads, looking out at him with a year ahead of us and nothing, nothing to eat.

(Persephone returns to herself. Pause. They stare at each other.)

DEMETER
Senseless.

PERSEPHONE
(In her own voice) They steal the eggs from the seabirds' nests in the cliffs, boil the seaweed and the nettles, and chew all day long until it's soft enough to swallow. They would lie down if they could, but the hunger drives them on, so they wander like broken birds until they drop into ditches when the night comes, welcoming the warmth of the fever, the little door that opens to the furnace of death where they can sleep without memory, beyond hunger at last.

(Pause. Birdsong, the sound of spring.)

They made such beautiful music once, these people. But I haven't heard them sing, not once, in years.

(Pause.)

Will the crop fail again this year?

(Demeter can't meet her eyes.)

Too many, too many, and now more to come. The staring forests of them standing in the Underworld. The silence of them. They ask for nothing and receive nothing, their empty mouths open, past words, past want. So still. Even the dead are frightened of them.

DEMETER
(Taking her hand) Let us meet this poisoned spring and see it through.

(They exit.)

Demeter waits as the darkness lifts. Heat and wind, perhaps the sound of insects. Sound of a distant truck in bad repair approaching. It stops. We hear a rusty door being opened, then slammed shut. Persephone walks on, wearing a patched and threadbare sweater. She is covered in a coating of fine dust. They embrace.

DEMETER
Will you ever be clean again?

PERSEPHONE
Don't start with me.

DEMETER
The richest grassland anywhere, seas of mesquite, wildflowers. And what do they do with it?

PERSEPHONE
I know.

DEMETER
All the dirt of the southern plains is airborne now but still they dig their tractors out and go on plowing.

PERSEPHONE
I know, they realize that now.

DEMETER
Do they? I don't think they do, my darling.

PERSEPHONE
You're the one who told them to stay put, to put their faith in the
blessed land—

DEMETER
This isn't farming! This is mayhem!

PERSEPHONE
Love your fields you said, treat them well, plow and thrive. That's
what you said, Mother. They're only following your advice.

DEMETER
Those aren't fields! That's prairie. I never told them to plow the
prairie. What kind of idiot thinks that's going to work?

PERSEPHONE
They've put their lives into those fields, Mother, they still think—

DEMETER
Well, they're wrong. How many dust storms will it take for them
to learn? They squander all their soil and then sit there on the
bones of the land they've destroyed, holding their hands out,
waiting for rain.

PERSEPHONE
You don't understand them.

DEMETER
No I don't, I've lost all patience with them.

PERSEPHONE

They sing, even dead they sing, and it's always songs about homesickness.

DEMETER

Homesickness? They've turned their land into the face of the moon. What can they miss?

PERSEPHONE

They remember the fields when they were fruitful, they remember the sky.

DEMETER

They don't deserve their land, they've destroyed it. All that soil, the skin of the world, lost forever now. What is the point of my gift to such people when they don't have the sense to leave the prairies alone? They had no business plowing them.

PERSEPHONE

But they could, there was enough rain, they could farm them for a while.

DEMETER

But of course it wouldn't last, droughts will always come, they must have known that. Don't they know their own history?

PERSEPHONE

No. They always think they can lick it. That's what they say.

DEMETER

Human beings. The blind, idiot optimism of them.

PERSEPHONE

You have to listen to them. Their voices. It's different if you can hear them.

DEMETER
All right, who's this?

(She reaches out to touch the sleeve of Persephone's sweater. The sound. Persephone enters a character.)

PERSEPHONE
(Young Kansas woman) The dust storms, they kept on coming, week after week, they came and well, they just blew the fields away. Our houses, everything we had was buried in the dunes of it. It was just long times, long times of only dirt. You wake and taste it in your mouth, on your teeth edge, burning in your eyes, the grit, we were never rid of it. And we heard that the way to draw the rain down was to kill a snake and hang it belly-side up along the fence and so you see the fences strung with snakes all over, but the worst dust storms come with Easter then and Jesus is hanging from the cross and the snakes are hanging from the fences, white bellies up against the brown sky, and the dust is still blowing.
But so then there was the new way of plowing, where there might be a way to hold down the earth and keep it from blowing, and we think, well, maybe, and you know we *did*, we had a crop come up at last in '39. So fine to see that little haze of green color coming up through the brown after all that. And in that little breath of time, there it was: hope. And it was that same week, after trying and trying, that I could finally tell Joe that we were going to have a baby of our own. For six mornings, I woke up every day with the happiness. The corn up once more and a baby in my belly. But then on the seventh day, my lord, the hoppers came, the rattling clouds of them, I can hear it now, the sound of them falling on the fields, the oceans of them weaving, it was a kind of evil it seemed like, crawling and throwing themselves around on the fields of little corn we'd finally got up, brand new, the first crop we'd had for six years, and they're eating everything, everything there was, and when they got done with what we had growed they're gnawing at the fence poles, the clothes left on the line. It's just

a world of eating hunger and we had nothing left, nothing left for them to eat but they're still eating. And you can't stand looking at it because they might as well be eating you too, crawling up your insides, their mouths going and going. So next thing is we're out there, standing in the moving sea of them with the black poison. We're poisoning the fields, our own fields, the fields we'd spent our hearts on bringing back, we're painting them with the sticky black molasses and strychnine, and this is the thing we can't believe now, but we're doing it, we're poisoning our own land. Because, because, well, there was nothing else to do. But we're watching ourselves doing it, and there's our hands, our own hands painting the poison, buckets and buckets of it, and the rattle of the hoppers is all you can hear and you're doing it, you're putting the poison down onto your own sweet fields, killing them again, because you can't think what else, what else to do.

(Birdsong, sound of spring. Pause.)

DEMETER
How did she die?

PERSEPHONE
The dust pneumonia. It took her baby too.

(A shift in the wind, they look up.)

DEMETER
You think?

PERSEPHONE
Hard to believe, but it could be.

DEMETER
It wouldn't *solve* anything; they've lost the soil at this point.

PERSEPHONE
But it sure would be lovely. Just to feel it on your skin.

DEMETER
The taste of it.

(Sound of distant thunder; they smile at each other.)

Welcome home, my darling.

PERSEPHONE
It's another creation story, Mother.

DEMETER
Born again. Made of mud.

(Sound of a sudden, drenching rain. They hold hands and walk off, faces raised to the storm.)

Demeter waits, as always, in a kind of expectant darkness,
but something is different this time. Suddenly, bright fluorescent
lights go on and Muzak woozily comes up, piped from speakers,
as if a supermarket manager had just arrived at dawn to throw
all the switches on. Demeter is pained and bewildered, shivering
in the air conditioning. The swoosh of sliding doors is heard, and
Persephone enters, wearing a huge hoodie, many sizes too big for
her, open over her dress. They embrace.

DEMETER
What is it you smell of? Gasoline?

PERSEPHONE
Plastic? Is that a smell?

DEMETER
Some kind of poison, it's everywhere they are.

PERSEPHONE
Yes, they track it down to me in eternity; even death won't release
them from it.
Why are we meeting here, Mother?
It's so cold.

(Persephone wraps the enormous hoodie around herself against the chill of the air conditioning. Demeter watches with distaste.)

DEMETER

The size of these people. What killing abundance they have now.

PERSEPHONE

Yes, it's a different kind of starving they're doing now. They starve in plain sight, starve inside their fat, aching with a kind of hunger that can't be fed by the feedings of sugar and corn and sugar made of corn.

DEMETER

(Looking around her at the supermarket) They're such strange berries now, the ones they have created, such needy things, like babies, heads lolling on their stems, wreathed since their birth in a chemical mist so dense and strong that they have never felt the dance of insects. No bird has ever sung to them, no shadow of a leaf or a rabbit has ever moved upon them.
I see the shining rows in the sun, the humans crawling beside them lifting them gently with their naked human hands so as not to bruise them, coughing quietly behind their masks as they tend the combed bright seas of their spectacular nothingness.

PERSEPHONE

Why here, Mother? Are there seasons here? Can spring be brought to such a place?

DEMETER

No, they are done with all that. It's all gone too far now. This was the richest soil in the world but now it's the most poisoned soil in the world, and the millions of tons of chemicals they poisoned it with are washing into the rivers and then the sea where they kill the last fish swimming, and stain the waters all the wrong colors. They have defiled everything, everything.
Look at what has happened to the dearness of the world.

PERSEPHONE
(Indicating her hoodie) This woman is not to blame for that.
All she wanted was what they all want, the taste of things,
the sound of her children's voices, rain, sun . . . life.
What you hate them for is not done by the people who are dying,
it's done by the people who are killing them.

DEMETER
They are all the same to me now. These, these human beings.
Enough.
This is not nature anymore, their circles of dead dirt with the
coddled, perfect rows of made-up plants. I gave them nothing like
this.
The world is too good for them.

PERSEPHONE
Mother—

DEMETER
Oh, I know what you will say, my darling, "Listen to her, just this
one story." As if I owed her that.

PERSEPHONE
But you do.

DEMETER
Why?

PERSEPHONE
Because she is your creation.

DEMETER
Never. This is none of mine. No.
Agriculture? My gift? Look at what they have done with it.
I have reached the end of my tolerance. They have sickened me.

PERSEPHONE
She died in the fields, in the midst of plenty.
She is what your gift has given them. This kind of death. She is
yours.

(Demeter takes a handful of the front of the hoodie—we hear the sound of the character entering Persephone.)

DEMETER
What did you die of?

PERSEPHONE
(As a migrant farmworker) Berries. They killed me. Berries.

DEMETER
How? You mean you ate the berries and . . . ?

(Her hands go in reflexive revulsion to her gut and she shakes her head violently.)

PERSEPHONE
No, no, no, never. Not once. No, it was the chemicals. I picked for
thirty years. I never eat them. But the chemicals they spray on
them, they *(Her hands move from her gut up to her throat)* . . .
they eat *me*. From the inside out. And by then my hands don't
work anymore, so the picking is . . . so hard. But most of all my
back, oh, my back. The years of agony. I can't remember not one
day without pain since I started picking the fruit that killed me.

DEMETER
Thirty years of picking it and you never ate it?

PERSEPHONE
(Her hands go to her mouth in horror as she shakes her head)
Oh, no. To put such a thing in my mouth . . . oh, no, not that.

(Demeter turns away from her in despair, still holding the hoodie.)

Can I ask you . . . ?

DEMETER
What?

PERSEPHONE
The fruit I see in the land of the dead, do I have to pick it too?
Will it kill me again?

(Pause as they look at each other.)

DEMETER
I'm sorry. *(She releases her hold on the hoodie and then smooths it gently on Persephone's chest)* Whoever you were. I'm sorry.

(Demeter walks a few paces away, looking out, as Persephone returns to herself. Pause.)

Oh, my darling girl. You were right.
They should have died out with the mammoths, all the beasts they hunted to extinction. They should never have known. I should never have helped them. It was a mistake.

PERSEPHONE
But, Mother, what is to be done?

DEMETER
I had a dream. It was a night not long ago that I slept in the shell of the dead nuclear reactor at Chernobyl, cold now for a human generation. The people can't come back, they say, for twenty thousand years, and so the forest and her creatures have taken over the abandoned ruin for themselves alone. There was a kind of silence I don't hear anymore—broken only by owls, a darkness I haven't seen for centuries, in which the only light was from the stars. I fell in love with it, the sweet pitch-black peace. Inhuman.

The land had restored itself somehow. Trees, marshlands, frogs, otters, wolf packs running in rippling smudges over the toppled fences, through the new forests.
I didn't miss them.

PERSEPHONE
People?

DEMETER
No. I thought, this is better.
And then I let myself imagine it. If they all just . . . left. It needn't be painful. Just a blinking out of humanity like so many bubbles, pop, pop, pop, by the billions. All their voices, all their lights in the darkness just embers falling into blackness and silence. And then, well, it wouldn't take long. Years, centuries, perhaps, but not long. It would be the triumph of the unspeaking world. The rise and dominion of everything else, animals, insects, the great world of wildness, my beloved green, exultant.
I saw the human creations, the strange, fragile crops, defenseless without their human protectors, coming up to be eaten by whatever creature came by, or just to wither, then be flung by the wind to sow themselves in ditches to bristle into tough complexity once more as the years go by. I saw the weeds return in their fierce disorder and insistence. The spiders holding sway again, the beetles and ants making their palaces unhindered, tending the dirt as it spends the centuries washing itself of the poisons they poured into it.
Whales would mate and sing in the ocean as it recovers from its long centuries of being plundered and polluted, schools of fish would delight in the passage through a world without nets.
I dreamed of the death of machines. Sprinklers gone silent in the great circles of crops. Oil rigs and threshers, backhoes and sawmills stopped forever, rusting, done.
I dreamed of the silent cities, forests rising through the memory of buildings, perpendicular lines tilting, bending, falling, returning to the earth.

I saw the bells that would never ring again in all the bell towers.
And in every town square I saw birds make their nests inside all
the stopped clocks.
Clocks that would never tell the time to anyone again.
I saw the seas rising and the storms, no longer remarked upon,
wending their way along the shorelines, plucking away the houses
one by one; it will take some time, dismantling the coastal cities.
And when the black tornadoes twist along the southern plains
where the prairie grass will have put the soil to rest again—there
would be no one to fear them anymore.
The terror they knew would die with them. Their knives, their
guns, just bits of metal to be buried in sand and grass and forgotten.

PERSEPHONE
(A new thought) There would be . . . there would be no more war.

DEMETER
None of their mayhem, none of their cruelty, none of their
suffering. Their particular violence would vanish with them.
It would soon be as if such things never were.
The planet would forget them.
Forget the noise of them, the unending yammer of them
explaining themselves.
Instead and forever, the sounds would be the sounds of wind and
of birdsong.

PERSEPHONE
I have loved them, but even so . . .

DEMETER
These people . . . oh, these people . . .

PERSEPHONE
The peace that would descend.

DEMETER
The quiet.

PERSEPHONE
No music, no stories. No art . . . no words.

DEMETER
The quiet of the world without them.

PERSEPHONE
None of the questions, none of the awe, none of the human sorrow or joy that once punished and exalted this battered world.

DEMETER
The world I gave to them. The world I would take away from them if I could.

PERSEPHONE
I know you would, Mother.

DEMETER
It would be safe. My world, my beautiful world.
Safe from their damage,

PERSEPHONE
their love,

DEMETER
their greed,

PERSEPHONE
safe at last from their terrible, marvelous minds.

END OF PLAY

ELLEN McLAUGHLIN's plays have received numerous national and international productions. They include *Days and Nights Within, A Narrow Bed, Infinity's House, Iphigenia and Other Daughters, Tongue of a Bird, The Trojan Women, Helen, The Persians, Oedipus, Ajax in Iraq, Kissing the Floor, Septimus and Clarissa, The Names We Gave Him, Penelope, Blood Moon, Mercury's Footpath,* and *The Oresteia.* Producers include: The Public Theater, The National Actors Theatre, Classic Stage Company, Ripe Time, Prototype Festival, One Year Lease, Flux Theatre Ensemble, and New York Theatre Workshop (NYC), Actors Theatre of Louisville, The Actors' Gang (LA), Intiman Theatre (Seattle), Almeida Theatre (London), The Mark Taper Forum (LA), Oregon Shakespeare Festival, the Getty Villa, Guthrie Theater, and Shakespeare Theatre Company (D.C.), among other venues.

Grants and awards include: Helen Merrill Award for Playwriting, Great American Play Contest, Susan Smith Blackburn Prize, the NEA, the Writers' Award from the Lila Wallace–Reader's Digest Fund, the Berilla Kerr Award for Playwrighting, and the TCG/Fox Foundation Resident Actor Fellowship for *Ajax in Iraq* at the A.R.T. Institute.

She has taught playwriting at Barnard College since 1995. Other teaching posts include Bread Loaf School of English, Yale Drama School, and Princeton University.

Ms. McLaughlin is also an actor. She is most well known for having originated the part of the Angel in Tony Kushner's *Angels in America,* appearing in every U.S. production from its earliest workshops through its original Broadway run.